The Turning Point

How Persons of Conscience Brought About Major Change in the Care of America's Mentally Ill

Alex Sareyan

HERALD PRESS
Scottdale, Pennsylvania
Waterloo, Ontario

Note: The authors have worked to ensure that all information in this book concerning drug dosages, schedules, and routes of administration is accurate as of the time of publication and consistant with standards set by the U.S. Food and Drug Administration and the general medical community. As medical research and practice advance, however, therapeutic standards may change. For this reason and because human and mechanical errors sometimes occur, we recommend that readers follow the advice of a physician who is directly involved in their care or the care of a member of their family.

Books published by the American Psychiatric Press, Inc., represent the views and opinions of the individual authors and do not necessarily represent the policies and opinions of the Press or the American Psychiatric Association.

Library of Congress Cataloging-in-Publication Data
Sareyan, Alex, 1913-
The turning point : how persons of conscience brought about major change in the care of America's mentally ill / Alex Sareyan.
p. cm.
First ed. published: American Psychiatric Press, 1994.
Includes bibliographical references and index.
ISBN 0-8361-3596-2
1. Psychiatric hospital care—United States—History—20th century. 2. World War, 1939-1945—Conscientious objectors—United States. 3. Mentally handicapped—Institutional care—United States—History—20th century. 4. Psychiatric hospital patients—United States—Abuse of. 5. Civilian Public Service. I. Title.
RC443.S26 1994b
362.2'1'097309044—dc20 94-26396
CIP

The paper used in this publication is recycled and meets the minimum requirements of National Standard for Information Sciences—Permanence of Paper for Printed Library Materials, ANSI Z39.48-1984.

THE TURNING POINT

Trade paperback edition published 1994 by Herald Press, Scottdale, Pa. 15683, released simultaneously in Canada by Herald Press, Waterloo, Ont. N2L 6H7
Library of Congress Catalog Number: 94-26396
International Standard Book Number: 0-8361-3596-2
Printed in the United States of America
Paperback cover design by Gwen M. Stamm

03 02 01 00 99 98 97 96 95 94 10 9 8 7 6 5 4 3 2 1

Contents

Foreword

Robert S. Kreider, Ph.D.

This is the story of three thousand men, conscientious objectors in World War II who helped change the world of mental health care in the United States. They were agents of change unawares. One-fourth of all the twelve thousand conscripted COs in the United States volunteered to work in sixty-one state mental hospitals and training schools for the mentally retarded. The men were joined by hundreds of women COs—wives, friends, and summer volunteers.

These conscientious objectors served primarily as attendants on the wards—the bottom rung of the hospital staff hierarchy. Rarely given formal orientation, they were handed keys and often deposited on wards with instructions to look after a hundred patients. Wartime was the "snake pit" era of institutional care: aging buildings, overcrowding, depleted staffs, cramped budgets, and penal-custodial attitudes toward the patients, often called "inmates." Alex Sareyan, the author, himself a CO in the front trenches of this service, is one among scores of COs whose concerns were sensitized in wartime alternative service and who have devoted lifetimes to the cause of improved care and understanding for the mentally ill.

In the first chapters of *The Turning Point,* Sareyan has gathered the stories of the CO experience in mental hospitals and training schools. One can hear it now: the clank of iron doors, the rattle of attendants' keys, the hissing of steam pipes, the babble of hundreds of voices, the angry bark of weary employees. One can smell it now: the urine-soaked clothing and bedding, the odor of herded-together bodies, the fetid air of toilets with clogged drains. One can see it now: cots row on row, disheveled patients on benches against the walls, wet slippery floors, nondescript blobs of food dumped on metal plates. Sareyan brings to vivid memory the ugly side of the American institutional experience. All is not pathology in this study. The author gives reports of those in the system who had a vision, were committed to radical change in patient care, and welcomed the COs as collaborators in institutional renewal.

The conscientious objectors entered this institutional world as amateurs, yet learned fast and developed concerns. This was a crash program in consciousness-raising. Sareyan weaves together the stories of how COs stumbled into roles as agents of change. *The Turning Point* is a source book on how in a variety of ways little people, the powerless, can effect radical social change.

The major contribution of the COs in producing change in this complex and formidable environment was simply their dependable quality service: thoughtful, sensitive, gentle, caring. They viewed the patients as persons in whom there was hope for recovery—intimations here of a new kind of therapeutic community.

COs effected change by telling the truth. The author relates how many attendants not only worked on the wards but observed carefully and reported sensitively what they saw. It was not a pretty picture that was exposed at Cleveland State Hospital, Eastern State Hospital in Virginia, Hudson Valley State Hospital, and other institutions. These allegations led to headline articles in the press, formal investigations, several shake-ups in hospital administrations, and heightened public awareness. They did not point fingers of accusation so much as they sadly recorded the problems that plagued the system.

In particular hospitals, COs brought a breath of hope that an old institution could reform itself. Sareyan draws on his experience at Connecticut State Hospital, where he and his CO colleagues innovated programs to encourage communication among staff and, most importantly, the patients. In addition, they launched a varied statewide program to enlighten the public toward fresh, positive understandings of mental illness.

An amazing story of creativeness and coalition-building is told in the chapter "The Turning Point." At Philadelphia State Hospital

(Byberry), four bright and energetic COs launched a movement to improve health care at the basement level—on the wards. Each month they published *The Attendant* (later entitled *The Psychiatric Aide*), focused on raising sights and empowering the attendants in hourly contact with patients. Soon it had a national circulation. They established a data-gathering center that provided an information bank for journalists writing articles published in Life and *Reader's Digest* and for the development of the influential book, *Out of Sight, Out of Mind* (1947). COs with training in law worked with the American Bar Association in preparing model legal codes to protect the rights of the mentally ill. Step-by-step they put together a coalition of psychiatrists, hospital administrators, politicians, and public-spirited citizens that became the National Mental Health Foundation, opening a new era of understanding for the mentally ill.

Meanwhile, the Mennonites, led by COs motivated through wartime hospital experience, established across the country a series of psychiatric centers that modeled the new wave of community-based care for the mentally ill.

The Turning Point is a celebration of how a few people—considered by some to be politically marginal—can profoundly effect change in the grim, gray institutions of our society. This is a voice of hope. Further, this volume is an informative grassroots treatise on the art and the delights of building coalitions of diverse and kindred people to achieve change in flawed public institutions.

Foreword

Don W. Hammersley, M.D.

Herein is a rich account of World War II service by a group of conscientious objectors in state institutions for the mentally ill and retarded and the subsequent significant roles of members of this group in postwar developments in mental health care.

Rejecting war as a way to resolve conflict in the face of a national flood of patriotic zeal to fight takes high moral courage to withstand rampant ridicule and abuse. To opt also to spend a time of alternative service caring for mental patients in the "snake pits" of the nation took an added level of courage. Remember that dismal and dehumanizing conditions existed in most state mental hospitals at the beginning of World War II and were getting worse.

This group of (3,000) conscientious objectors not only accepted these challenges but served with distinction. Further, they provided the documentation of conditions in the hospitals that led to major exposés in the national media and provided leadership in the advocacy and reform movements that followed. Many of them took up lifelong careers as mental health educators, clinicians, and administrators and were nationally recognized leaders in their endeavors.

Alex Sareyan does yeoman service to bring all of this together in logical sequence with careful documentation from a broad range of sources. He also gives us interesting highlights of questionnaire responses from over 400 members of the group 40 years later.

In this book we find out what inside leadership emerged at which location to carry out new ideas that helped shape the dimensions of needed reform. We also learn of significant help that came from state and national public figures in fostering improvement in mental health care in the postwar years. We learn of the Mennonite Church leadership in sponsoring new and pioneering mental health programs in the postwar period.

Historical summaries regarding the care of mentally ill people in the United States after World War II sometimes understate or ignore the significance of this group of conscientious objectors. From this book we can achieve a more balanced and inclusive view of their many contributions.

Apart from the mental health issues discussed, we get a perspective on the conscientious objectors of that period and some of their ways of dealing with problems. They were well educated or in the process of becoming so. Many had wives who took jobs at the same institutions as their husbands and who were no doubt an important support to them. The basic pacifist beliefs they held as members of one of the "peace" churches–Mennonite, the Brethren, or Quaker–seem to correlate well with their caring humanistic approach to the mentally ill. Then such caring was the primary therapeutic modality to which patients responded. This is still of basic importance today as it was then, the present-day array of psychotropic medication notwithstanding.

With each war in which the country engages, the public debate about conscientious objectors is rekindled. In World War II the option that evolved for service in state institutions for the mentally ill and mentally retarded proved to be a win-win-win all the way, for the country, for the mentally ill people, and for the "persons of conscience" who elected to serve their country in this way.

Civilian Public Service is an experience in democracy . . . such as no nation has ever made before . . . to find out whether our democracy is big enough to preserve minority rights in a time of national emergency.

General Lewis B. Hershey, before the U.S. Senate Committee on Military Affairs, 78th Congress, February 17, 1943.
Sibley and Jacob, *Conscription of Conscience*

PREFACE

During World War II, a very small band of men refused to bear arms for their country at a time of international crisis because of their religious beliefs and convictions. Excluding those who elected to serve in the military services in noncombatant roles (primarily as medical corpsmen), there were at most 15,000 or so young men for whom military service could not be reconciled with their conscience.

The stance of approximately 3,000 of these individuals was so absolute that they either refused to register for the draft or, once having been processed by their local draft boards, refused to report for "work of national importance" under civilian direction. This was the concession granted by the U.S. Congress in 1940 for accommodating the religious beliefs of conscientious objectors. Congress made this concession in response to the prodding by the nation's three main peace churches (the Quakers, the Brethren, and the Mennonites) and other religious bodies. Virtually all of the men who held to this absolutist position were tried in federal courts and sentenced to prison terms of up to five years each.

Those approximately 12,000 conscientious objectors who felt comfortable with their 4E draft classification were all assigned to the Civilian Public Service program under the general supervision of the three peace churches and a few other religious agencies. As detailed in the story that follows, these men were directed to report to one of the 70 base Civilian Public Service camps scattered throughout the country. Once arrived, they were put to work on projects under the technical direction of such federal agencies as the National Park

Service, the Soil Conservation Service, and the U.S. Forest Service.

Eventually, other service opportunities were offered in a variety of detached service settings such as the Agricultural Experiment Stations, the Coast and Geodetic Service, the Office of Scientific Research and Development, the Weather Bureau, the Office of the Surgeon General, and 65 of the nation's public mental hospitals and state training schools for the retarded. It was in this last group of hospitals and schools that some 3,000 conscientious objectors fulfilled their commitment to work of national importance.

In the past 45 years many book-length accounts of the Civilian Public Service program have been published. Some of these were written by men who had experienced the program firsthand, whereas others were written from an outsider's perspective. Although many of these books included segments about the Civilian Public Service mental hospital experience, none before *The Turning Point* dealt exclusively and in such depth with this subject.

The Turning Point tells the story of the conscientious objectors who worked in the hospitals and training schools. Many of these individuals continued to play principal roles in the postwar mental health scene. The Civilian Public Service mental hospital experience triggered the most significant crusade on behalf of the mentally ill that has occurred in this century. One of the main objectives of *The Turning Point* is to document this achievement—not just from my viewpoint, but from the perspective of all who participated in this program.

In documenting this story, I have drawn on many resources, including the personal observations and reflections both of the people involved and of people who were touched by the program in one way or another. The developing Civilian Public Service mental hospital program was grist for the mill of countless news reporters, science specialists, editorial writers, and contributors to the "Letters to the Editor" columns in the nation's dailies and weeklies. Where appropriate, relevant excerpts from many of these items are sprinkled throughout the text.

Because of the diverse vantage points contained within *The Turning Point,* the transitions from one chapter to the next may sometimes leave the reader a bit up in the air. But be assured there is a logical development to the story from the time it opens in "bedlam"-like settings to the point where it describes how the conscientious objectors became acclimated to their new world and discovered that they had been placed in a perfect laboratory situation where they would soon be able to test the efficacy of their pacifist beliefs. From that time onward they were able to demonstrate that love was a more powerful force than violence in dealing with interpersonal tensions. It was this exposure to the unreal world of the mental hospital that in time motivated these men to launch a campaign that stimulated America to do something constructive about its long-neglected mentally ill.

In recent years many highly respected mental health professionals have acknowledged the part played by World War II conscientious objectors in bringing about a new era for the mentally ill. Perry Ottenberg, M.D., Clinical Professor of Psychiatry at the University of Pennsylvania, recently reinforced this conclusion after reading a manuscript version of this work. This is what he wrote:

> . . . *The Turning Point* provides an historical review of the social resistance to change encountered by this group of internally motivated people of conscience. To have the personal strength to take on one's entire society can represent the very best in human maturity. Without the truth there is little resistance to dehumanization on a vast scale. These courageous few, religiously motivated COs fought their own quiet battle during the war and deserve all of society's thanks.

For those who took part in the story that is revealed in the following pages, it was a time of unprecedented personal growth and maturation. The experience also served to strengthen their convictions that their pacifist ideals were solidly embedded in reality.

Alex Sareyan

Acknowledgments

Several individuals and organizations played important supporting roles in the development and preparation of *The Turning Point*.

First and foremost, I want to express my deep appreciation to the more than four hundred men who were gracious enough to respond to a survey, the replies to which helped provide the underpinnings of *The Turning Point*. All of these men participated in the Civilian Public Service mental hospital and training school program during World War II. A complete list of these individuals, except for a few who chose to remain anonymous, can be found in Appendix C. Many of these persons also made financial contributions to help cover the costs associated with the preparation of this book, and they too are acknowledged in the appendix.

It is very doubtful whether the effort that led to the completion of *The Turning Point* could have been sustained had it not been for the generous financial support of several donors. These included The Anna H. & Elizabeth M. Chase Fund Committee, Maurice Falk Medical Fund, Mary Livingston Griggs and Mary Griggs Burke Foundation, Ittleson Foundation, Mrs. Patricia Kind, Mennonite Mental Health Services, and The Thomas H. & Mary Williams Shoemaker Fund.

Equally vital to the completion of this book were the helpful suggestions of several colleagues as the manuscript moved from one stage to the next. Among those in this group were C. Lloyd Bailey; Chandler B. Grannis; Richard Hunter; Arthur Jost; Robert Kreider; Charles Lord; David McAllester; Jack Nether; Roy Simon; Delmar Stahly; and Frank L. Wright. Highly useful historical and anecdotal material was provided by Calhoun Geiger, Robert M. Cox, Clyde Weaver, and Wilton E. Hartzler.

Among others whose advice and counsel proved highly useful were L. William Yolton, Executive Director, National Interreligious Service Board for Conscientious Objectors; and Richard Reuter, a senior staff member of the National Service Board for Religious Objectors, the agency that coordinated the Civilian Public Service program during World War II.

Gathering the essential background material for *The Turning Point* would have been impossible without the generous assistance of the personnel at several archival collections. These collections include the Swarthmore College Peace Library, the Mennonite Archives at Goshen College, the Archives of the Brethren Service Committee, Governor Luther Youngdahl Records at the Minnesota Historical Society, and the American Friends Service Committee Archives (Jack Sutter, Director).

Several esteemed psychiatrists were especially helpful in the final stages of preparing *The Turning Point* for publication. Among them were Don Hammersley, M.D.; Perry Ottenberg, M.D.; Lucy Ozarin, M.D.; Mabel Ross, M.D.; George Tarjan, M.D.; and Dallas Pratt, M.D.

One of the greatest challenges I faced in tackling this subject was locating the present whereabouts of the 3,000 conscientious objectors who participated in the specific experience that is the focus of the book. Fortunately, I obtained current mailing addresses for 1,200 of the above men with the assistance of Wilmer Tjossem and Mel Zuck, both affiliated with the American Friends Service Committee; Hazel Peters, staff member of the Brethren Service Committee; and Marilyn Langeman, an administrative assistant with Mennonite Mental Health Services.

Without the generous and patient help of my son, Andy, in guiding me through the intricacies of modern-day word-processing technology, the manuscript for *The Turning Point* might never have seen the light of day. And to my wife, Mildred, and daughter, Roslyn, I am eternally grateful for the encouragement and inspiration I needed as I tried to fulfill one of the most important tasks of my life–the completion of the story chronicled in the following pages.

Alex Sareyan

Chapter 1

Conscientious Objectors in the United States: 1775 to World War II

> . . . It is gratifying to learn that out of the 5,000 conscientious objectors so far recorded in this country, at least 200 have already engaged in relieving the war-caused manpower shortages of at least two general hospitals, one in New York, one in Chicago, as well as in six different state institutions for mental patients.
>
> . . . And what could be more welcome to the patients in our institutions and to their relatives and friends, than the knowledge that, war or no war, their interests will not be forgotten by their fellow men?
>
> Excerpt from an editorial that appeared October 16, 1942, in *The Hartford Courant*

The passage of the Selective Service Act in September 1940, authorizing the conscription of all 20-year-old men for one year of military service, was a major historical event. It marked the first time in United States history that

---

Some of the background material appearing in this chapter relating to the early planning and development of the Civilian Public Service program was drawn from an unpublished doctoral dissertation by Cynthia Eller titled "Moral and Religious Arguments in Support of Pacifism: Conscientious Objectors and the Second World War," presented in 1988 to the faculty of the Graduate School, University of Southern California, Los Angeles, California.

conscription was authorized when the country was not at war. Equally noteworthy was the fact that it granted persons who had conscientious objections to military service the option to meet their obligations by participating in a work program of national importance under civilian direction.

During World War I, Congress had passed a conscription law that granted noncombatant service only to those men who were members of the historic peace churches: the Quakers, the Brethren, and the Mennonites. Persons recognized as conscientious objectors (COs) under this law were inducted into the army. They were to be limited to noncombatant roles.

Conscientious Objectors in the United States: A Brief History

Before reviewing the various ways in which the "work of national importance" developed during World War II, it may be helpful to review briefly how COs were treated in earlier wars in which the United States was engaged.[1]

In 1775, busy 70-year-old Ben Franklin tacked an amendment onto the Pennsylvania Assembly's military budget. The bill provided that troops were to be raised by conscription to go to the aid of the colonists who were fighting the British in Boston. Franklin's amendment provided for military exemption for those "persons who from religious belief are scrupulous of the lawfulness of bearing arms." He noted that his intent was to respect the consciences of the thousands of Quakers and Moravians in Pennsylvania.

Military conscription had begun in the new United States. And thanks to Ben Franklin, so had exemption for COs. Some type of militia service was required in many of the colonies: Quakers and Mennonites underwent severe hardships because of their refusal to bear arms. Much to George Washington's disgust, conscription was applied only half-heartedly in many of the colonies and not at all in some. Most of the Revolution was fought with volunteers.

When ratifying the Constitution, Virginia, North Carolina, and Rhode Island recommended that it be amended to provide exemption from military service to "every inhabitant of the state of any religious denomination, subject to military duty, but from scruples of conscience could not bear arms except in time of insurrection or invasion, on paying annually, the sum of $2.50 for such exemption."

Both the War of 1812 and the Mexican War were fought with volunteers, and the question of COs never surfaced. During the Civil War, both the North and South had conscription laws in place. Initially, the South had no provision for exempting COs. But subsequently, an order was issued exempting Quakers, Mennonites, Dunkards, and Nazarenes if they paid an exemption fee of $500 or presented a substitute and if they could offer a statement from an official of their church that they had been members of that church as of October 11, 1862.

COs in the North experienced problems similar to those in the South. A $300 tax bought complete exemption. This revenue was used in treating the sick and wounded. Eventually, the Federal Conscription Act was amended to permit members of the Society of Friends who took the CO position to be assigned to noncombatant roles and to work in hospitals and among the freed slaves. Many who were unable to pay the tax to qualify for exemption were turned over to the military services, where they suffered harsh treatment.

It wasn't until the onset of World War I that the problem of securing exemption from military service for COs surfaced once again. The 1917 Selective Service Act recognized CO status only for those men who were members of the historic peace churches. As soon as a draftee received word to report for induction, he was considered to be in the army. COs were exempted from combatant duty only. But it wasn't until one year after the draft had been enacted that any official definition of what constituted noncombatant duty was issued. In the interim, many of those who had been drafted as COs experienced great hardships, as reported in the following pages.

In an article appearing in *The Compass,* a magazine published by COs during World War II, Howard Moore eloquently recounted his experiences as a CO during World War I.[2] A condensed version of this article follows:

A CO's Experiences in World War I, by Howard Moore

It must be admitted that the treatment of COs so far in World War II has been, in some respects, different from that accorded COs in World War I. Then, at least in the beginning, the only alternative to combatant or noncombatant service was prison or death, or both, as was the case in many instances. . . .

Men who refused to register under the Selective Service Act for the last war and made such refusal known, were arrested and tried in the civil courts. Those who registered as COs and attached detailed statements of their positions to the questionnaires either reported to their local draft boards voluntarily when called, or were taken there by force and castigated as slackers, cowards, and draft dodgers. . . .

In spite of my refusal to sign papers, or submit voluntarily to physical examination, I was automatically registered as fit to stop a bullet and was soon on my way to Camp Upton on Long Island, where I was to be assigned to a battalion as a private in the army.

As soon as we registered at Camp Upton, we were taken to be supplied with uniforms. Until this time I had simply made my protests known all along the line as gentlemanly and nicely as possible. . . . Epithets and abuse of the foulest kind were heaped upon me for refusing to accept a uniform. Returning to the barracks, I sat on my bunk, ignoring the whistles and shouts to line up for reveille and retreat.

When these ceremonies were over, a lieutenant and two sergeants appeared. The latter grabbed me roughly and threw me out through the second-story window. I landed in the cinders of the company street. Aside from some bruises, I was unhurt and was immediately taken before the company's commanding officer, a former Episcopalian minister, who boasted of his prowess as an expert bomb thrower. He scanned the papers in my case and, after a short conversation, dismissed me as a disgrace to his company and said he wouldn't have me in it. He immediately arranged for my transfer to a company of men suffering from venereal diseases, where officers constantly threatened me with willful infection.

So far, I had neither known nor met any COs. Here there were several. Among them was Harry Lee, a labor organizer. He told me of going through nights of terror, of bullets passing through the floor near his bunk from rifles discharged "accidentally" by soldiers from the floor below.

Other COs, like myself, in civilian clothes were soon contacted as we walked about the camp. Eventually, all of us were transferred to a CO concentration barracks. No policy of dealing with us had as yet been formulated. We roamed the encampment at will. Soldiers were forbidden to talk to us on threat of court martial.

Ugly rumors began to reach us. Ernest Gellert, a CO, had been shot. An investigation revealed as nearly as I can remember, that Gellert and another CO, for no obvious reason, were taken to the outskirts of the camp by a squad of soldiers and ordered to dig what the men thought were to be their own graves. They refused to follow orders and were knocked unconscious. When they came to, they were stood up in the holes dug by the soldiers. Whenever they leaned against the side of these holes, they were prodded by bayonets. Water seeped into the holes, rose above their ankles and froze. At the end of the day, one of the men was taken back to his barracks. The next morning Gellert was found dead from a rifle shot. According to the report on the incident, Gellert had borrowed a gun from his guard and had shot himself as a means of calling attention to the plight of the COs.

The monotony of confinement was broken by the news that we were to be visited by a Special Board of Inquiry. Its members included Harlan Stone, then Dean of the Columbia University Law School, Julian L. Mack, Judge of the Circuit Court of Appeals, and a Major Stoddard. They had been asked to inquire into the sincerity of all COs. Those who were considered to be sincere were offered farm furloughs or the opportunity to be paroled to their homes with soldier status. Some accepted these options but the majority refused to cooperate and were regarded as stubborn and defiant. The Government was willing to provide an escape so that its dilemma in dealing with COs could be buried.

Shortly after our appearance before this Board, we were handcuffed in pairs, put in mule wagons, and taken to the railroad station for our journey to Leavenworth, Kansas, where we were to be imprisoned. Our transfer at the New York terminal gave our guard an opportunity to kick and shove us about for the benefit of spectators, before we were shackled to the arms of our seats in the coach.

At Leavenworth, we were placed in post barracks outside the prison proper. Here we met COs from all over the country, and learned from them of the brutalities in their camps. The stories of men being held down in feces of latrine pits until they nearly suffocated, and beatings into insensibility, were the most common.

The morning after our arrival, we were all led by a group of armed officers to an open field where a lot of army tents had been piled. When we were lined up, a major flipped the cover of his holster open and, resting his hand on the butt of his automatic, said: "Now I want you men to erect those tents which you are going to occupy. If there is anyone who refuses to do so, let him step forward." The line moved forward as one man. He then dropped his hand from the gun and said we were the most useless men he had ever seen.

In a few days we were shipped to Fort Riley, Kansas, and again taken to a field, except that this time, the tents were ready for occupancy. There were no sanitary facilities, and we were informed that if we wanted to eat, we would have to carry raw food in open mess kits from the commissary which was a mile away. We were then required to cook our food over open fires. Some tried to do this but several refused to do so and declared we were going on a hunger strike in protest.

Each day our camp was raided by squads of soldiers who tipped us out of our cots and scattered our belongings about like the tornado that eventually leveled the camp. At night we were subjected to a barrage of stones. Several of the COs were cut and hurt. Two to three weeks into the hunger strike, several of us collapsed and we were taken to the Fort hospital. We were tube-fed by orderlies who, on orders from the officer in charge of the section, pulled the tubes out of our stomachs so rapidly that it felt like a hot iron.

Eventually, Major Adler, the Army's chief psychiatrist, and his staff arrived to investigate. We were accused of having a martyr complex. Since we weren't going to be permitted to die, we were advised to eat voluntarily to avoid the inconvenience of being force-fed. But we were not seeking martyrdom, but staging a protest against the conditions into which we had been thrust.

After many hardships, Howard Moore, along with several of his fellow COs, was finally tried before a military court at Camp Funston. He reported that most of the men offered no defense at the trial but merely read prepared statements as a matter of record. A few of the men received sentences of 50 years. Four of the men were sentenced to death, but these sentences were later reduced to 25 years each. Because Moore had been helpful during a flu epidemic, he was given a five-year sentence. Ironically, although Moore had received the shortest of the prison sentences among those in his group, he was the last to be discharged when the war was over. The sentences for all the others had been commuted, and they never served out their full terms.

It was reported by the National Service Board for Religious Objectors that severe sentences were meted out throughout World War I to COs who refused to cooperate with military authorities. In all, 17 men were sentenced to death, 142 received life sentences, and 85 were given prison terms ranging from 25 to as many as 50 years. Another 301 were sentenced to prison for shorter terms. After the war, most of these sentences were commuted, and no one was executed.

In 1926, the army drew up contingency plans for a nationwide conscription in the event that the country once again faced the prospects of a military conflict. The proposed plans called for the same provisions for COs as had prevailed during World War I: noncombatant services for members of the historic peace churches who claimed conscientious exemption.

COs who felt they could accept this category of noncombatant service were classified 1A-O by their draft boards and were customarily assigned to the medical corps in the armed services. In these units, they were primarily engaged in evacuating the wounded and performing other related medical chores. In carrying out their duties, they were not required to carry guns. Perhaps the most celebrated of the men in this category was the well-known movie actor of that era, Lew Ayres. After a short stint in the Civilian Public Service (CPS) program he opted to volunteer for the 1A-O status and joined the armed services. After the end of the war he pursued a career as an ordained minister in the Congregational-Christian denomination.

The Option of Alternative Service

In July 1940, pacifist leaders flocked to Washington to ensure that a new draft law then under consideration by Congress provided COs with the option of alternative service under civilian direction, as well as the option for noncombatant service. When the Selective Service Training and Service Act of 1940 was finally adopted in September of the same year, the option of alternative service was extended to all persons who by religious training and belief could not in good conscience serve in the military. Of equal importance, the alternative service options were to be under civilian direction.

For many COs, noncombatant service was not an acceptable choice because it meant becoming directly involved as a participant in the armed services. To do so would have violated their belief that war was an un-Christian and unethical means for dealing with international conflict. However, those in this group did feel a sense of responsibility to the nation in a time of crisis and were willing to be conscripted to perform work of national importance under civilian direction. They were willing to comply with the law requiring them to register with local draft boards and to demonstrate to these bodies the sincerity of their convictions. Those who passed muster with their boards were given the 4E classification and were assigned to CPS.

In addition to those in the 4E category, there was another group of COs whose beliefs against involvement in the war effort were so absolute that they felt they could not cooperate with the government in any manner. Many of these men even refused to register as required by law. For these men prison sentences were meted out, generally for terms up to five years.

The story of securing alternative service from Congress did not end with the passage of the Selective Service Act. The act specified nothing about the alternative service program except that it be "work of national importance under civilian direction"; the rest was left to the direction of the president and his duly appointed deputies. The three peace churches represented by the American Friends Service Committee, the Brethren Service Committee, and the Mennonite

Central Committee, along with representatives of other church and peace groups, jointly established the National Service Board for Religious Objectors to serve as their liaison with Selective Service and other governmental and technical agencies through which the CPS program was to be carried out. Initially, the three peace churches offered to bear all the expenses of administering the alternative service program, at least for their own young men. They also intended that, as evidence of their dedication, those men serving under their respective auspices would refuse to accept any pay.

The National Service Board for Religious Objectors worked out a detailed proposal, suggesting that two types of service be made available: 1) work for government agencies with a commitment on the part of the peace churches to be responsible for maintenance costs and wages for the COs and 2) work for private agencies, with the agencies bearing the costs of the program for those COs who chose this type of service. Eventually, they agreed on an arrangement under which camps were to be financed and operated by the church organizations, with the projects subject to governmental direction. The peace churches also agreed to accept all men assigned to the projects under their administration. At a later date Selective Service undertook to manage a number of camps on its own to accommodate those who chose not to serve in camps under the auspices of the peace churches for personal reasons, or those who were transferred to these facilities for disciplinary reasons.

Under the CPS program, each individual project was under the control of a single church agency, whereas the National Service Board for Religious Objectors handled general administrative matters and relations with federal agencies. Approximately 12,000 COs served in the CPS program during World War II. While addressing a Mennonite audience during a U.S. speaking tour in the summer of 1945, The Honorable Rhys J. Davies, Labor member of the British Parliament, observed that there had been 12,000 registered COs in England during World War I and 65,000 during World War II. He went on to predict that this number would reach a half a million should World War III occur within 10 years.[3]

The first projects were all work camps, modeled on the Civilian Conservation Corps camps established in the early 1930s. They had been designed to provide training and gainful employment for young urban men, for whom job opportunities were virtually nil during the severe economic depression of that era. These camps housed groups of 150 to 200 young men in barracks-type facilities under the aegis of the U.S. Forestry Service, the Soil Conservation Service of the Department of Agriculture, and other similar federal agencies.

By the late 1930s, the Civilian Conservation Corps camps had been phased out because they were no longer needed. They were reopened at the outset of the CPS program and continued to function under the technical direction of federal agencies such as those noted above. The agency responsible for overseeing work assignments in these camps provided supervisory personnel, equipment, tools, and supplies. Activities in these base camps included building roads, cutting timber, planting trees, dredging waterways, fighting forest fires, manning observation towers, and other related tasks.

It was the responsibility of the peace churches to feed, clothe, and supervise the men in their off-duty hours. The churches were also responsible for maintaining personnel records for Selective Service. In addition, they provided health services for the men under their charge. During off hours, the churches tried to maintain a religious atmosphere in the camps. Classes were offered on a wide variety of topics, including Bible study, societal issues, preparation for work assignments in relief and reconstruction programs, and the creative arts. Many of the nation's prominent pacifists and clergymen made the rounds of the CPS camps in the role of visiting lecturers. They made important contributions in stimulating the religious and intellectual climate of the camps, and they were especially valuable in sustaining the morale of the campers.

Who the COs Were: Some Background Data

As mentioned earlier, approximately 12,000 men participated in the CPS program in World War II. Another 2,000 to 3,000 men whose applications for CO status had been turned down by local draft boards or who chose to ignore their orders to report to duty in the

CPS program were picked up by the authorities. After legal procedures, these men received prison terms of up to five years.

Of the former group, almost 7,000 were drawn from the ranks of the three major peace churches: the Quakers, the Brethren, and the Mennonites. The remainder represented more than 200 separate sects and religious bodies. Prominent among these groups, in descending order, were the following: Methodist; Jehovah's Witness; Congregational-Christian; Presbyterian, U.S.A.; Church of Christ; Northern Baptist; and German Baptist.[4]

In a 1947 study that described the characteristics of COs in World War II, it was stated that COs came from two main religious groups: 1) the three historic peace churches in which pacifism is taught as the traditional "correct" attitude and 2) the various denominational and other religious groups that do not emphasize pacifism as their official church position. The report observed that "men who come from the former churches, accept their pacifism more often as the group norm, whereas men from the latter group more often reach their conclusions through individual thinking and experience."[5]

The authors of the study went on to point out that men who had been drafted to serve in the CPS program under the administration of the American Friends Service Committee were not only older at the time of their induction, but had had considerably more educational experience than men who had been drafted into the armed services. Over 68% of the COs had either graduated from college or had had some college education, whereas the comparable figure for men drafted into the military was slightly more than 11%.

Beginning of Detached Service Projects in Response to Need for More Meaningful Work Assignments

Although the camps (70 in all) scattered throughout the United States remained active throughout the war, a demand quickly grew for alternative work projects that offered opportunities to participate in services more meaningful than those being offered in the base camps.[6] Selective Service also began to be pressured by health and social agencies whose programs were being seriously jeopardized by acute labor shortages stemming from the war economy. In response, Selective Service began approving detached service projects that then became available to men in the CPS camps on a voluntary basis.

Many detached service units were approved for assignment to agricultural schools and to the farming industry, where COs were able to use their skills in conducting significant research projects, dairy testing, and a variety of essential crop-related activities.

In Florida, a detached service unit was made available to the Public Health Service to aid several rural communities in combating hookworm infestation that was plaguing the health of farm laborers. Another unit, assigned to a poverty-stricken Puerto-Rican community, was instrumental in helping to establish a sorely needed medical service where none had existed before.

COs volunteered as participants in at least 50 different scientific experiments, largely done under the Office of Scientific Research of the Office of the Surgeon General. In many cases, the men served as "guinea pigs" in experiments related to alleviating diseases such as influenza and jaundice. Others submitted to starvation diets, subsistence on salt water, dehydration experiments, sea and air sickness episodes, and many others.[7] These experiments were generally done in hospital or university settings. Some were conducted in base-camp settings where men who participated were quarantined for extended periods of time.[8]

"Guinea Pig" Projects

The national edition of *The New York Times* for May 29, 1989, carried a story about a reunion of several members of Civilian Public Service Unit 115R, which had been stationed at the University of Rochester's Medical School during World War II. The 20 COs who had volunteered for this unit were subjected to a variety of unusual experiments to test the human body's tolerance for extreme temperatures, high altitudes, and diets with different protein levels.

From the fall of 1943 until the spring of 1946, unit members endured numbing cold, blistering heat, and life-threatening decompression tests, all in the name of science. Raymond Stanley, one of the members of the unit, recalled the first of the experiments to which they had been subjected: "We'd go into a room that was 130 degrees and stay in there for as long as 12 hours until we had lost 10% of our body weight."

The men in the Rochester unit were also subjected to diets in which wheat germ, cottonseed flour, or sunflower flour was the test source of protein. Nutrition experts at the university were trying to find an inexpensive source of protein to help countries stricken by famine after the war.

Men were subjected to high-altitude tests to determine whether pilots could soar to more than 40,000 feet and still function effectively if aided by oxygen masks. In another study, in which hypothermia was the focus, men stripped to their shorts would be asked to ride stationary bicycles for eight hours at a time.

In another landmark guinea pig study, Dr. William Davis of the Rockefeller Foundation recruited 30 COs assigned to a CPS Forestry camp in the Pemigewasset Valley of New Hampshire. The volunteers for this experiment were infested with lice in the interest of finding an effective insecticide powder to curb epidemics in war-weary Europe.

Those who volunteered for this experiment were taken to a remote wilderness setting, given lice-infected items of clothing, and ordered not to take them off day or night. After a period of 10 days, the men were given various insecticide powders and sprays to determine which were effective. In its issue of October 19, 1942, *Time* magazine reported that "results are a war-time secret; but if the anti-louse powders are as effective on the conscientious objectors as they were on laboratory animals, this new method of typhus control might save millions of lives in the next few years."

Many editorials and news stories appeared in the nation's press in response to the various experiments in which COs participated during this period. In one of the editorials published at that time, the *Tribune Journal* in Sioux City, Iowa, had this comment:

> In any nation at war, it is so customary to glorify deeds of fighting men that it is rather generally assumed there is no other form of heroism than facing danger and death at the fighting front. . . . The role of a CO with the courage of his convictions is particularly unenviable. . . . Considering this situation there seems reason to say

> a word of commendation for the more than 100 COs who are voluntarily serving as "human guinea pigs."

The New York Times story of 1989 reported that the "experiments not only helped American soldiers survive exposure in North Africa and aided fighter pilots in battle, but also pioneered the development of modern respiratory medicine." Dr. Marsh Tenney, a physiologist affiliated with the Dartmouth University Medical School, commented that the findings resulting from the experiments to which the COs were subjected at the University of Rochester "remain as landmark research."

As the nation became almost totally absorbed in its commitment to World War II, serious disruptions began to be felt in the delivery of services to the nearly 600,000 persons confined in public mental hospitals and state training schools for the retarded. Many of these institutions had lost so many members of their nursing and attendant staffs to the war effort that they were on the brink of having to close their doors. In many instances, they had turned to recruiting their own patients to help in meeting their staffing needs. As the state agencies administering these services began learning of a possible labor pool in the CPS camps, feelers were directed to Selective Service to see whether this manpower resource could be tapped.

Meanwhile, Selective Service was being besieged by a large number of other social and service agencies for access to this labor pool. In June 1942, General Lewis B. Hershey, director of Selective Service, authorized the establishment of the first CPS mental hospital unit at the Eastern State Hospital in Williamsburg, Virginia.

Before the year was out, eight additional mental hospital units had been approved for assignment to state hospitals for the mentally ill and state training schools for the retarded. By the time the CPS program had been dismantled at the end of the war, over 3,000 COs had volunteered to serve in 61 of these state institutions.[9]

Before requesting assignment to one of these detached service units, COs were required to spend the first 90 days after their induction in one of the regular base camps. Transfer to a detached service project was on a purely voluntary basis, subject only to the approval of the director of the special project.

The introduction of COs as a labor force in the nation's mental hospitals and training schools triggered a major reawakening of the country's interest in its mentally ill and mentally retarded. Using documentation provided by the COs serving in these institutions, the media spread the shocking account of the inhumane and neglectful treatment of the nation's mentally ill in bold and blaring headlines from coast to coast. But more about this later.

In 1988, the author of this book conducted a survey of 1,200 of the 3,000 COs who had participated in the mental hospital program. The purpose of the survey was to ascertain what changes, if any, this particular experience had made in their postwar lives. The findings from the survey are included in Appendix B.

Of the more than 400 COs who responded to the survey, one out of three individuals reported that their postwar careers had been redirected to the helping professions as a direct result of their experience in the CPS mental hospital program. Some of these men went on to play major roles in establishing community-based mental health services. Others took on leadership roles in the citizens' mental health movement at the local, state, national, and international levels. Many went on to assume key leadership roles in the delivery of mental health services under the aegis of governmental agencies. Some used their talents in educational activities to help the public better understand the importance of mental health as an essential component of their well-being, and to help to eradicate the myths and stigma associated with mental illness.

Before proceeding with the main body of this story, a few facts about the backgrounds of those who were in the CPS mental hospital program may be helpful. Some of the facts gleaned from the 1988 study deserve mention at this point, as they offer additional insights into the kinds of men who were drawn into this phase of the CPS experience.

Whereas the individuals enrolled in the CPS program represented more than 200 different religious affiliations, those specifically enrolled in the mental hospital program came from only 20 religious affiliations. The Mennonites accounted for 40% of the men in the hospital program. The Brethren, the Methodists, and the Society of Friends each accounted for 13% of the men in this program.

The CPS mental hospital program itself only lasted a few years. But some 45 years later, its legacy continues to fulfill the expectations of two physicians, Robert A. Clark, M.D., and Alex M. Burgess, M.D. In an article that appeared in *The Psychiatric Quarterly,* they wrote:[10]

> For the first time . . . intelligent, educated, and humane observers were placed on the wards of mental hospitals. . . .
>
> It was inevitable under these circumstances that further developments should take place. . . . Publicity concerning the conditions in public mental hospitals began to appear and spread. . . . Then came a more organized effort to obtain better conditions. . . . by reaching community leaders, legislators, and the public. Before long, actual improvements followed in the form of changes in administration, and larger appropriations. . . .

The mental hospital experience to which COs were exposed during the war was a major contributing factor not only to igniting a revolution in the care of the mentally ill, but also to the emergence of a new and enlightened public attitude toward mental illness and mental health. What follows is the story of how it all came about.

Chapter 2

Out of Sight, Out of Mind

We Americans cannot justly be proud of the way we have dealt with our nation's most important health problem. Mental disorders affect more of us than cancer, tuberculosis and infantile paralysis combined. . . . Yet most of us have been sadly unaware of its extent, falsely confident that adequate care is generally available, and blindly indifferent to its disastrous effects, both social and economic upon our national life. . . ."

Owen J. Roberts, Chairman
National Mental Health Foundation
June 1947

In the May 6, 1946, issue of *Life Magazine,* an exposé of conditions in U.S. mental hospitals appeared under the headline:

BEDLAM 1946: Most U.S. Mental Hospitals Are a Shame and Disgrace

---

The indictment contained in that headline had been inspired by the collected reports of some 3,000 conscientious objectors (COs) who had volunteered for assignment as attendants in 65 state institutions for the mentally ill and mentally retarded during a period when the operation of these facilities was severely threatened by critical personnel shortages during World War II.

Albert Q. Maisel, noted science reporter of that era, had been commissioned by the editors of *Life Magazine* to write a graphic and chilling account of the deplorable conditions under which most of the nation's several hundred thousand mental patients were being cared for during the war era. Some glimpse of the details divulged by Maisel may be gleaned from the following introductory paragraphs of his story:[1]

> In Philadelphia, the sovereign Commonwealth of Pennsylvania maintains a dilapidated, overcrowded, undermanned mental hospital known as Byberry. There on the stone wall of a basement ward appropriately known as the "Dungeon," one can still read, after nine years, the five-word legend—"George was kill here 1937."
>
> This pitiful memorial might apply quite as well to hundreds of other Georges in mental institutions in almost every state in the Union, for Pennsylvania is not unique. Through public neglect and legislative penny-pinching, state after state has allowed its institutions for the care and cure of the mentally sick to degenerate into little more than concentration camps on the "Belsen" pattern.
>
> Court and grand-jury records document scores of patient deaths following beatings administered by brutal attendants. . . . Hundreds of instances of abuse, falling just short of manslaughter, are similarly documented. And reliable evidence, from hospital after hospital, indicates that these are but a tiny fraction of the beatings that occur. . . .
>
> Yet beatings and murders are hardly the most significant of the indignities we have heaped upon most of the 600,000 guiltless, patient-prisoners in over 180 state mental institutions.
>
> We feed thousands a starvation diet. . . . We jam-pack men, women, and sometimes even children into hundred-year-old firetraps in wards so crowded that the floors cannot be seen between the rickety cots, while thousands more sleep on the bare floors. . . .
>
> Thousands spend their days . . . locked in devices euphemistically called "restraints." . . . Hundreds are confined in . . . bare, bedless rooms, reeking with filth and feces. . . .
>
> Thus thousands who might be restored to society linger in manmade hells for a release that comes more quickly only because death comes faster to the abused, the beaten, the drugged, the starved and the neglected. In some mental hospitals, for example, tuberculosis is 13 times as common as in the population at large. . . .

. . . Some outstanding superintendents have managed to raise their institutions to a decent level despite low pay scales and heavy overloads. . . . Some have succeeded not merely in discountenancing beatings and restricting the use of restraints and solitary confinement, but in eliminating these relics of the dark ages entirely.

The sad and shocking fact, however, is that these exceptions are few and far between. The vast majority of our state institutions are dreary, dilapidated excuses for hospitals. . . .

Charges such as these are far too serious to be based solely upon the observations of any single investigator. . . . In addition to court records and the reports of occasional investigating commissions, there is now available for the first time a reliable body of data covering nearly one-third of all the state hospitals. . . . A by-product of the war's aggravation of the long-existing personnel shortage, this data represents the collated reports of more than 3,000 conscientious objectors, who, under Selective Service, volunteered for assignment as mental hospital attendants.

. . . Supported as they are by other official data, their reports leave no shadow of doubt as to the need for major reforms in the mental hospital systems of almost every state.

COs Establish Clearinghouse to Gather Information on Conditions and Practices in Mental Hospitals

In the spring of 1944, during their off-duty hours, four COs then serving at The Philadelphia State Hospital established a clearinghouse through which they and their fellow COs in the Civilian Public Service (CPS) program could share information and concerns about the institutions in which they were serving. This operation, initially called the Mental Hygiene Program of CPS, also made it possible to share constructive ideas for handling patients, as well as information on prevailing conditions at their hospitals. It was this latter body of data that two years later was to provide the stimulus for the publication of the *Life Magazine* story cited earlier. The value and truthfulness of these reports were attested to by Dr. George Stevenson, Medical Director of the National Committee for Mental Hygiene, then one of the nation's leading authorities on the institutional care of the mentally ill. He observed:[2]

> No one can deny that members of the Civilian Public Service Program have firsthand knowledge of conditions in our mental hospitals. Since they know whereof they speak, their voices may well be hearkened to, and their influence in their communities may well break down the lethargy of the public in regard to present conditions in our mental hospitals.

The more than 1,400 reports collected by the COs provided the stimulus not only for Maisel's article, but also for similar exposés by many other crusading reporters who had been deeply stirred by the reports. Notable among this group were Albert Deutsch and Mike Gorman, both of whom later received special tributes from the American Psychiatric Association for their journalistic efforts on behalf of the mentally ill.

Book Based on COs' Reports Is Published

After his discharge at the war's end from the CPS mental hospital service program, Frank L. Wright, Jr., took on the task of preparing a book based on the same body of reports used by Maisel for his *Life Magazine* article. Wright's distillation of these CPS Mental Hygiene Program reports appeared in 1947 in a book titled *Out of Sight, Out of Mind,* published under the auspices of the National Mental Health Foundation.[3] This was the nationwide citizens' organization established by the COs in the spring of 1946 to carry their Mental Hygiene Program forward into the postwar period. A fuller account of the tremendous impact made by the National Mental Health Foundation on the mental health scene in the United States appears in Chapter 8.

In the foreword to *Out of Sight, Out of Mind,* Owen J. Roberts, the distinguished former U.S. Supreme Court Justice who had agreed to serve as chairman of the National Mental Health Foundation, noted:

> Mr. Wright's forceful book cannot fail to shock us, to awaken us, to impel us to action. . . . Americans should read it, for unless these facts are faced frankly, and the problem solved satisfactorily, many thousands of mentally handicapped persons will continue to be "out of sight, out of mind." . . . No one should doubt the authenticity of this book.

Here then are some of the factual accounts that Wright selected for inclusion in his book. In the preface to this work, he wrote:

> . . . You will find herein a number of graphic incidents, each a short story or character sketch unto itself, each undeniably true and accurate, each representing hundreds of similar incidents that are occurring all over the country today, and giving you some new insights into the problems of mental patients and mental hospitals. . . . Names of persons and places have been altered for purposes of publication. Nevertheless, I hope you know that it is real flesh and blood which you are meeting in these pages. . . .

> Careless medical practice should never be tolerated by the mental hospital administration. . . . Failure to investigate the somatic side of the problem is careless psychiatric practice.
>
> William A. Bryan, M.D.
> Superintendent, Norwich State Hospital
> From *Administrative Psychiatry,* New York,
> W. W. Norton & Company, 1936

"Aren't you going to remove the gallbladder?" asked the young doctor assisting at the operation.

"We'll just wipe it out and leave a drain in it. That's best," replied the senior surgeon who performed most of the operations at the state hospital.

The young doctor—McMasters by name—showed his amazement even through his operating mask. He knew that for at least 20 years, it had been standard procedure to remove inflamed gallbladders. He knew that removal was the only thing to do in this case. But he also knew that his suggestion held no weight against the clumsy confidence of Dr. Spellman, the senior surgeon.

Still he could not hold his tongue when he saw that Dr. Spellman was going to close the incision with just one row of wire suture—it needed to have at least three different closures if it was to heal. "The peritoneum is ready for closing," Dr. McMasters suggested.

But Dr. Spellman disregarded the suggestion and quickly closed all of the layers of the abdominal wall with the single row of stitches. "Finished," he announced.

That night the inevitable happened. A few stitches broke through the tissue, and the wound reopened. At 3 A.M., the night nurse found the patient with his intestines spilled out of the abdominal wall and the wound wide open. Knowing that such a catastrophe required immediate restitching, she called Dr. Spellman at his apartment on the grounds, and reported what had happened. Dr. Spellman gave directions that a heavy dressing be drawn tight with adhesive tape to hold the intestines in. "I'll stop in to see the patient in the morning at 8:30," he concluded, and hung up.

When Dr. Spellman stopped by in the morning, the patient was dead.

Dr. McMasters and Dr. Spellman met again over the patient's open abdomen at the autopsy. Signs of negligence were plainly evident.

"Well, after all, what could you expect?" Dr. Spellman commented. "He was just a poor dope."

Dr. McMasters turned on his heel and left the room. He had heard it said before, but now he believed it. Some doctors instead of being in the Hippocratic tradition, were most certainly in the "hypocritic" tradition. (Based on Mental Hygiene Program report 772.)

While the ward physician is not directly responsible for the ward routine which is carried on by the nursing and attendant personnel, yet his attitude toward his patients will determine, more than any other factor, the attitude of the nursing personnel toward the patient.

George W. Morrow, M.D.
Superintendent, Kankakee State Hospital

"Bright morning, Mr. Pisky, isn't it?"

Mr. Pisky looked up from the bowl of unsweetened cereal he was eating, and blinked at the attendant standing there. A little smile broke on his face. "Yeah bright! More cereal?" he asked. "Sure enough. I'll bring it right over." And the attendant went away smiling, to try to scrape just a little more paste oats out of the tin.

Those were the first words Pisky had spoken in two weeks. During most of that time he had been so depressed that he had to be told to eat every mouthful. This morning he had gotten out of bed by himself and had dressed himself. (That is, he had done everything but button his shirt—all its buttons were torn off, and he had let another patient tie it together with a string.) Now he was actually asking for food, and eating it as if he enjoyed it.

As soon as the attendant and his 63 patients were back on the ward, Pisky presented himself again. "Say, do you s'pose I could have my glasses and something to read?"

"Sure, you can have this magazine to read. But we'll have to ask the doctor for your glasses. He should be along soon, so you watch for him. Okay?"

"Hokay!" said Mr. Pisky.

Pisky had been around long enough—he had been in the hospital 15 years—to know that the doctor didn't spend much time going through the ward. He took up his vigil right at the door of the ward and watched carefully for the doctor's appearance.

The attendant was down at the other end of the ward when Dr. Klemm swept in on his daily dash through the wards. One hour—10 wards—700 patients—not much time.

Pisky stepped up timidly behind the doctor and touched his shoulder. "Please sir. . . ."

Dr. Klemm whirled around, pushed Pisky roughly onto a bench and cursed him roundly. "You ______! Who do you think you are, putting your hand on me?"

Pisky quivered on the bench a moment, slid to the floor, and ran for the toilet, where he crouched in a corner, crying.

Dr. Klemm strode out the door at the other end of the ward, muttering: "If I ever get fired or want to leave this hospital, I'll beat the hell out of that patient before I go." (Based on Mental Hygiene Program report 283.)

> Rules and regulations about treating patients kindly have no effect upon ward personnel, unless it is evident that supervisor and superintendent support these rules wholeheartedly through their own actions and attitudes.
>
> Willard C. Hetzel
> Director, Legal Division,
> National Mental Health Foundation

Attendant Alden sat on the porch keeping guard. All the patients except Blozo were out in the enclosed yard. Blozo sat on a bench near Alden. A worker-patient began to sweep the porch. As he came near Blozo, Alden yelled:

"Blozo, get your lazy hulk off that bench. Let the man sweep." Blozo didn't move.

Alden seized the inch-wide restraining strap at his side, leaped on Blozo and beat him on the face and head, shouting, "Get up! Mind me, you ______!"

The patient still didn't move. Then Alden noticed that he was strapped to the bench and couldn't move.

"You fool, why didn't you tell me?"

"You put me here," said Blozo.

"Well you didn't get anything you didn't deserve."

"I'll ask the doctor about that."

"You tell the doc about this and I'll beat you within an inch of your life."

Blozo knew that might be true. Nevertheless, he met the doctor at the door when he came in later that morning, and began to tell him what had happened and what threats had been made. Alden came up with the strap in his hand and said, "I told you you'd get it if you told the doc," and without a moment's hesitation, began beating Blozo about the face and head again.

The doctor, without a word, turned on his heel and stepped out the door.

Alden then stripped Blozo of his clothes, gave him an excessive dose of epsom salts, and strapped him in bed. Blozo lay there for a full day and night, naked and beaten, in his own filth. (Based on Mental Hygiene Program reports 1334 and 1342.)

> There is a type of psychological abuse of mental patients which may be more disastrous than any kind of physical abuse. By this I mean the tactless treatment of the patient, the refusal of small desires and requests, and the abuse of power that is necessarily conferred upon the individual who is in charge of a ward of mental patients.
>
> William A. Bryan, M.D.
> Superintendent, Norwich State Hospital
> From *Administrative Psychiatry,* New York,
> W. W. Norton & Company, 1936

"Mr. Finney, has my newspaper come yet this morning?"

Big John stood timidly outside the attendant's office. His sightless eyes rolled from side to side. His mighty body towered in the doorway. His big hands rested gently on the back of Peter's wheelchair.

Big John and Peter were never seen apart. John, big, black, and powerful, was blind. Peter—tiny, blonde, a paralyzed Swede—had no legs. Together, they were alive. But apart, they were little more than dead, John entombed in his world of darkness and misunderstanding, Peter in his world of immobility and persecution.

They had one real pleasure every day—the morning paper. Big John had a small pension from the government, and he had ordered a paper delivered to the ward each morning. As soon as it came, —the paper was always delivered promptly at eight o'clock—John and Peter would retire to a sunny corner of the ward and spend the entire day going through the paper. Peter would read every word and describe every illustration. Then Big John would ask questions, and the two friends would talk on and on about what was happening, what would probably happen tomorrow, and why things were turning out as they were.

Big John had asked for his paper three times already that morning. It was nearing noon now, and still he hadn't received it.

"I sure would like my paper, Mr. Finney," he said again.

"Get out of here, you blind ape!" shouted the attendant. "Can't you see I'm busy?"

Big John started to move away, but Peter's fingers held the wheelchair still. Peter could see that Mr. Finney was playing solitaire, and the prized paper was lying on the table. "Give us that paper," he said.

"Why you sawed-off little shrimp! I'll beat your two-bit brains out!" yelled Finney, leaping out of his chair.

But John had the wheelchair under way now. Big tears rolled down his ebony cheeks.

"Don't hurt my li'l Pete. Don't hurt my li'l Pete," he pleaded as they fled to the other end of the ward. Peter's palsied arms shook in impotent rage as he guided the chair.

Big John patted Peter's arm. "Don't bother, Pete. You jus' tell me 'bout Sweden once more." (Based on Mental Hygiene Program report 685.)

Certain technical things help to create the desired atmosphere of confidence and reassurance in the hospital and assist in rebuilding mentally sick patients. There is always a degree of exhaustion, both physical and mental, which must be counteracted by external measures such as ultra-comfortable beds, attractive and well-ventilated rooms, easy access to toilet facilities, and appetizing, nourishing food.

Karl Menninger, M.D.
From *The Human Mind,* New York,
Alfred A. Knopf, 1966

The tree-lined drive and the colonial-type buildings reassured Walter considerably. Ever since the doctor at the admission hospital in the city had told him he was going to be transferred to a state hospital, Walter had been dreading what he might find there. But now, as he arrived, it looked quite nice. The rolling lawns, the spacious verandas, the spreading trees—everything looked calm and serene.

The car stopped in front of the main building, and the attendant who was transferring Walter said, "Well, here we are." They got out and went into a blue-tinted waiting room. Comfortable leather chairs, bright pictures and a rug on the floor made Walter feel at home. He had lost all his fear by the time the doctor had come in, talked to him, and put him in the charge of an attendant.

Walter said goodbye to the attendant who had brought him, and accompanied the new one through a short sunny hall to a locked door, marked Ward C. The attendant opened the door with his key and waited for Walter to enter.

Walter gasped and started back. Stale air, laden with a collection of repulsive odors, assailed his nostrils. His eyes looked into a long, dark hallway in which half-dressed men were wandering up and down, muttering to themselves.

The attendant's hand pressed insistently on Walter's back. He moved across the threshold, and the door shut on the sunny hall. Walter had arrived.

Walter went through the rest of the admission procedures automatically, without speaking or thinking. He only observed. He found that the walls were dark gray here and there where the plaster had fallen. The only furniture consisted of dark brown benches and one table. The part of the smell that didn't come directly from the 200 unbathed, poorly clothed men came from the wooden floor. The seams and pores had opened up over the years so that everything that touched it—spoiled food, dirty laundry, human waste—left a little of itself behind.

He also found that the ward bathroom contained three toilet stools (all without covers or seats), one tub (no showers), and one deep sink. The sink served variously as a urinal, drinking fountain, wash tub for bedpans, mop rinser, and dishpan for food plates.

Having made these observations and having taken his bath (which made him feel dirtier) and put on hospital clothes (which made him feel more undressed), Walter turned his attention to his fellow patients. He found it difficult to think of them as people. They seemed more like animals: a big herd of them penned up in one corral, milling about and making queer noises, unmindful of others except for an occasional push or snarl.

As these thoughts were going through Walter's mind, two attendants passed by making plans for taking the patients upstairs to dinner. One attendant said: "You go ahead. I'll drive the critters up."

Walter let out a bawl that sounded just like a steer on the way to the slaughterhouse. The attendants looked at each other and shook their heads.

Walter had arrived. (Based on Mental Hygiene Program reports 141 and 976.)

Fire-protection was the one thing that was stressed when a new attendant came to work in Building J. And well it might be, for the building was known to be a firetrap, and it was rumored that it had been condemned four years ago. Be that as it may, the building still housed 700 mental patients, and attendants were told to take special precautions to prevent fires.

Mrs. Tolan read the rules and regulations carefully when she started to work in Building J. The fire hazard struck her especially, since she was to work on Ward 6 on the third floor. There were 253 patients on that ward, and the only exits were locked stairways at either end of the building, and a special fire escape—also reached through a locked door. She was duly impressed with the fact that she alone carried keys to open any of these exits—patients could not get out except with her help.

The first morning on Ward 6 passed quickly for Mrs. Tolan, and it was soon time for her to go to lunch. But it didn't seem right to just go off and leave 253 patients locked on the ward. She called the supervisor's office.

"Do you lock the doors on Ward 6 when you go to lunch?" Mrs. Tolan asked.

"Certainly! Never leave the ward without locking all the doors."

"But then the patients can't get out."

"That's exactly the idea, Mrs. Tolan. The patients aren't supposed to get out."

"Oh, I know. But I meant in case of fire."

"Oh that! Well don't worry about that. There are three hours a day and an hour each night when the ward is left unattended. No one relieves you; just go off duty when the time comes."

"Alright, but it seems funny."

"Don't worry about it. If fire breaks out on the ward when you're not on duty, you won't be held responsible for it."

Mrs. Tolan replaced the receiver on the hook.

"Well, that's nice," she thought. "I suppose that should put my mind at ease." (Based on Mental Hygiene Program report 113.)

Nurses and attendants should be encouraged to keep some type of behavior notes on their patients. Appreciation should be expressed by the ward physician for notes containing pertinent information.

George W. Morrow, M.D.
Superintendent, Kankakee State Hospital

Cleaning up the music room was a tedious but interesting task. The hospital had been without any musical activity for several years, and a lot of junk had collected in the meantime. Miss Moran made all sorts of interesting discoveries among the piles of music and boxes.

She drew out one box labeled, "Property of James Doerr—Patient." Inside she found a large assortment of music, from Bach and Mendelssohn to Cohan and Berlin. But most interesting of all were several pieces of music written by James Doerr himself, as well as a number of original arrangements and orchestrations. Several printed programs and posters in the box showed that he had appeared with a troupe of entertainers in England and Scotland several years previously. Miss Moran made a mental note to look up James Doerr and to get him into her new music program if it was at all possible.

A week later, she had an opportunity to refer to James Doerr's record. She found that the diagnosis of the investigating physician included this note: "Delusions of grandeur; believes he has written songs; believes he has been to Europe where he played before important personages." (Based on Mental Hygiene Program report 1125.)

> The personnel of mental hospitals are, on the whole, gentle and kindly people. . . . Abuses are rare exceptions. Indeed it is astonishing, in view of the dangers to which attendants are continually exposed, that instances of physical violence are not more common.
>
> Edith Stern
> From *Mental Illness: A Guide for the Family,* Arlington, VA, National Mental Health Association, 1968

The blisters on Mr. Dunn's hands were so painful that he decided he'd better rest a day or two before going back to shoveling coal. He didn't want to give up his job on the coal pile—anything was better than just sitting on the ward all day long. But he had been an accountant before he entered the hospital, and shoveling coal was hard work for him.

When the powerhouse foreman came to collect his worker-patients, Mr. Dunn said, "I would like to be excused temporarily from outside work, Mr. Grace."

"Come on you loafer. We've got to unload today."

"But, my hands—."

"Quit bellyaching," Mr. Grace ordered, as he pushed Dunn through the door. Then he called to the ward attendant, "Okay, I've got my men," and closed the door.

The rough handle of the shovel bit into Mr. Dunn's blistered hands. Tears of pain blurred his vision, but he kept working, slowly but constantly. This was occupational, he was sure—but could it be therapy?

He didn't even wince when he heard Grace shout, "Dunn! Get a move on." He slowly urged his shovel under a pile of coal, gritted his teeth, gripped the handle, and lifted the shovelful into a wheelbarrow. He lowered the hand of his shovel again, started to repeat the process. Then the flat of a shovel hit him heavily in the back, and he buckled under the blow.

Grace swung the shovel once more at Dunn's back and called for two other attendants to help him. The three of them drew Dunn to his feet, punched him a dozen times in the stomach and ribs, and knocked him down again. They then rushed him off to the violent ward.

The next day, Dunn was sent to the medical ward and given an X ray. Eighteen bruises were noted on the supervisor's report, and three ribs were listed as apparently broken.

Two days later, Mr. Dunn died. His postmortem report read: "Cause of death: unknown." (Based on Mental Hygiene Program report 1328.)

> Let me emphasize that none of the good hospitals uses straitjackets or other forms of mechanical restraint, except in rare cases; nor do they resort to sedative drugs and seclusion except as a last resort. Force, which would excite and arouse even sane people, has given way to psychology and patient effort.
>
> Inis W. Jones
> From "Man's Last Specter:
> The Challenge of Mental Disease,"
> *Scribner's Magazine,* December 1938

"Hilda, if you open your mouth just once more, you'll go right into the 'strip' room. I'm sick and tired of your godawful talking and singing."

Hilda, of course, could no more stop talking and singing than a woman with a sprained ankle could stop limping. It was a symptom of her illness. But Mrs. Gladwyn, the attendant, slammed the magazine down on the desk and said, "By God, I'll show you!"

She unlocked a small, barred room which was entirely empty except for a young girl who lay naked on a torn piece of blanket in the corner. Mrs. Gladwyn seized the nude girl by the hair and gave her a sudden pull.

"Come on, goon-child. It's the bench for you tonight. We've got a customer for your room."

The girl awkwardly got to her feet and was led off without protest. Mrs. Gladwyn then got a bath towel, wet it, rolled it, and sneaked up behind the singing Hilda. Quickly she whipped the towel around Hilda's neck, pulled it tight, and began to twist. "Now me proud wench! To the 'strip' room." Punctuating her words with jerks and twists on the towel, she half-pushed, half-dragged Hilda to the room just emptied. Once in the room she gave one final, tighter twist, and let Hilda fall to the floor unconscious.

She then removed Hilda's single garment, took the piece of blanket from the room, slammed and locked the door.

"Now," she said, "I guess we'll have some peace and quiet around here for a while." (Based on Mental Hygiene Program report 976.)

In mental hospitals, as elsewhere, the employee's satisfaction in his job depends to a large extent on prevailing practices of personnel management. . . . If his work assignments are indefinite or confused, if constructive initiative on his part is ignored or actively discouraged, the effect on the employee's morale is often catastrophic. Each employee should be told exactly what is expected of him, and should be helped to understand the function and importance of his particular role in the hospital's program.

Earl D. Bond, M.D.
Administrative Director, Pennsylvania Hospital
Philadelphia, PA

"Well, Don, I'm leaving this outfit." Jack was standing over his bag, packing his clothes, when his roommate came in.

"Can't say that I blame you much," Don answered. "I've been working around this hospital for almost 10 years, and I've wanted to leave nearly every day of it. But I haven't packed my bag yet. What's starting you off?"

"It's nothing special," Jack replied, "just more of the same old thing."

"Was 'Old Ramrod' on a rampage today?"

"Not much worse than usual. I don't mind being the bottom man on the totem pole. But when the guys on top starting kicking the patients in the teeth and acting holy about it, then I quit."

"Yeah? Go on and tell me about it while you pack."

"It's not just that we eat that lousy stew over in the cafeteria while the doctors and nurses get served classy chops in their dining room. And I certainly don't give a hang that we're not allowed to speak to nurses except in the line of duty. I can almost stand it that we have to ask the 'Old Hen' when we want to stay out after 11 P.M. But darned if I can take it when they obviously don't give a hoot about the patients. Take today, for instance. You know that special diaper I worked out to keep old Louis from removing his catheter? Well, Dr. Graves saw that outfit this morning and ordered it removed immediately."

"No foolin'!"

"Yeah. It had been working perfectly for three weeks, and now we've had to put Louis back into a straitjacket again, to keep him from bothering the thing. You know his bladder is so bad he has to have one in there all the time."

"Yeah."

"I suppose I should have expected something like this. When I first suggested using a diaper, Miss Lodge told me I'd better not do it even though it did sound like a good idea. 'The doctor will condemn you for your presumption,' she said. 'You just do what the doctors say, and forget about anything else.' But when I could save the patient a lot of pain and keep him out of a jacket at the same time, I went ahead anyway. Well, Graves noticed it today—after three weeks of use—and I got bawled out for not minding my own business. Which seemed to mean, waxing floors and keeping the ward clean."

"Well sure, Graves is a little unreasonable, but—."

"But phooey! It's the same way about everything. Did you ever see Dr. Bancroft on the rare occasions he's in his office? He's like a paunchy potentate holding court up there. All his little lieutenants come running in and out: plumber, gardener, farmer, carpenter, chauffeur, doctors, and nurses. They all come in to get their daily orders from Bancroft. You know I can't even get toilet paper on my ward unless he signs the order. The way everybody flits around to do his bidding, you sort of expect to see them salute, click their heels, and say, 'Heil Bancroft!'

"But did you ever see him when the state examiners come around? Then, it's just the opposite. The paunchy potentate bows and scrapes to the state officials, shows them how low he's keeping the budget, and sends them away saying, 'Bancroft makes a good hospital superintendent.' Gad, I wish they could see that stinkin' hole where my 70 patients live—or die!

"I don't wonder that most fellows who stay around here so long, get to saying, 'Why worry,—and who cares?' Everybody from the garbage collector to the staff surgeon feels the same way."

"I'd go along with you, Jack, only—."

"Yeah, I know, Don. It's the patients who pay. And you've got a soft spot in your heart for the poor devils. Well—so long and good luck." (Based on Mental Hygiene Program reports 267, 272, and 276.)

In the concluding pages of *Out of Sight, Out of Mind,* Wright again reminds us that every one of the incidents reported in the book—all 63 of them—were based on firsthand, "on the spot" reports from COs assigned to public mental hospitals during World War II. He also observes that many of the reports were based on information provided by other hospital personnel, including physicians, nurses, and attendants.

Wright makes it clear that the abuses he describes in his book are not isolated instances:

> Incidents similar to those reported in the book are widespread. . . . There is no public mental hospital in the country that lives up to its possibilities. . . . An important corollary of this fact is that there is no hospital that is all bad—that has no redeeming features. . . . The proof of this is that our state mental hospitals discharge, as recovered or improved, thousands of patients every year. . . .

Wright then suggests that some might attribute the disgraceful state of affairs in the nation's mental hospitals to the exigencies related to pressures resulting from the war economy then in place. However, he notes that when one administrator of welfare in an eastern state complained to the governor that the poor conditions in the state institutions were the result of wartime controls imposed by the federal government, many newspapers obtained statements from several hospital superintendents indicating that conditions had been just as bad before the war. And several prominent journalists, writing for national publications in the late 1930s and early 1940s, were cited by Wright as having confirmed that many state hospitals in those periods were struggling to meet the needs of their patients under tremendous handicaps.

In the concluding pages of his book, Wright reminds the reader that U.S. Surgeon General Dr. Thomas Parran had observed that "mental illness is America's number one health problem." To illustrate the lack of public support for research, education, and prevention efforts concerning mental illness, Dr. Parran reported that while public contributions for infantile paralysis were estimated at $94 per victim annually, the corresponding figure for each victim of mental illness amounted to less than half a cent per year.

To reinforce his message, Wright cited a statement attributed to Dr. William Menninger, Chief Psychiatrist of the Army Medical Corps during World War II, in which he said: "Why is it that we have become so responsive to a cause like poliomyelitis, and have ignored so completely a problem like mental illness—one thousand times greater in magnitude?"

Chapter 3

A View From the Lion's Den

In February 1942, Warren Sawyer, a 22-year-old Quaker whose classification as a conscientious objector (CO) had been approved by his local draft board, was ordered to Marion, North Carolina, to serve in a Civilian Public Service (CPS) camp under the jurisdiction of the National Park Service. Sawyer and about 150 other COs sent to that camp were assigned to various tasks that involved maintaining the parklands under that agency's supervision.

At about the same time, Selective Service, responding to pressures to provide more meaningful service opportunities to COs than those offered in the CPS base camps, agreed to permit COs to volunteer as attendants in state mental hospitals then facing acute staffing problems because of the war economy. Over the next four years, about one in four of the 12,000 young men classified as COs was granted permission to volunteer for assignment to one of the 61 state mental hospitals and state training schools for the retarded.

In accord with his wishes, Sawyer was transferred to the CPS unit at Philadelphia State Hospital in September 1942. He remained there until his discharge in January 1946. This chapter contains excerpts from letters that he wrote home throughout his stay at Byberry, the familiar name by which the hospital had come to be known. These letters were selected as an integral feature of *The Turning Point* because they provide an intimate glimpse of what it was like to be a CO working in a state hospital during a particularly stressful period. At that time, Byberry more closely resembled the notorious Bedlam of the eighteenth century than an institution of the enlightened twentieth century.

Sawyer's letters capture, poignantly and accurately, the conditions that approximately 600,000 mental patients in the United States were forced to endure at that time. Many institutions did not sink to the levels of degradation that prevailed at Byberry in the 1940s. But in all state hospitals at that time, custodial care—not treatment—was the overriding concern. The average per capita expenditure for patients in state hospitals at that time was less than $4 per week!

In the pages that follow, Sawyer reveals the specter of fear and aura of punishment that hung heavy in so many state hospitals. He chronicles the almost continual daily confrontations with physical violence that both patients and attendants faced from morning to night. He brings to light his endless frustrations in trying to provide the patients in his care with such daily essentials as soap, clothing, bedding, toilet tissue, and a host of other simple needs. Then, too, there were times when impending outbursts of violence were thwarted by expressions of tender loving care. Glimpses of these experiences are also shared with the reader.[1]

1942

September 24th

. . . I have been very busy getting rearranged in my new work. This hospital—Philadelphia State Hospital, also known as Byberry—is the second largest of its kind in the U.S.A. It has 6,100 patients in residence. Before the war, it was staffed by over 65 doctors. Now there are only 18, plus a few interns. Similarly, there was one attendant for every 25 patients; now there is only one attendant for every 500 patients. As you can see, the hospital is severely understaffed.

My hours yesterday and today were from 7 A.M. to 4:30 P.M. Tomorrow I'm assigned to the infirmary where my hours will run from 2 P.M. to 11 P.M. Within these hours, we're entitled to have our meals. For the next eight weeks, we're to be given six hours off from our ward duties each week to attend classes designed to help us understand the nature of mental illness. In these sessions, presided over by a hospital physician, we're given a chance to observe patients as well as listen to lectures and observe demonstrations. This is the first time that the hospital has ever conducted such classes for its attendant staff.

The buildings for the most part are only two stories high. To house so many patients, you can imagine how extensive the grounds must be. With so much walking to get to work, to class, and back home again, my feet are taking a beating. It's a mile each way and we have to do this routine several times a day. And when we're on ward duty, we're on our feet all the time.

Our quarters are very nice. The beds are all in one room. The reason for this is that the men sharing these quarters are all on different shifts. Our dressers and clothing are in a different room so as not to annoy those who may be sleeping.

Saw a patient die tonight of senile decay. He was really just skin and bones. I never had seen a human skeleton before. His waist was less than three inches from front to back. And he weighed but 35 pounds!

September 27th

Thursday, we had a meeting with Dr. Zeller, the hospital's superintendent. He remarked that since the COs had arrived, he had noticed a distinct improvement in cleanliness throughout the hospital. He also observed that patients were receiving better treatment since our arrival. "There was far less beating of patients by attendants," he noted. He expressed the opinion that the regular attendant staff had been influenced by our behavior and were beginning to use a kindlier approach in dealing with patients. I do like the work here and have tried to understand the feelings and problems of the patients with whom I come in contact. . . . I must also add that the morale of the men in our unit is high.

October 11th

Everything here is going well. . . . Before I go off night duty at 7 in the morning, I have to see that all the beds on the ward are clean and made up. One other fellow is on duty with me, and we have 50 beds to take care of between us. The other night when changing beds I became nauseated from the stench and smells of dirty linen.

This week, I am going over to Building A which is where 350

incontinent male patients are housed. . . . Nearly all the patients on this ward are naked from morning to night. A worker-patient does nothing all day but continually mop the filth from the floor. The rumor is that a group of men from our unit is to be given complete responsibility for staffing this building.

October 17th

I can't be home for Christmas, but I have 14 days furlough coming to me. I will try to get there over New Year's Day. . . . Last night I learned how to wrap a body for the morgue. At first it seemed like a repulsive job. But after I got up my nerve to touch the body and closed the eyes and mouth, it was not so bad. . . . Received my uniform today—white coat and tailored pants. . . . I'm now working on a ward with another CO. Before that I was sharing responsibility for the ward with one of the regular attendants. He had absolutely no compassion for the patients. When moving patients from one side of the bed to the other, he would yank them as if they were paralyzed, or had broken hips, or some other major disability. . . . It made me angry to see him treating the patients in this manner so I reported him to our supervisor. Within two days he was transferred to another building where he no longer works directly with patients.

November 8th

Some of my patients are beginning to show real improvement. They're beginning to ask for a bottle or bed pan. One of the patients with diarrhea has learned to go to the bathroom. When we first arrived, the patients seemed to be in a constant state of fright. They were especially afraid of the physical abuse to which they had been subjected by uncaring attendants. Since we've taken over the ward, and this is also true of other wards and buildings for which we are in complete charge, the patients have come to trust us and have become responsive to our requests.

November 22nd

Thank you for the dollar, Aunt Jane. It will be used for Christmas, and will have to cover a lot of territory. . . . Do the kids back home know about my stand as a CO? . . . One of my fellow COs whose

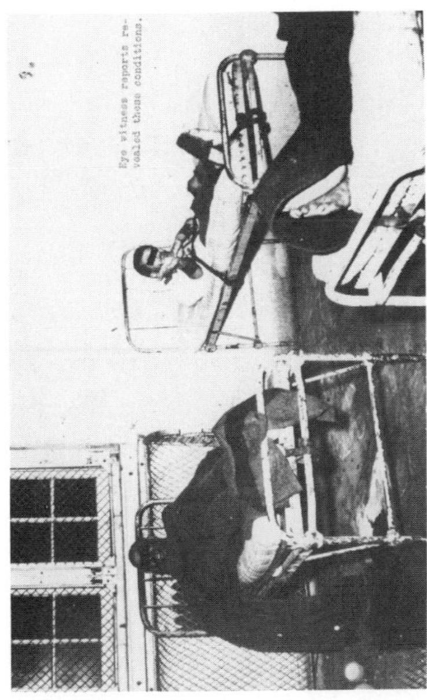

Scenes from Philadelphia State Hospital (Byberry) between 1942 and 1946. Photographer: Charles Lord.

home is in Florida can't visit there because the last time he was there, the neighbors ran him out of town. He's vowed not to go back home until after the war ends. . . . Many of the Quaker families in the vicinity of the hospital have extended Thanksgiving Day invitations to members of our unit.

December 15th

. . . I've been trying hard to make some money to help pay for my visit home next month. Our monthly $2.50 allowance from the hospital doesn't stretch very far, so when I learned that I could get $7.00 for giving a pint of blood, I went downtown to do so. I used $2.00 for the remaining presents. This left $5.00 to help pay for the round trip to Aurora. . . . The physician in charge of the physical well-being of the men in our unit is undertaking a study designed to understand the traits and characteristics of those like us who have volunteered for service in mental hospitals. Right after the first of the year, we're expecting another 15 men to join our unit.

1943

January 23rd

The first night back on duty after my furlough, we had a terrific struggle with a patient. He was a huge fellow and had had an epileptic seizure. He had managed to grab the night supervisor by the neck and was choking him. Several other attendants, hearing the commotion, came just in time to rescue him. In all, it took six of us to calm him down. The struggle went on for nearly an hour, but we finally succeeded in immobilizing him with cuffs and restraints. . . . A case of small pox has been reported in one of the buildings. We've all had to be vaccinated. Though the hospital has been quarantined, and no visitors are allowed to come to the institution, the staff is allowed to leave the grounds.

February 7th

I've been transferred to day shift duty. A great deal of my time is spent changing bandages on patients with bed sores. . . . My co-worker on this ward is also a member of our CPS unit, but we have very different approaches to our assignment. His primary concern is in the physical appearance of the ward and the patients. He shows little or no interest in the patients as individuals. On the other hand, I want to spend time talking with them so I can relate to them as persons. This difference in attitudes toward our patients is generating tension between us.

March 22nd

The big news I had hoped to pass on to you today was that our monthly allowance of $2.50 had been increased to $12.50. But we received word from Harrisburg, it was not to be so. . . . I've been promoted to Charge Attendant. In this capacity, I will be serving as the key staff person on the ward to which I've been assigned.

April 5th

Our unit's strength is still limited to 27 men. The administration has been experiencing difficulty in getting additional COs because the employees' union is raising a rumpus. It's their feeling that our presence is undercutting their bargaining status in seeking higher wages. But it is nothing of the sort. The hospital could easily use 300 more attendants if they were available. Most of the male wards are covered by at least one attendant. However, there are several buildings where there is only one attendant on duty for several wards. The situation is far more critical on the female wards. In many instances, there is only one attendant on duty for an entire building. . . . Lately, I've been spending considerable time bandaging broken jaws received by patients in Building B, living quarters for those patients who are considered prone to violence. Many of the injuries sustained by patients were caused by attendants on duty while trying to maintain order. In this entire building, the normal complement of attendants should be 12. But at any one time, there are only three on duty.

April 27th

Last week I was assigned to work in Building A where the incontinent patients are housed. Earlier this week I was placed on duty in

Building B which I described in a previous letter. I was asked to take the 2 P.M. to 11 P.M. shift, and agreed to do so on a temporary basis. In one struggle to separate two fighting patients, my glasses got bent. This is a perfect setting in which to demonstrate the superiority of pacifism over brute force in handling tense situations. If you can convey to patients that you're not afraid of them and respect them as individuals—even though you're shaking in your boots—they return your respect. A few attendants have had their jaws smashed, but they're usually the ones who approach troublesome patients with broom handles and other similar weapons. When patients sense that you feel safe and have the situation in command without the threat of force, they are much more amenable to following instructions. I've already broken up several fights using this technique, and it works.

May 3rd

We've just learned that Selective Service has approved sending an additional 70 COs to Byberry. Twenty of the new arrivals will be coming to participate as guinea pigs in an experiment designed to test new approaches in treating yellow jaundice. They will be injected with the jaundice virus and then monitored over an extended period of time. The remaining 50 men will be assigned to hospital duty.

May 10th

Under the auspices of the American Friends Service Committee, a unit of 25 young women, with pacifist views similar to ours, will be arriving shortly to assist in easing the acute shortage of attendants on the female wards.

May 24th

Thursday, I was called to the phone and told to report to the farm at 1 P.M. the next day. I was placed in charge of a crew of worker-patients. For the rest of the day, we weeded onions. It was an exhausting and tiring afternoon, and I got a bad sunburn on my arm, to boot. The next day it rained, but our crew went out anyway and we weeded more onions. The following day, we shoveled 100 tons of coal from two box cars. There were 12 patients in my crew, five of whom were from the so-called violent ward. Over a two-day period, two of the patients in my crew managed to escape.

June 14th

A week ago, I went along with three other fellows from our unit to Norristown State Hospital (about 30 miles west of Byberry) to visit a Mennonite-sponsored CPS unit stationed there.

There are 93 COs in that unit. In addition, 100 regular attendants are employed to cover the male wards with a patient population of 2,100. With nearly 200 attendants to service these patients, Norristown is in a far superior position than Byberry to cover their wards. We only have 100 attendants to care for 3,500 male patients. Their incontinent ward was remarkably clean. Even more startling was that almost all of their patients were wearing suits and ties. Our patients are lucky if they have a pair of pants—let alone one that fits. . . . Word has come down from Selective Service that approval has been given to a $15 monthly allowance for all men working in CPS mental hospital units. Because of procedural red tape, it'll probably take a few months before it takes effect.

August 9th

We're still waiting to get our approved $15 monthly allowance.

August 16th

Last Wednesday, we celebrated the opening of our CPS unit here at Byberry a year ago. The dinner was provided by the hospital and attended by several members of the medical staff. Also joining us were several guests from the American Friends Service Committee, the official sponsoring agency of our unit.

Today, I had a run-in with the man who's in charge of the hospital farm. He has a consuming hatred toward all the fellows in our unit. He thinks we're cowards and "yellow-bellies"—no doubt because he has a son in the army overseas. Shortly after my assignment to the farm crew, he ceased to deal directly with me and instead gives his orders to me through an assistant. . . . He has little or no regard for the worker-patients whose labor is so essential to running the farm. In wet weather, the worker-patients who are ill-clothed to begin with are given no rubbers and are expected to work in muddy soil that reaches up to their knees. And to make matters worse, upon returning to their wards after a long day in the fields, are given no change of clothing.

August 31st

For the past five weeks, my farm crew and I have dug up 5,000 bushels of potatoes from this 40-acre plot. We still have three more potato fields to harvest, the largest of which covers 25 acres. . . . Our $15 monthly allowance is still tied up in red tape and Selective Service has advised the state agency responsible for oversight of Byberry that our unit will be transferred elsewhere if the matter is not promptly resolved.

October 1st

Yesterday I was told that the Jaundice Project was about to get under way. An army doctor who is conducting this experiment came to Byberry to visit me and another fellow CO, the first to be enrolled in the program. He took us to University Hospital where the experiment will be conducted. We were each given a few tests and then a battery of injections. After taking our medical histories, we returned to Byberry. My knowledge of jaundice is very scant at this time. We were told that they tried to run the experiment with animals as guinea pigs, but the results were unsatisfactory. The possibility of those of us in the experiment becoming ill with jaundice is slight, we were advised. We were asked not to spread word around about this project for security reasons.

October 11th

In further preparation for the jaundice experiment, we've had to be injected with a dye-like substance. We've also had to drink some vile-smelling, ink-like liquids which are supposed to facilitate reading X-ray tests to which we will be exposed.

October 29th

Last evening I escorted several worker-patients to a Halloween dance. The costumes were concocted from the funniest combinations of colors and designs. Though I had attended dances for the patients on previous occasions, I had never danced with any of those attending these affairs. Last night, however, I did join in and had a grand time. The worker-patients do so much for the hospital and get so little in return that it was a pleasure to see them having such a good time. Without their help, the institution's services would lapse into utter disaster.

November 29th

No, I haven't come down with jaundice yet. But I was really sick on Thanksgiving Day. All night long, I felt weak and had difficulty in breathing as well as becoming nauseous. But when I called Dr. Neefe, the physician in charge of the experiment, he didn't think I had come down with the disease. On Saturday, I was back to normal. Because of my assignment with the experiment, I was given a new responsibility. I'm now serving as secretary to Miss Veach, the head nurse of a building with 1,100 patients. I had done some typing for her on a previous occasion. She told me she liked my work and wanted me to take on this new chore on a permanent basis.

1944

January 11th

Our unit's strength has been increased to 125 men. In my current work assignment, I'm learning quite a bit about the inner workings of the hospital. In reviewing requisitions for last year's supplies, I discovered that not a single pair of socks, or even a shirt, had been ordered to replace those that had been worn out. Even now, many of the poorer patients do not have either socks or shirts. . . . Because of the attendant shortage on the female wards, which is so acute, the administration is considering assigning some of the male attendants to the female wards.

February 7th

Still no signs of jaundice. Every time I report to the University Hospital, I find myself getting edgier and edgier as I anticipate the four or five needle jabs I have to endure. My skin has become punctured so often that it seems to be getting resistant to the needles.

February 21st

I've decided to work one night a week in a settlement house located along the waterfront in downtown South Philadelphia. Juvenile delinquency has skyrocketed in many of the city's slum neighborhoods and members of our unit have been asked to consider serving as part-time workers in settlement houses. Our transportation is paid, and in addition we receive a modest fee for our labors. . . . You'll be pleased to learn that Dr. Neefe does not expect me to contract jaundice. He said that I had had slight symptoms of the disease a few weeks ago.

March 14th

This morning, while on my way to University Hospital for my jaundice tests, I noticed that someone had scribbled "COs won't fight" in large bold letters along one side of the bus. As the war drags on and the casualty reports begin escalating, I expect we'll be seeing a lot more of similar bursts of hostility directed at us. . . . The local newspapers have been running quite a few stories about COs both pro and con. I've been saving them. Twenty years from now, it'll be interesting to read them.

March 22nd

Byberry is really going to pieces. On Monday, a large piece of the ceiling in the violent ward dayroom collapsed, leaving a hole at least three feet square. From the first floor, you can look up through the beams holding up the second floor. The roof was exposed. Of course, when it rains, the roof leaks and the water pours right down to the floor of the dayroom. In Building C, where most of the patients with epilepsy are housed, the floor is so bad that the patients can pull the boards right out of the floor. The roof is so leaky there that when it rains, the water not only floods the dayroom, but also reaches the basement. Many of the fellows in our unit have the feeling that nobody seems to care about the rampant decay that is ravaging the institution and its inhabitants. The chief steward of the hospital has assigned all the carpenters on the payroll to remodeling his house. Four of the girls in the women's volunteer CPS unit have cracked up under the terrific strain to which they've been exposed.

Instead of installing locks on broken ward doors, all that the maintenance men can do to forestall patients from escaping is to nail the doors shut. Lights keep going out because of failures in the electrical system. And when that happens at night, especially on the ward with the violent-prone patients, and you're the only one on duty, which is usually the case, you've got a big, big problem.

Because of critical shortages during the war, most suppliers are unable to handle orders of the magnitude that Byberry needs. So when supplies are unavailable, as is usually the case, attendants are forced to wash sheets manually and then hang them over radiators to dry. Drains and toilets are constantly getting plugged up. It takes the maintenance crew so long to get around to fixing them that patients often find themselves living in the midst of stinking puddles. One of the physicians got so fed up with the daily hassles in getting needed supplies and services that he resigned. Members of our unit are now deployed in virtually every department of the hospital. The only exceptions are the laundry and the garage. . . . Incidentally, I've decided to drop out of the jaundice experiment.

May 15th

We're about to undergo the farce and mockery of a state investigation. In anticipation of the visit, we've been advised that the hydrotherapy service, which has been in disuse since our arrival two years ago, is to be reactivated. When the examiners have departed it'll no doubt be mothballed, once again.

May 23rd

The Investigating Commission descended on the hospital this week. It *was* a farce. Before their arrival, the Personnel Director made the attendants in Building A put up a scaffolding so that the ceiling in the dayroom could be cleaned. Shoes were brought to the building so that every patient could have a pair. For many of the patients, these were the first they had worn in months. Each of the patients was also given a clean shirt, the first they had seen in weeks. And to top it all, the staff in Building E was asked to send over 350 bedspreads so that there would be one for each patient's bed. As soon as the inspection was over, the spreads were ripped off the beds and returned to where they had come from.

July 6th

Earlier this week, we had a serious flare-up in Building B. One of the patients assigned there had previously been serving time in prison because he had tried to knife a police officer. The patient had pulled a knife on one of the attendants and had cut his thumb. An attendant who had come to his aid had his hand injured, and a patient who had come to their rescue suffered cuts on his head. . . . Our unit has set up a series of weekly meetings that are aimed at preparing us for the postwar era when we'll be free to reestablish our civilian careers. Those who are planning to go into the teaching professions are facing some real problems. In several states, laws have been enacted or are in the process of being considered which contain provisions effectively barring COs from employment in public school systems. I recently heard that one of my former campmates, who had been released from the CPS program by Selective Service, had been run out of his hometown when he applied for a teaching post in one of the local schools. He landed a bookkeeping job in another state. In a letter describing his ordeal, he wrote that he had come close to being beaten before he managed to escape.

August 8th

The attendants in Building A wanted to take the patients outside for a walk today. But because they didn't have enough trousers, or even underpants for their charges, they were stymied. Had they drawn on the scant supply of these garments, then the patients who have visitors on the two regular weekly visiting days would have had nothing to wear for these occasions.

August 21st

. . . We now have our full complement of 96 men. . . . On Saturday, a murder was narrowly averted on the violent ward. The situation there has reached a state of bedlam. Patients are removing restraints from each other. Window screens are being torn off windows. . . . The toilets and urinals keep flowing constantly, flooding all the floors. Those in our unit assigned to this building are reaching the breaking point because of the constantly prevailing state of strain and tension.

There's a hospital rule that all outgoing mail from patients must be censored by the nursing staff before it can be sent. If the nurse reviewing the letter disapproves of its contents, it's usually put into the trash. The tragedy is that if the patient's letter doesn't pass inspection, he or she is never told. Byberry is supposed to be a hospital where patients are to receive care and treatment, yet in many respects they are treated as if they were criminals.

August 29th

One of the significant developments that has emerged from the presence of our unit here at Byberry is the publication of a periodical called *The Attendant.* It's a modest publication which features constructive suggestions for handling mental patients. The articles for it are being provided by men in various CPS units throughout the country. Selective Service has been so impressed by this development, as well as a corollary effort by four men in our unit to establish a clearinghouse through which men in all units can share their experiences and constructive suggestions, that it is now considering assigning these four men to carry out this program on a full-time basis.

This week, the hospital's Chief Nurse issued a directive to all patients' services throughout the institution. The attendants in Building A had conniptions when they read the instructions. As you will remember, this is the building housing the incontinent patients. The instructions stipulated that in the case of incontinent patients attendants must be sure to take bedpans and urinals to each of their patients every two hours. The entire building only has two serviceable bedpans and not a single urinal. The orders go on to state that patients must have their teeth brushed at regular intervals. Patients in this building haven't seen a toothbrush since they first arrived. The directive also calls for trimming patients' fingernails and toenails at regular periods. Since neither clippers nor scissors have been provided to the attendants, no instructions are included as to how these duties are to be performed. Is it any wonder that our exasperation-quotient keeps rising?

September 27th

A week ago one of the patients in Building A was observed to have swallowed a spoon. He was taken to X ray where they discovered he already had three other spoons in his stomach.

October 2nd

I've just learned that Dr. Stokes, who was responsible for initiating the jaundice experiment, has been asked to go to Italy to report on his findings from this program. He is expected to be involved in setting up a prevention program based on the results from the experiment. I feel grateful to have had an opportunity to participate in this project.

October 10th

Two nights a week from now 'til Christmas, I will be moonlighting to earn some extra money at Friends' Hospital, a private psychiatric hospital. This place is a hospital in the true meaning of that word. I've been assigned to the so-called most difficult ward. In all, there are 11 patients on this ward, only one of whom is incontinent. The floor has rugs—there are stuffed chairs throughout the ward, along with floor lamps and tables with plenty of reading matter. Patients are referred to as guests. The fees for their care and treatment run about $60 a week. They come from a wide range of backgrounds. One was formerly the superintendent of a school for the blind; another is a former college professor who has traveled extensively throughout Europe, and can speak fluently in five languages. The others are equally fascinating.

October 15th

One night last week when I was on duty at Friends' Hospital, the patient who had been a college professor came up to me and said: "I'm so glad for the nights you're on duty because you give me so much cheer." . . . The size of our unit at Byberry has just been raised to 135 men, making it the largest of any of the CPS units serving in a state hospital or state training school for the retarded.

November 26th

For several weeks now, I've been trying to take a few courses at the University of Pennsylvania during my free time. When I was on the office detail, I was able to handle the subjects. But now that I've been reassigned to the wards again, it's been difficult to do justice to both my job and studies.

1945

January 4th

. . . I'm seriously considering applying for a transfer to a CPS hookworm project operating in Florida. The CPS unit there has done an excellent job of aiding several poverty-stricken rural communities in building privies to forestall hookworm infestation that had been prevalent in their neighborhoods.

January 21st

In the last two weeks, one of my co-workers had his jaw splintered when a newly admitted patient attacked him. The teeth on one side of his jaw may have to be pulled. . . . I, too, was another victim of violence when a patient hit me in the mouth. There was some bleeding, but fortunately, it was only a minor injury. One of the serious disadvantages under which we work is that if we are seriously injured or incapacitated, none of us in the CPS units is covered by insurance or workmen's compensation.

February 5th

Today is my day off. And coincidentally, it's my third anniversary in CPS. Much has happened to the world in the last three years, and much has happened in my small world. I've learned a lot about people and, more importantly, how to get along with people. And I've learned that there is more to living the life of a CO than simply being opposed to war and violence. Here in the hospital with its almost cynical disregard of human values, I've experienced how love and understanding can touch and move even the most irrational among us. Since I was transferred out of my office job, I've been working in the building for incontinent patients. In normal times, about 15 attendants were assigned to this service. Now there are just three of us. We're supposed to bathe the patients daily. But four weeks ago, the plumbers removed the old showers and we're still waiting for replacements. You can imagine what the dayroom must smell like during such an extended lack of bathing facilities. . . . Fridays are when patients normally get shaved—by other patients. Some of them manage to do a creditable job. It's almost like seeing the patients thrown to the lions. Everywhere you see faces scarred with nicks, and blood oozing from cuts and scratches. It's a ritual the patients dread.

February 22nd

Today we received the first black CO addition to our unit. Because of the institution's long-standing prejudice against hiring blacks he may run into some flak. I sincerely hope not.

March 18th

The assistant superintendent has ordered that new showers must be installed on our ward by tomorrow. Many of the patients have had to do without showers for several weeks.

April 14th

It was quite a shock today when we learned that President Roosevelt had died. I can't imagine how Mr. Truman will be able to take his place. . . . The good news today was that I was transferred back to office duty where I had previously been assigned.

May 1st

Last Friday evening I enjoyed a new experience. Our CPS choral group was invited to sing and entertain at a detention camp for enemy aliens, just outside Camden, N.J. After singing for them, we sat around and had a chance to converse with them. The facility had a very grim, prison-like setting. The windows were barred and the entire building encircled with a high wire fence. Fifty of the inmates were women about evenly divided between Germans and Italians. A few other nationalities were represented among the 90 or so male detainees.

May 7th

A few days ago, a tragic event occurred in the building set aside for patients with epilepsy. The attendants discovered that one of the patients was missing more than half of one of his ears. Teethmarks on the lacerated ear indicated that another patient had been the culprit. This isn't an everyday occurrence, but the incident reflects the constant state of fear that permeates many of the institution's wards. . . . This morning we learned that Germany had surrendered.

June 4th

The women's unit is beginning to fill up now that summer is upon us. The girls who volunteer for this unit are recruited from various colleges by the American Friends Service Committee. Similar units are being recruited by the Mennonites and the Brethren for those institutions for which they have administrative responsibilities.

June 11th

The really big news this week is that Ruth and I have formally announced our engagement. As I've told you on recent visits home, she comes from a wonderful Quaker family. She teaches school and is in complete empathy with me and my stand as a pacifist.

August 6th

This week, a decision was made by the authorities to make a thorough search of the entire building for hidden knives, razors, and other hazardous implements that could easily become lethal weapons in the hands of the wrong patients. I won't burden you with the entire list of dangerous articles that were confiscated but they included such items as a hacksaw hidden in a mattress, pieces of razor blades in a patient's mouth, and knives hidden in clothing. One patient who is almost constantly strapped in bed had a knife blade secreted on his body. These and other similar items are often smuggled into the hospital by parole patients, visitors, and others.

September 25th

The discharge situation is looking bright. . . . There is an excellent chance that my release will take place next February. It appears that Selective Service may have reached an understanding with the church agencies administering the CPS program, that discharges of CPS men can get under way if they are not accompanied by undue publicity.

October 17th

The big day in our lives—our wedding day—has come and gone. It was a day that Ruth and I will cherish forever.

November 20th

The staff situation is getting real grim now that men from our unit are being discharged and returning to their homes. Those who have accumulated furlough time are going on leave so as not to lose what they had earned. . . . The other day, one of our co-workers found a patient on his ward gagging for breath. It turned out that in an attempt at suicide, he had tightly tied a shoe lace around his neck. Fortunately, he was saved in the proverbial "nick of time."

December 5th

I've received word that I'm on the list of those to be discharged next month. Men who worked here as attendants before the war are beginning to return to take up their previous assignments. One of the first of these returnees was an attendant at the time of my arrival at Byberry. I recall one incident when he pushed one of the patients in his charge down the stairs and then proceeded to kick him on the head. Several of the regular attendants who've been here through the war have been on a drunken binge for the past few weeks. Under these circumstances, trying to get the wards adequately staffed has become an almost impossible task.

1946

January 7th

Rumors have been floating around the hospital that a reporter and photographer from *Life Magazine* are coming to the institution to do a picture story on Building A, which houses most of the incontinent patients.

January 21st

My discharge arrived on the 14th and I'm finally a free man! . . . For the time being, I've decided to stay on at the hospital in the office position I've been holding down in the recent past. I was given a grade A rating and will be earning $81.50 per month plus room and board.

At the end of a few months, when I will have accumulated some much-needed money, I expect to apply for a cattle-boat project sponsored by the Brethren Service Committee. They are recruiting ex-CPS men to assist in transporting cattle and horses to Poland. The fellows are needed to care for the animals while they are on the high seas. Each trip lasts about six weeks, and those who participate in the program receive $150 for their services.

Several of the fellows still in the CPS unit at Byberry are initiating a campaign to publicize the truth about the hospital. We're hoping to get the cooperation of the Philadelphia newspapers in this effort. . . . Our intent is to avoid putting the blame on individuals but focus instead on such issues as difficulties in staffing the hospital because of the low prevailing wages, persistent problems in getting adequate supplies for the patients, and the horrendous delays in getting a response to breakdowns in the institution's infrastructure. In this context, we plan to reveal how state hospitals in some other states like California, New York, Michigan, and others are responding to the needs of their patients. Our ultimate objective is to arouse public pressure on the state legislature to increase the budgets for state facilities like ours so that patients may have access to more enlightened care and treatment.

February 5th

We're noticing an increased attention being given to news about state hospitals in this area by the local newspapers. In particular, concerns are being voiced by readers through letters to the editor.

February 11th

Yesterday morning, the *Philadelphia Record* ran a front-page story concerning problems rampant at Byberry.

February 19th

As a result of the press coverage that has been directed at Byberry in the past few weeks, the head of the State Department of Welfare, the agency that administers state institutions like ours, paid the hospital a visit. She has had little or no use for the men in our CPS unit. As she was inspecting Building B, she turned to one of our men on duty and muttered—"You fellows seem to have more time to write letters to the newspapers than to clean the floors." Just prior to the time of her visit, one of the patients in restraint had urinated on the floor. For close to a year, no mops have been available for any of the wards in our service. We have had to resort to using towels to handle such problems, but towels are chronically in short supply.

March 18th

Today I will be leaving Byberry at long last. . . . I'm certainly glad to be leaving this place after three years and five and a half months. As I take leave, I have a wonderful sense of relief and release. At the same time, I leave with a deep sense of frustration that the patients whom we've tried so hard to serve under the most difficult circumstances are little better off than when we first arrived. I must close with one final observation—what an even more tragic place Byberry might have been in this war period had it not been for the presence of our CPS unit.

Chapter 4

Agents for Social Change: Part One

> Even admitting that all conscientious objectors are not alike, most of them exemplify qualities of mind and heart that no people ever will get too much of. . . .
>
> Excerpt from an editorial that appeared October 16, 1942, in *The Hartford Courant*

The first suggestions for establishing Civilian Public Service (CPS) units in state mental hospitals during World War II came from a group of conscientious objectors (COs) then assigned to two U.S. Forestry Service units. These were located at Royalston and Petersham, Massachusetts. In their attempt to seek more socially significant work for their labors, they had sought the help of a YMCA secretary in a nearby community. He in turn had addressed their request to the superintendent of nearby Gardner State Hospital. Dr. Charles Thompson, then superintendent of that institution, brought the idea to the state commissioner of mental health. After a series of lengthy negotiations, approval was forthcoming for establishing a CPS unit at the hospital. It was officially slated to open April 1, 1942, under the auspices of the American Friends Service Committee.[1]

Less than 10 days before the scheduled opening date of the unit at Gardner, the executive committee of the Massachusetts Department of the American Legion met and condemned the assignment of the COs to the state hospital as "un-American." They proposed instead that COs be sent abroad to do "menial work for the soldiers—to give aid to the wounded—bury the dead—and to dig latrines."[1] In response to this reaction, the proposed project was abandoned just as the first contingent of the CPS unit was preparing to leave for Gardner.

At the same time that the Gardner unit was in the formative stages, a similar unit was in the process of organizing for placement at Elgin State Hospital in Illinois under the auspices of the Brethren. Like other state hospitals throughout the country, the Elgin facility was experiencing the same critical staff shortages and was eager to tap into this unexpected labor pool. The Elgin CPS unit had been scheduled to open on January 21, 1942, after a prolonged series of negotiations. Men who had been selected for this unit were already en route by train when word was received that the project had to be abandoned because of adamant protests by the local chapter of the American Legion and the labor union representing staff personnel at the hospital.

The first CPS mental hospital unit finally did become operative at the Eastern State Hospital at Williamsburg, Virginia, in June 1942, under the auspices of the American Friends Service Committee. This hospital had the distinction of being the first state mental hospital in the United States.

As one CPS mental hospital unit after another became operative, Mary E. Corcoran, R.N., a staff member of the U.S. Public Health Service and consultant to Selective Service concerning this program, made this observation:[2]

> The patients in many mental hospitals are receiving very considerate care by the COs who have volunteered to work in these institutions. . . . The majority of the men I have seen on the wards of the 12 state hospitals I have visited are doing well by their patients. In some cases they present very good examples in personal behavior to the other employees.

As the men in these units began to experience firsthand the miserable existence into which so many of the nation's mentally ill and developmentally disabled had been thrust, they were dumbstruck with disbelief. They had expected to find themselves amid the therapeutic milieu of a hospital. Instead, they quickly learned that their primary function was to maintain some semblance of order among those entrusted to their care. Almost without exception, men assigned to these units were given little or no training before or after they reported to their ward assignments. It was not at all unusual for a member of the CPS unit to find himself the lone attendant on a ward with 100 or more patients on his first day or night of duty. This was an especially traumatic experience for those who happened to be assigned to the 11 P.M. to 7 A.M. shift with only a flashlight for support.

In at least one institution, the CPS men were issued blue uniforms with brass buttons, attire more typical of that worn by prison guards of the era. Even the women attendants were garbed in gray, striped uniforms such as those worn by matrons in prison settings. But no matter what kind of uniforms prevailed, state mental hospitals in the mid-1940s had a prison environment. Virtually all state hospital wards were locked. Attendants were the gatekeepers. Windows were invariably barred. When patients were taken out of the wards for any purpose, they were accompanied by one or more attendants. At these times, especially when large numbers of patients were involved, it was a regular ritual to count the patients as they left the wards and again on their reentry to be certain that no one had eloped.

Roots of the Problem

To understand why so many state hospitals and state facilities for mentally retarded people fell so far short of fulfilling their mission to care for and treat their patients, one must be aware of the difficulties they faced at that time. First and foremost, the war effort had drained away so many physicians, nurses, occupational and recreational therapists, social workers, and attendants that these institutions could barely provide custodial care—let alone their customary range of medical and nursing services. In many institutions, it was not unusual for one physician to be responsible for 1,000 or more patients. In many instances, few—if any—remaining members of these institutions' medical staffs were certified as psychiatrists.

Trained attendants were even more scarce in this period. In some institutions, the situation was so severe that only one attendant would be on duty to oversee entire buildings housing as many as 500 patients. To provide some semblance of coverage, virtually every state institution had to rely on worker-patients to fill the void for attendant personnel. In most instances, these were individuals whose mental illness was in a state of remission and for whom discharge was not a viable option as they had no families to accept responsibility for them. To comprehend fully the enormity of the personnel problem during that period, compare it with the current-day situation at state hospitals, where there is roughly one attendant for every two or three patients. In many such facilities, the attendant staff outnumbers the patient census.

The acute personnel shortages during that period were reflected by the conditions that prevailed at the Philadelphia State Hospital (Byberry). In early 1941, it had approximately 1,000 employees. It had been designed to accommodate a caseload of 2,500 patients, but could handle as many as 3,500 patients if necessary. As of October 1942, its employee staff had dropped to 200, while its walls bulged with 6,000 patients in residence. Most similar institutions at that time were just as critically understaffed.

In this same era, the average cost of treating and caring for mental patients in state institutions ranged from a low of about 40 cents per day to as much as 90 cents per day. In private mental hospitals at that time, the comparable per capita cost was about $7 per day. By the early 1990s, per capita costs for patients in state mental hospitals had climbed to about $200 per day, and comparable costs in private mental hospitals were considerably higher.

Other factors that discouraged able and qualified persons from applying for positions as ward attendants in the 1940s were the long work week to which they had to submit and the abysmally low wage scales then prevailing. At that time the average work week was six days. Attendants were required to work a minimum of 54 hours and up to as many as 80 hours. In many instances, they also were required to work split shifts, during which they would report for duty from 7 A.M. until noon, then be off duty until 4 P.M., at which time they would go back on duty until 9 P.M. when they would be relieved by the night shift. For such a schedule, their monthly salaries ranged from a minimum of $40 to a maximum of $90, plus room and board.

For the most part, state hospitals of that period were isolated from the communities in which they were located. Fences usually surrounded the cluster of buildings that comprised the patients' quarters. Even more insidious was the invisible wall of fear and ignorance that kept these institutions hidden from public concern and awareness.

It was an era in which if you happened to be a black person with a serious mental illness, the only available option was the state hospital. The welcome mat was not out for black individuals seeking treatment in a private psychiatric hospital. Although black persons were accepted at public institutions, more often than not they were assigned to segregated wards or placed on wards where they were often subjected to discriminatory behavior. As for qualified black persons seeking employment in mental hospitals, the doors—almost without exception—were closed.[3]

But the doors of these same state mental hospitals were wide open to white persons seeking employment as attendants. Practically no one who applied for an attendant's position was turned away. Many of these applicants were drifters, also referred to as "bughousers." They would stay just long enough to accumulate enough money to pay for an orgy of drinking and carousing. When the party was over—usually within a month or several weeks—they would move on to the next-nearest state institution for their customary brief period of employment. It was not uncommon for some of these drifters to brag about having worked in as many as 100 or more state hospitals from coast to coast.

Once a new employee was hired as an attendant, he or she would customarily be assigned to a ward by the nursing office without having to undergo any training or orientation. The overriding concern was to fill as many vacancies as possible, with little or no regard for the person's qualifications. Not all applicants could be described as drifters, or bughousers, but those who fitted this category were defined in the following way by Leo Baldwin, a member of the CPS unit at Western State Hospital in Fort Steilacoom, Washington, in a newsletter published by his unit:

> The bughouser bases his attitude toward mental patients upon the age-old argument that in order to control a person, you must first establish authority over him. . . . This is especially true with mental patients because they are not rational. . . . You can't do business with a mad person unless you are prepared to render him practically helpless, and then tell him what to do, and when to do it.

Needless to say, the bughouser's philosophy of patient care violated all basic tenets for providing the kind of therapeutic milieu so essential to the well-being of mentally ill people. Not all attendants in the 1940s subscribed to the above philosophy, but enough of the regular attendant staff did to make it the prevailing attitude of ward personnel at the time when the CPS units began making their appearance in mental hospitals.

What Set the COs Apart

To understand the reactions of COs to the mental hospital scene, it is important to understand what set them apart from the rest of the institutional staff.

First and foremost, COs had been required by their local draft boards to demonstrate satisfactorily that their grounds for claiming exemption from military service were based on religious training and belief.

Another significant factor that set the CPS men apart was that, as a group, they were well above the average employee in intelligence, education, and job experience. In the CPS units administered by the American Friends Service Committee, the men averaged 15 years of formal education. At the time of their induction, many of the men had been employed as teachers at the high school or college level. Quite a few had been trained as research scientists, lawyers, artists, and musicians and in other similar professions. Except in a very few instances, the capabilities that men in the CPS mental hospital units brought with them were never used.

In an article published in *The Psychiatric Quarterly Supplement* in 1948, two physicians, Robert A. Clark and Alex M. Burgess, had this to say about what differentiated the COs assigned to state mental hospitals during World War II from the regular rank and file of attendants.[4]

> Besides intelligence, education, and skills not often found, most of these men brought to their positions a high level of idealistic humanitarianism. Since they volunteered for hospital service, they were largely self-selected. As they were at the bottom of the state hospital hierarchy, they had unparalleled opportunities for continual and close observation. . . .
>
> Very soon after they began working, it became obvious to the men in the CPS mental hospital units that not only was their own orientation and training insufficient, but also that the care of the patients was woefully inadequate in nearly every respect. This inadequacy resulted in almost general neglect and not infrequent brutality. There was overcrowding into old and dangerous buildings.
>
> In many hospitals there was an absence of a minimum standard of medical care. Nowhere was there an approach to the maximum medical need because of shortages in trained professional staff, as well as for medicines and medical equipment. Consequently, even good custodial care was seldom being given. Though these conditions were accentuated by the war, it was evident that in many institutions much the same state of affairs had existed before and would continue afterward. In some hospitals, conditions were worse than in others, but in none were they ideal.
>
> First the COs began comparing notes among themselves, then seeking methods of reaching the public with their findings. Articles began to appear in newspapers and magazines, written or inspired by men in the CPS mental hospital units, and often illustrated by photos taken by them. Sympathetic superintendents often helped with, or gave permission for these articles. . . .
>
> Probably the most far-reaching event in its effects was the publication in *The Cleveland Press* in the fall of 1943 of a series of articles concerning the Cleveland (Ohio) State Hospital. Discovering unusually bad conditions there, the men in the CPS unit at first

complained to their supervisors, then to the physicians and the superintendent. Getting only rebuffs, they carried their concerns to Walter Lerch, a staff reporter for *The Cleveland Press,* who in turn prepared a series of articles for publication.

COs Help Expose Bad Conditions at Cleveland State Hospital

Walter Lerch's hard-hitting and graphic accounts of the state of affairs at Cleveland State Hospital began appearing on October 7, 1943. For the next two months, over 20 news stories and special front-page features brought home to the Cleveland community the shocking state of affairs that prevailed at their state hospital. Lerch's vivid accounts of goings-on at the institution were introduced by blaring headlines such as the following:

Mental Patients Here Beaten and Shackled

Food for Mental Patients "Revolting"

Seeks to Fire Eight in Hospital Probe

Lerch's persistence in bringing to light the many ways in which the hospital failed to meet its obligations to serve mentally ill people committed to its care sparked the indignation of many of the leading citizens of Cleveland. Foremost among these was the Reverend Dr. D. R. Sharpe, a highly respected Baptist clergyman. It wasn't long after the newspaper began its relentless exposé of conditions at Cleveland State Hospital that a grand jury investigation of conditions at the hospital was authorized. Dr. Sharpe was named as leader of the grand jury.

In several editorials, *The Cleveland Press* called for the resignation of Dr. Hans Lee, Superintendent of Cleveland State Hospital, who had been directing the hospital administration at that time.

In mid-1944, Dr. Lee was transferred at his request to another assignment within the state. But before leaving his post, Dr. Lee made arrangements with Selective Service to close out the 23-man CPS unit at the hospital. The men were transferred to other state hospitals where they were readily accepted. Within a year, the new administration at the institution had requested the placement of a new CPS unit, and Selective Service complied with the request.

When the findings of the grand jury investigation were finally released, the highly respected journalist Albert Deutsch used them as the basis for a series of syndicated articles, originally published in the spring of 1946 in the New York City newspaper *PM.* In his account Deutsch reported:

> One of the strangest and most terrible indictments in American legal history was handed up in 1945 by the Regular Grand Jury of Cuyahoga County, Ohio. The presentment resulted from an official investigation of the Cleveland State Hospital, a state-owned facility for mental patients. . . . No single individual was indicted in this presentment. An entire community and a whole social system were indicted. The indictment read as follows:
>
>> The Grand Jury is shocked beyond words that a so-called civilized society would allow fellow human beings to be mistreated as they are at the Cleveland State Hospital. No enlightened community dare tolerate the conditions that exist at this institution. . . .
>>
>> It would be a prison for the well. It is a hell for the sick. . . .
>>
>> We indict the uncivilized social system which in the first instance has enabled such an intolerable and barbaric practice to fasten itself upon the people and which in the second instance permits it to continue.
>>
>> We are told these inhuman conditions have long existed. If this be so, we indict all who have abetted, or even tolerated, such foul treatment of these unfortunate ill, even as history will indict us if we fail to redress this ancient and inexcusable wrong.
>>
>> The Grand Jury condemns the whole socio-political system that today allows this unholy thing to exist in our State of Ohio. The responsibility is widespread and it must be met.

CLEVELAND, MONDAY, OCTOBER 25, 1943

Mental Patients Here Beaten and Shackled

By WALTER LEACH

Wielding bare fists or wet towels, attendants at Cleveland State Hospital in recent weeks have beaten mentally ill patients into submission.

This is a violation of both criminal laws and Ohio Welfare Department regulations.

Other patients who resist the brute force method of mental "mistreatment" are kept for days in solitary confinement in strong rooms or placed in shackles to restrict their movements.

On a typical day anywhere from 50 to 6? patients may be under restraints at the hospital, which cares for 285? persons in ivy-covered, gray stone and brick buildings at Broadway and Turney road.

The Press obtained first-hand information on a few of the recent attacks by attendants on patients. It has reports on several others which indicate the beatings are not isolated instances.

The Press also obtained an up-to-date review of food and housing conditions now existing in the scattered buildings on the 10-acre plot of wooded land.

Governor Bricker at Columbus today promised to correct conditions at Cleveland State Hospital and punish any person guilty of mistreating patients if an official Welfare Department investigation "substantiates charges made in The Press story."

After reading the story, Mr. Bricker said:

"I hope the paper is not taking statements of irresponsible persons and publishing them as absolute facts. It seems incredible to me that anyone would be guilty of physical mistreatment of any mentally sick or incompetent patient."

Even with the bright reddish-brown background of falling leaves the mental hospital community known as "Newburgh" to Cleveland residents has a forbidding look to passersby.

A trip through patients' wards, kitchen, dining halls and wardrooms does nothing to change this impression. In succeeding articles, The Press will report on the food situation and also on overcrowding and other serious conditions in the present quarters.

The general theme of these stories—brutality, bad food and poor housing—is not new. It has been reported many times in the last few decades.

Dr. Lee also admits confining patients in strong rooms and keeping leather shackles around the wrists of others.

These events occur today when the accepted method for treating mental patients calls for emphasis on kindness and tolerance. Dr. Lee knows this and so do his superiors in the Ohio Welfare Department at Columbus.

Mentally Ill Patients Beaten and Shackled

(Continued From Page One)

word of several patients is better. But evidence from a sane witness is best of all."

"Resign" for Clear Record

But, even when competent witnesses are available, the offending employees are not fired. They "resign," and with nothing to mar their civil service record, they are free to obtain similar jobs at other state institutions.

Dr. Hans P. Lee

Release of Mental Felons Up to Court

Governor, Parole Board Have No Say in Matter

Press State Service

COLUMBUS, Oct. 26—Neither the Pardon and Parole Commission nor the governor of Ohio have anything to say about the release of mental felons committed to Mansfield Reformatory under provisions of the Ascherman Act.

This was revealed today by State Welfare Department officials who pointed out these regulations concerning commitment of such cases:

To gain freedom, an Ascherman prisoner must first serve the minimum of what normally would have been a sentence for the crime committed. For example, a mental defective sent to the reformatory following conviction on an unarmed robbery charge must serve at least one year of the one-to-25-year term prescribed by statute.

If the reformatory's medical staff, upon observation of a prisoner, believes there is a noticeable improvement in his mental condition, it may recommend to the superintendent of the institution that the man be released.

The superintendent forwards this recommendation to the court that committed the prisoner to the reformatory. The court's own psychiatrist examines the prisoner and reports his finding. Final authority to release the prisoner rests, therefore, with the court.

WEDNESDAY, NOVEMBER 10, 1943

On Record!

SECOND SECTION

TUESDAY, OCTOBER 26, 1943

Mooney Plans to Investigate State Hospital

State Welfare Director to Check "Beating," Other Charges

Psychiatrist Calls Hagert Insane

Grants Confessed Slayer Could Be Feigning Lunacy

Mental Patients Given Bad Food, Little Meat

(Continued From Page One)

TOMORROW: Patients' food ration points used by staff.

Food for Mental Patients "Revolting"

By WALTER LERCH

Meals prepared for nearly all mentally ill patients at Cleveland State Hospital are "revolting and inadequate."

Average patients don't get a fair share of meat and other war-rationed foods obtained by the institution under the OPA "point pool" system.

Staff doctors, other employees and a few "privileged" patients get the best food in separate dining halls. Many

A statement by Ohio Welfare Director Herbert R. Mooney, pledging investigation of "reports of mistreatment of patients" at Cleveland State Hospital, appears on the First Page, Section Two.

openly boast: "We get steaks once or twice a day." The patients get none.

These facts were disclosed in The Press' survey of the big mental institution in Newburgh Heights.

Staff members obtaining their rationed foods through the OPA allocation made directly to the hospital also held individual rationing books until recently. These were withdrawn after the OPA received complaints against the practice.

As in the case with reports on brutality and other abuses against the mentally deranged inmates, Dr. Hans P. Lee, the hospital director, today admitted that facts described by persons interviewed by The Press were essentially correct.

"I suppose the patients don't get all they are entitled to under the food rationing system," he said.

"The food for patients is substantial, but not always as appealing as home cooking. Yes, we have a special dining room for employees. I admit the patients don't get the same food as the employees and doctors.

"At present we are serving vegetables harvested on state farms. But I know that during the summer the food was not as good as we served before the war."

Although psychiatrists say nourishing ... im-portant factor in keeping up morale and recovery of mental patients, this and o... treatment appear to be neglected in State...

A food expert familiar with operations... kitchen reported the food served to patie... both in proteins and vitamins.

Proteins are needed for the mainten...

Turn to First Page, Section Tw...

The Cleveland Press
October 26, 1943

Lauds Hospital Aid of Objectors

Cleveland Press

Mental Expert Surprised at Removal Here

Nov. 15, 1943

By WALTER LERCH

Scores of mental hospitals throughout the nation use conscientious objectors as emergency attendants, and find them among the most reliable workers they have had, Dr. George S. Stevenson, executive secretary of the National Committee for Mental Hygiene, said today.

Dr. Stevenson

Dr. Stevenson came here from New York City at the request of the Cleveland Welfare Federation to assist in arranging final plans for establishment of a local Mental Hygiene Association.

According to plans, the local association would not only deal in educational and preventative work to reduce the incidence of mental disorders, but would maintain a constant check to insure a high standard of treatment for patients committed to mental hospitals.

Dr. Stevenson said he was surprised that officials at Cleveland State Hospital were dismissing their entire unit of conscientious objectors after some members of the unit had protested against the beating of mentally-ill patients.

Dr. Stevenson said state officials ...ve an obligation to see than men...lly-ill patients get the type of ...atment a sick person should have.

...he national organization which serves grew out of ...reatment of mentally-ill person... Connecticut hospitals more tha... ars ago. The conditions expose... by Clifford W. Beers, a patie... ater recovered, were similar reported recently at Clevela... Hospital.

Stevenson met at noon ...llerton with public offic... members of the Cleve... ociation and the Acac... ine. John A. Greene, c... the Welfare Federa... committee, presided.

...ard A. Bolt, chairm... health education co... under the federati... Mental Hygiene A... be set up as a ... ie Welfare Feder...

...trustees will m... a request for an... ance for the ... for 1944 of ... Edward D. Ly... ary.

Church Group Asks Action in Mental Probe

Cleveland Press
Nov. 22-43

Demand Impartial Investigation of Care at State Hospital

By WALTER LERCH

Aroused by reports of brutal treatment of mentally-ill patients at Cleveland State Hospital, a representative group of Greater Cleveland residents today called upon Governor Bricker to appoint immediately an impartial, objective fact-finding committee.

The plea for early action by the governor came last night from more than 100 persons attending the Sunday Evening Religious Hour at Euclid Avenue Baptist Church, presided over by Dr. D. R. Sharpe, executive secretary of the Cleveland Baptist Association and president of the Cleveland Church Federation.

Dr. Henry C. Schumacher, director of the Cleveland Guidance Center, cited the need for an "unbiased committee to sift out fact from rumors" after telling the audience:

"The present situation is undoubtedly bad. I know from personal experience that conditions never were good in state hospitals. Things may be worse now under wartime conditions. I have every reason to believe that some of the reports on treatment of patients are true."

Guard to Appear

Meanwhile, Leonard Booth, 50, a former Cleveland State Hospital attendant, appeared late today in Municipal Court on assault and battery charges. Booth is accused of beating a shackled, mentally ill patient last Sept. 25. Bond was fixed at $1000 and a hearing set for tomorrow.

Although invited to attend the meeting personally or send representatives in their behalf, Governor Bricker and other state officials did not appear at last night's church session.

"Gov. Bricker, a long time friend of mine, has not replied to my letter," said Dr. Sharpe. "I hear he ... for president. I think

Hospital to Oust "Objector" Staff

Group Includes Witnesses in Beating Expose

Nov 13, 1943

By WALTER LERCH

Despite a serious personnel shortage here, the entire unit of conscientious objectors serving as emergency workers at Cleveland State Hospital will be removed Dec. 1.

Ouster of the complete unit came at the request of Dr. Hans P. Lee, hospital superintendent, shortly after he ordered the immediate removal of eight of the original members. Among these eight were two witnesses to an assault by regular attendant on a mentally-patient.

Col. Lewis F. Kosch, director the camp operations division Selective Service at Washing... confirmed reports that Dr. Lee dismissing all the conscientious jectors. The unit is under su... vision of the American Fri... Service Committee, and had be... service here since last Decemb...

"There's too much bad feelin... tween the regular hospital sta... the conscientious objectors," Col. Kosch. "We put these in there at the hospital's r... and now they are not wanted...

"Under the circumstanc... might as well put them i... other hospital where they ca... We want their services ... utilized. Cleveland State ... is the only place in the co... my knowledge where we h... this difficulty."

...conscientious ob...

Shifts 8 in Mental Probe Tomorrow

Cleveland Press

Hospital Head Dismisses Men Needed as Witnesses

Nov. 12, 1943

By WALTER LERCH

Eight conscientious objectors employed as attendants at Cleveland State Hospital today reported they were notified by Dr. Hans P. Lee, hospital superintendent, to return to work camps tomorrow morning.

Included among these eight men were two witnesses in an assault and battery case now pending against Haden Blake, 23, a regular attendant. Blake fled Nov. 4 shortly after the warrant was issued, and is now being sought by police.

Dr. Lee informed Leland C. Bullen, leader of the conscientious objectors unit, of the effective time of the transfer order shortly after Governor Bricker said he would oppose any attempt by hospital officials to get rid of any witnesses" who might testify concerning beating of patients at the hospital.

Reached at Columbus, Governor Bricker later said he would not oppose removal of the men, and said he believed their transfer "would have nothing to do with their ability to testify against any other employees at the hospital."

Mr. Bullen, whose transfer is not being sought by Dr. Lee, said he accepted the superintendent's notice to other members of the unit under protest.

Dr. Lee could not be reached for comment on the transfer order. He previously had accused one member of the C. O. (conscientious objectors' unit) of making disparaging remarks to another regular attendant who was a veteran of World War I. He did not disclose the nature of his complaints against the other seven conscientious objectors.

Mr. Bullen, who originally received word that Dr. Lee intended to order the transfer, said he was informed by Dr. Lee that "all eight of you are trouble-makers and obnoxious."

Commenting later on Dr. Lee's statement, Mr. Bullen said:

"If, by this, Dr. Lee means that we refuse to co-operate in beating patients and also refuse ... lent when other ... tients. ...

> Our Governor, the State Legislature, the Welfare Director, the Commissioner of Mental Diseases, the hospital superintendent, the least attendant, and we the people—all must share in the guilt for this social crime against these innocent and helpless people. All must share in the responsibility for instituting immediate redress.

Deutsch then went on to state some of the grand jury's specific charges:

> Cleveland State Hospital is not a hospital; it is a custodial institution in which we have incarcerated the sick. It presents a case history of brutality and social criminal neglect. Patients have died shortly after receiving violent attacks from the hands of attendants or other patients, made possible only by the lack of proper supervision. In other cases patients have died under circumstances which are highly suspicious.
>
> Frequent active assaults have resulted in broken bones, lacerations, bruises and a consequent deterioration of the mind. Favorite weapons have been the buckles of heavy straps, the loaded end of heavy key-rings, metal plated shoes and wet towels which leave no marks after choking.
>
> Violent patients have been used for "strong-arm" purposes by attendants who persist in running the hospital as a penal institution. The atmosphere reeks with the false notion that the mentally ill are criminals and sub-humans who should be denied all human rights and scientific medical care.

Deutsch concluded his story on Cleveland State Hospital with the following words:

> The Grand Jury investigation of Cleveland State Hospital resulted from a chain of events paralleled in many other communities in present-day America. A group of COs assigned to the hospital by Selective Service to help relieve the desperate shortage of ward attendants was horrified by the conditions unfolded daily before their eyes. They kept diaries; they drafted reports. They contacted a modest, young, and extremely able and social-minded reporter named Walter Lerch. This reporter was no nine-day sensationalist;

he ran a long series of well-documented exposés of the hospital that shocked the decent people of Cleveland into organizing an effective reform movement, stimulated by the Grand Jury inquiry.

Evidence laid before the Grand Jury included documented statements by the CO attendants and some of their wives who served as attendants on the female wards at Cleveland State Hospital. Some read like Torquemada's medieval inquisition chambers or like inside stories of Nazi concentration camps. Remember, the victims were all sick Americans, entitled to proper medical care and treatment.

The CO attendants reported several specific instances where patients, male and female, died soon after brutal beatings. They complained repeatedly to the superintendent as well as the supervisor of male attendants about these abuses. One particularly sadistic attendant, an ex-convict, was later convicted for assault and battery on a patient. Another worker who had been fired from several state hospitals for brutality was allowed to resign after charges were formally made against him.

CPS Unit at Virginia's Eastern State Hospital Sparks Probe That Leads to State Investigation

A scenario very similar to that involving the CPS unit at Cleveland State Hospital took place at the Eastern State Hospital at Williamsburg, Virginia, site of the first CPS mental hospital unit authorized by Selective Service in June 1942. Shortly after arrival at the Williamsburg institution, the men in the CPS unit began to be concerned about the prevailing bedlam-like conditions to which the patients were being exposed. Van Cleve Geiger, one of the COs in the unit, described his feelings of frustration about conditions at the hospital in a communication addressed to his former fellow campers at the National Park Service CPS unit at Buck Creek, North Carolina:[5]

> Soon after the first members of our unit arrived here a year ago, it became clear to us that we could not condone much that went on here. Several of us came near to returning to camp, feeling that we could not take part in serving such an institution. But most of us

stayed. We did not feel responsible for the evils represented at the hospital. We believed that we needed to make an effort to improve matters. If we could not accept this challenge, then we could not in good conscience continue to stay here.

We also agreed that we had to be patient. If we were going to succeed in our efforts to bring about change, we had to be fully aware of the facts, and we had to learn how to be skillful in bringing about meaningful change with our supervisors and fellow workers.

In trying to support a better life for the patients, we made many mistakes. On the wards to which we were assigned, we were successful in creating a pleasanter atmosphere. But overall, the hospital was still mired in budgetary constraints and the welfare of the patients was at the bottom of the heap.

Several months ago, we became acquainted with Marshall Suther, Jr., a friend of one of our fellow-CPS men. While waiting for his draft call, he decided to join the attendant staff. Although he is not a CO, we learned to respect his sincerity. In late June, he learned that his draft call had been scheduled for the latter part of July, so he resigned and decided to visit a friend before leaving for his army assignment. His friend, aware of conditions at Eastern State Hospital, had long been wishing that something might be done about improving the situation. Marshall's friend introduced him to a lawyer-friend who had also expressed concerns about the pressing problems at the hospital.

As a result of Marshall's visit to his friend, the following events took place. Marshall visited several of us at the hospital and invited as many of us as could do so to join with him in a meeting with his friend and the lawyer to explore next steps. We were asked to supply them with particulars about conditions at the hospital which they could then draw upon at a planned meeting with the state's chief executive, Governor Darden.

Governor Darden listened sympathetically to Marshall's report on affairs at the hospital and arranged for him to meet with Dr. Henry, the State Hospital Commissioner. He in turn arranged for Marshall to meet with the State Hospital Board. At that meeting, the Board decided that a formal investigation of Eastern State Hospital was in order and set in motion steps to convene a formal hearing.

The meeting opened on July 29th and continued over until

August 3rd. Sixteen of the 33 men in the CPS unit testified at the hearing and were given every opportunity to describe conditions at the hospital as they had observed them, and to make any special comments we felt like contributing.

Among the various incidents reported at the meeting was the following.

> Some of the patients eat in a basement dining room, commonly called the hole. I helped supervise feeding the patients the first morning I was there. As the patients finished their meal and began returning to their ward, one lagged behind to pick up his clothing. The charge attendant became highly irritated, slapped the patient and knocked him down. He then bent over and slapped him again. Next he lifted the patient's leg by his ankle and kicked him several times in the seat of his pants. The patient begged him to stop and finally the attendant let him go with the admonition—"that'll teach you to move the next time I speak to you."

> Another [CO] contributed the following incident: Six of the patients on his ward normally slept on a tile floor which was usually wet with urine. For lack of mattresses or blankets, some of these patients often had to wrap themselves in rubber sheets. Two of these patients were discovered in such a weakened condition that they became ill with pneumonia. After transfer to another ward, one of the patients recovered. The other, transferred to a different ward, died with advanced tuberculosis.

Geiger then reported to his former camp mates that after the testimony by the COs, the hospital administration was invited to give its side of the story. During this period, all instances of brutality toward the patients were denied. A host of explanations and excuses were offered for the various shortcomings imposed on the patients.

The *Richmond Times-Dispatch* gave extensive press coverage to the state hospital board hearings from their onset in July well into mid-September when they were concluded. Many of the accounts turned up on the front pages under banner headlines. Editorials in support of the need for change followed. Equally important and

Brutality Charges Aired As Asylum Probe Opens

By James Latimer
Times-Dispatch Staff Writer

WILLIAMSBURG—An investigation of complaints alleging neglect and "brutality" in handling some patients, unsanitary conditions, overcrowding and lack of proper medical treatment in the Eastern State Hospital here was begun yesterday by the State Hospital Board.

Four witnesses—one former attendant, recently inducted into the armed forces and three attendants now serving among a group of conscientious objectors assigned to the hospital for wartime service—testified at an all-day hearing which the board indicated was just the beginning of an exhaustive, fact-finding inquiry.

Still unheard when the board ... page brief filed with the board by yesterday's principal witness, Marshall E. Suther, Jr. Hospital authorities, headed by Dr. George W. Brown, superintendent, also have yet to present their side of the charges. They made no statements yesterday, but Ashton Dovell, counsel for Dr. Brown, closely cross-examined the four witnesses.

The board will meet again here at 10 A. M. Tuesday to resume the investigation.

Opening of the investigation was the result of complaints taken to Governor Darden and the hospital board here several days ago by Mr. Suther.

Taking the witness stand yesterday, Mr. Suther testified that the complaints arose from his observations and experiences in the ... months' serv- ... t at the hos- ... beginning last

... 5, Column 2

Charges of Brutality At Hospital Are Denied

RICHMOND TIMES-DISPATCH-AUG.4

By James Latimer
Times-Dispatch Staff Writer

WILLIAMSBURG — Charges of brutality, neglect and the inadequate training of attendants, made by various witnesses in the State Hospital Board's investigation of the Eastern State Hospital were denied categorically last night by witnesses for the administration of the nation's oldest mental hospital.

Several officials and attendants testified before the board after numerous complaints had been registered earlier in the day by a dozen individuals, chiefly conscientious objectors assigned to the hospital as attendants and caretakers.

Affairs of the Western State Hospital were injected into the hearing briefly yesterday morning, when Miss Wilma Virginia Clark, secretary to the registrar of the College of William and Mary for the past eight years, told the board that her brother had been mistreated at the Staunton institution and at the hospital here.

The board agreed to hear Miss Clark's testimony relative to alleged conditions ... State Hospital, but no other witnesses were called in connection with that institution and the board announced that it has not determined whether the probe will be extended to the Staunton hospital.

Miss Clark told of having tried to pay her usual weekly visit to her brother while he was at the Eastern State Hospital, when she was informed that she could not see him because he had become violent, struck an attendant and knocked his teeth out.

"On a later visit, I asked my brother why and if he had struck the man," she said her brother told her, she added that he had asked for an aspirin to ease the pain of a sinus infection and that after he had been refused several times, he was told by the attendant that if he made another request for aspirin he (the attendant) would knock him down, "My brother made the request again, and the attendant struck him in the face. My brother struck him back and knocked several of his teeth out."

The witness said that she had been reluctant to testify because

State and City

Darden, Goode, Henry Oppose Removal Now of Objectors Serving in State Hospitals

Demands of Dr. George W. Brown, superintendent of the Eastern State Hospital at Williamsburg, that conscientious objecters serving as attendants at the institution be removed met with rebuffs yesterday from Governor Darden, the State Hospiltal Board and Dr. H. C. Henry, State hospital commissioner.

Both Governor Darden and Senator Morton H. Goode, chairman of the hospital board, sent telegrams to the State convention of the American Legion in Danville urging that body to exercise caution in its consideration of the matter and Dr. Henry directed a letter to Dr. Brown taking sharp issue with the superintendent over a statement he issued in Williamsburg last Saturday.

Meet With Governor

The Darden and Goode telegrams to the Legion convention were sent after a brief conference in the Governor's office and Dr. Henry's letter to Dr. Brown went out by mail later in the day, which opened in Danville Sunday.

Coincident with these resolutions adopted by the American Legion posts, one of which is located in Williamsburg, Dr. Brown issued a lengthy public statement Saturday demanding removal of the objectors from his institution, asserting that they had been guilty of mistreating the patients they are assigned to attend.

Senator Goode made it clear in his telegram to the Legion convention that the hospital board has no objection to the adoption by the convention of a resolution "opposing the general policy of the Federal government in regard to conscientious objectors," and asserted that the board "no doubt would agree with your position."

However, the Senator pointed out, the board doesn't want the mental hospitals of the State singled out as the target for Legion resolutions condemning the policy of handling the conscientious objectors.

Dr. Brown Attacks Use Of Objectors

Inmates Treated Badly, He Says

RICHMOND TIMES-DISPATCH AUG. 2

WILLIAMSBURG, (AP) — Dr. George W. Brown, superintendent of the Eastern State Hospital here, charged last night that conscientious objectors serving as attendants at the hospital had mistreated inmates and "must be immediately removed."

His charges were contained in a statement which took the form of a counterattack against charges recently leveled at the hospital administration by a group of conscientious objects who had served there.

Their complaint brought an in- vestigation b Board in op liamsburg. T the hearings studied by tl

Legion

The Penin the Americar in a resoluti Dr. Brown's conscientious removed fro and replaced of the preser

"We call tion of the E to rid itself and in the promptly d placed under long as the Eastern Stat lution stated ordered pre Legion conve ville today.

Dr. Browr the board c "only severa for the pres in defense c proportion r phasis given leged charg press report answers to

He said t timony wo charges of b ment of p "and, indeed ly denied by

C. O.'s A

"On the tinued, "fou C. O.'s adm treating pa accused by tious object

4 Witnesses Rap Methods Of Hospital

State Board Hears Williamsburg Men

Criticisms of treatment methods, of deficient training given attendants, of delegations of authority to untrained persons and other practices they said were common at the Eastern State Hospital were voiced by four witnesses at a hearing conducted by the State Hospital Board in Williamsburg Thursday.

Their testimony, which also cited cases of neglect and "brutality" in handling patients, was the first taken in the board's investigation of complaints regarding hospital conditions. The board, having expressed its determination to uncover all facts involved in the complaints, will resume its hearings next Tuesday.

Served as Attendants

The four witnesses who testified as the investigation opened have served as attendants at the hospital, where the State cares for white mental patients. Marshall E. Suther, Jr., who directed presentation of the complaints, left recently to be inducted into the Marines and will report soon for active duty. The other three are among a group of conscientious objectors assigned to wartime duty as attendants at the hospital. All are college-trained men.

In a 43-page brief in which they outlined testimony on their observations and experiences as attendants, they cited instances which they listed, among others, under these heads:

"Indications that the orientation of important members of the staff is away from the welfare of the patients and their possible recovery, and towards the 'efficient'. 'economical running' of a business institution.

Some on Staff Unsuited

"Particular personalities (among the hospital staff) are unsuited for various reasons to deal with mental patients.

"Authority and responsibility properly belonging only to a physician is delegated to untrained persons."

Attendant Richard Scott told the board he had heard the supervising nurse at Dunbar "attribute the acts and words of disturbed patients to 'just plain meanness'.

"She characterized the immobility of a patient diagnosed as a dementia praecox of the catatonic type as 'stubbornness' and made an effort, once, to move him by means of a switch which she broke from a convenient tree."

significant, the men in the Williamsburg CPS unit were given credit for initiating the probe.

The findings of the state hospital board led to the resignation of Dr. George W. Brown, superintendent of the hospital, as well as other key staff members. The hearings also led to plans to upgrade buildings at Eastern State Hospital, as well as recommendations for more equitable salaries for employees of the state hospital system and provisions for upgrading the quality of patients' services.

The state hospital board's inquiries into charges leveled at Eastern State Hospital were expanded to cover all of Virginia's mental hospitals. Major changes in the administrative staff of the Western State Hospital were recommended by the board, in addition to a proposal to plan for the development of a new mental hospital for the north-central region of the state.

In concluding the story of the investigation at Eastern State Hospital, it should be noted that two members of the CPS unit were licensed physicians who had applied for and received CO status from their local draft boards. These men were given medical responsibilities at the institution. Before their arrival, the hospital's medical staff was close to zero because so many of its physicians had resigned to join the army medical corps or left to take more lucrative positions elsewhere.

Throughout the state hospitals in which CPS units had been established, it was not unusual to find one or more doctors whose pacifist beliefs had led them to take the CO stand. Unlike the rank-and-file CPS assignees in mental hospitals, whose privileges (except for salary) were comparable to those of the regular hospital attendants, the physician assignees were customarily granted housing and meal allowances similar to those granted to the regular medical staff. However, these men received the same basic $15 per month allowance to which all COs in the unit were entitled.

CPS teams in many other state mental hospitals during World War II (such as those at the Hudson River State Hospital at Poughkeepsie, New York, and the Cherokee State Hospital, Cherokee, Iowa) found themselves drawn into the public eye under circumstances similar to those experienced by the COs at Eastern State Hospital in Virginia and Cleveland State Hospital in Ohio. In several instances, investigative bodies were convened to review allegations similar to those examined in Virginia and Ohio. In most cases, corrective measures usually followed suit, but none were as sweeping as those that occurred in these two states.

Forgotten Children

Of the 61 CPS units sent to state mental institutions, 14 units were assigned to state training schools for the retarded and one unit was assigned to a state school for delinquent boys.[6] On average, there were about 15 COs in each of these units—considerably fewer than those in state mental hospital units. Although the two kinds of institutions provided many similar services to their patients, there was one major, underlying distinction. Patients in mental hospitals were suffering from an episode of mental illness. With proper medical care and treatment, a significant number could be expected to recover and resume their normal life-styles.

On the other hand, the training schools were expressly designed to facilitate the training and rehabilitation of persons with various degrees of mental retardation. The mental impairment of many residents of these facilities was often so severe that the institution's primary responsibility was to provide them with as high a level of custodial care as was humanly possible. Those with less severe degrees of retardation could, with proper education and training, resume limited roles in society. During the war era, the nation's training schools were barely able to offer basic custodial services, let alone the educational and training services that they had been mandated to provide.

Because they were able to offer higher salaries, the war industries had lured many of the regular employees from the tedious, nerve-wracking work in these state training schools. The draft had taken away many other employees. It wasn't long before these facilities became unbearably understaffed and overcrowded. The Buckley State Training School in the state of Washington was complaining that although its patient capacity was limited to 400, it had been forced to extend its services to 600 patients with far fewer staff on hand than it had when it was serving 400.

In Pennsylvania, the Pennhurst State Training School, which had an already overburdened caseload, was struggling to care for 2,500 patients. Fifteen hundred more patients were lined up waiting to be admitted. Similar troubles were brewing in other training schools all over the country. Riots or near riots had become a common occurrence in training schools. To make matters especially difficult for these schools, delinquency was a commonly found trait among many of those institutionalized in these facilities.

A 1944 issue of *The Reporter,* published by the National Service Board for Religious Objectors, offers glimpses into some of the day-to-day activities of several training schools. Here are a few illustrations:[7]

> The day attendant in the Delaware State Training School at Stockley comes on duty after breakfast. He puts toothpaste on two dozen toothbrushes and sees to it that 24 of his feeble-minded charges brush their teeth. He sees to it that a higher-grade worker-patient sweeps the floor; another scrubs the floor; and another takes out the trash. As another worker is picking up papers, the attendant sees to it that the rest of the patients change into their day clothes. All this takes a good part of the morning. Comes noon, together with the worker-patients, he gets them off to lunch.
>
> During the meal, he keeps an eye on the patients to see that they get enough—that they don't steal anyone else's food—and don't give their food away. In the afternoon, the lower-grade patients go to the play yard, and the higher-grade worker-patients go back to work. The supper routine is pretty much the same as at noon. At bedtime, he checks to be sure that everyone is clean, gives medication to the patients with epilepsy, bandages cuts, stops fights, and then pretty much collapses as everyone finally gets to sleep.
>
> The COs in these training school units are also given a variety of other responsibilities depending on their skills and training. Some are given teaching assignments while others are engaged in such tasks as farming, maintenance, and clerical duties, among others. The work pattern for those in the unit at the New Lisbon State Training School is a typical example of those in other similar

> CPS units. Six of the men have half-day teaching assignments—two in physical education, two in music, one in handicrafts, and one each in the three "R"s and woodwork. Eight of the men work on the farm, supervising the worker-patients. Two others conduct psychological tests while the others are employed in the laundry, the hospital, the supervisor's office, the recreational program, and as cottage attendants.

Wives of the COs were eagerly welcomed at the state training schools where their husbands were assigned. At the Southern Colony and Training School in Wisconsin, 13 wives joined their husbands. They were employed as switchboard operators, office personnel, and cottage attendants.

In a report transmitted to the Mental Hygiene Program of the CPS, one of the COs assigned to the Mansfield Training School in Connecticut made the following observations about the patients at that facility and their attitudes toward the attendants:[8]

> An alert and observing attendant will discover these low-grade patients resemble a normal person, living in slow-motion fashion. Notwithstanding this constitutional make-up, these "little thinkers" are careful to preserve a spark of life. They seem far more human than many normal people. They seek satisfaction and contentment in "being a part of" and "belonging to" a group similar to their own understanding. They seek encouragement in their abilities and like attention. They seek consolation in their frustrated moments. And they seek security from the inconsistencies of their fellow playmates.
>
> Understanding the low-grade patient to be mentally dormant but highly . . . sensitive, the attendant must be very tactful in making impressions. Scores of glancing eyes are watching, most unassumingly, every movement he makes. Carefully, they tabulate the difference it makes to you if "Popeye's" left shoe is on his right foot, or if "Woodchuck's" clothes are soiled. They make a note of your reaction to Mickey's cut or bruise. Eddie may be homesick; Mike may have had a tough day; they are all trying to express their feelings. Caution is in order when they are . . . measuring your disposition.
>
> If an attendant is earnest and sincere, he will be concerned about

> the welfare of his "boys." The patients in return show their confidence in and respect for such an attendant. To gain this quality of respect from his charges, the attendant needs to simulate the kind of kinship that is characteristic of that found in a father-son relationship.

Some insights into what life was like in the state training schools during this period may be gleaned from excerpts of a letter written by Gordon Zahn to the Board of Visitors of the Rosewood State Training School after his discharge from that institution. Zahn had served as the assistant director of the CPS unit at Rosewood and had also functioned as a cottage attendant. In this latter capacity, he had had a firsthand opportunity to participate in and observe the day-to-day operations at Rosewood. Below is an edited description of what he and others in the CPS unit experienced at that facility, along with recommended changes for the board to consider.[9]

> I am writing you now because much of what I have seen is deeply disturbing to me as a citizen, and because I realize how difficult it is for . . . even the board member to know, in detail, the conditions which exist here. . . . I feel certain that by passing along my observations and detailed charges, you will see fit to correct the difficult situation under which inarticulate and unfortunate residents of this facility have been placed.
>
> My first contention is that the residents of this institution have been, and still are, subject to capricious, careless, and unjust disciplinary actions. Related to this observation is that Rosewood, nominally intended to be a training school, has in fact become, primarily custodial in emphasis and punitive in nature.
>
> Custodial care may be appropriate for those whose degree of mental retardation is so severe that any efforts directed at rehabilitation or training would likely fail. But this limited form of care is tragically inadequate for the vast majority of Rosewood's population, which is made up of those who are educable and trainable. It is in this group which you will find most of the "problem" children at Rosewood. To a great extent, these are products of a childhood within which punishment was a way of life for those who kept stepping out of bounds. In return, these children kept reacting with socially unacceptable responses. For this behavior, they were then

brought to Rosewood, not for punishment, but for training and correction. . . . But once they were admitted to Rosewood, these same individuals who had been unable to adapt to the pressures of daily life at home and in the community, once again found themselves in a setting where their behaviors were being controlled by punishment of one degree or another—or threats of punishment. All too often, the punishments imposed neither fit the "crime" nor the "criminal."

Rosewood is and has been sadly lacking in offering proper recreational programs and facilities for its residents. A weekly movie is one of the very few diversions it does provide. However, instead of being offered in response to a very real human need, admittance to this program is provided as a "reward" for good behavior. The children at the institution know that for the slightest misconduct they may be, and are often, deprived of their only pleasure for an entire week.

Recently, the institution held its first dance in several years. The children looked forward to this event as one of the most important in their lives. They talked of little else for weeks in advance of the affair. When the school principal in charge of the dance received the list of boys who had asked permission to attend, she deleted a large number of names. They were boys who for one reason or another were either "unworthy," or could not be trusted. One of these was a boy who had a reputation for "hanging around the cafeteria talking to one of the girls." Two weeks prior to the dance, he had been punished for such behavior and had promised he would refrain from doing the same in the future. The employee in charge of the cafeteria reported that he had kept his promise. But in spite of the improvement in his behavior his name was dropped from the list.

It is a regrettable fact that the majority of punishments meted out to the boys are not even reported to the doctor in charge. This places the child entirely at the mercy of untrained employees who more often than not are swayed by their emotional reactions to the misconduct which they have observed. One 14-year-old boy, an epileptic, became involved in an argument with another boy who had been sent to bring him back to his cottage. Upon arriving there, the disturbed epileptic kicked out the pane in the door. One of the staff doctors had informed members of our CPS unit that it is typical of epileptics to be generally irritable and unstable as a result of their affliction. The untrained attendant, probably unaware of this characteristic, punished him by taking away his movie privileges for an entire month.

Another boy was found guilty of tearing three hospital gowns. For this, he was punished by the nurse with the doctor's consent, by transferring him to the institutional prison cottage for an indefinite period. He remained there for two and a half months because both the nurse and physician had forgotten about the incident, and that the boy was still there.

The disciplinary frame of mind at Rosewood is not free from an element of vindictiveness. One boy was banished to the prison cottage for disobeying an injunction "not to go into town." While being escorted to his cottage after being apprehended, he complicated matters by making some uncomplimentary remarks about the school's business manager, who happened to be present. As a result, he was denied the daily two-hour exercise period granted to those in this particular cottage. He was not permitted to spend any time in the completely fenced-in porch accessible to others in this unit. He was also deprived of attending weekly movies as well as religious services. After seven weeks of this regime, he was permitted to be released each day for a 12-hour stint as a hospital work-boy. When the business manager learned of this change, the boy was remanded to full punishment status.

The continued use of the prison cottage as a method of disciplining those who step out of line at Rosewood runs contrary to an enlightened approach in dealing with behavioral problems, particularly for those whose capacity for growth and development has been stymied because of serious deficiencies in their mental capacities. Those confined in this punishment facility range from psychotics, helpless idiots, sex perverts, to runaways. Others are left to wander aimlessly for most of the day. Virtually no recreational opportunities are available. The atmosphere is loaded with fear.

Resources are so pitifully inadequate that it is not unusual for a group of boys wishing to play baseball to ask for a ball of twine as a makeshift substitute. Those wishing to play football are often found using a rusty tin can instead. Rosewood has a gym with facilities for basketball. Yet, it is used in the daytime for drying

> laundry. And when the office is asked for a basketball for an evening game, none is available.
>
> Rosewood has a dean of boys on staff. Most of his time is consumed on farm chores and in serving as the institution's chauffeur. All the while, the boys in the cottages have nothing to do but get into trouble. . . .
>
> At the present time, occupational programs in most state institutions are much closer to providing them with a source of unpaid labor than providing a useful service to their patients. My impression, based on the three years I've been here, is that the situation at Rosewood is much closer to the former than the latter. A few illustrations will support this point of view.
>
> For instance, several girls assigned to kitchen and cafeteria duty work a daily schedule, with some of them getting an occasional day off, while others get no time off at all. The same situation prevails for boys working in the power house, the dairy, as well as for all worker-patients assigned to cottage duties.

In the 1940s, the mentally retarded (or the developmentally disabled, as they are more commonly referred to in the 1990s) were popularly described as persons with a mental deficiency, or simply as the feebleminded. Because there was such a dearth of popularly written material about this condition, which affected nearly 2% of the population, the subject was clouded with ignorance and much misunderstanding. Acutely aware of this ignorance, the CPS unit at the Vineland Training School in New Jersey decided to try and remedy this problem. Under the leadership of Arnold Krause, one of their members, they prepared a manuscript titled *Forgotten Children*.

The manuscript was sent to the Mental Hygiene Program of the CPS as that group's contribution toward seeking public understanding for mentally retarded people. Subsequently, when the National Mental Health Foundation took over the Mental Hygiene Program, *Forgotten Children* was issued in an attractive pamphlet format. It was eagerly acquired by state agencies administering the training schools for the retarded, as well as by citizens' groups concerned about changing the public perception about the mentally retarded.

Forgotten Children concludes with these words:

Though the American people have been called the greatest philanthropists in the world and the best informed of all peoples, this generosity and understanding somehow hasn't extended to their feebleminded children. Too often they have been "forgotten children." When they have been remembered at all, it has too often been for the wrongs they do with no consideration of the wrongs done to them. Their greatest handicap is not their low mentality, but the public's lack of sympathy and understanding. Painstaking research over the past 100 years has found the key that can unlock the door to their welfare and happiness. Will we lose the opportunity? Or will we remember these "forgotten children"?

Chapter 5

AGENTS FOR SOCIAL CHANGE: PART TWO

> Perhaps in the rank of these men lie the hopes of the nation. They will be the single largest group outside of psychiatrists with valid and useful experience in dealing with mental cases. . . . The framers of the Selective Service Act were wiser than they knew when they provided that COs should be assigned to "work of national importance. . . ."
>
> William B. Hesseltine
> "Salvaging the War's Mental Wrecks"
> As cited in *The Reporter,* August 1, 1944.
> A publication of the National Service Board for
> Religious Objectors, Washington, D.C.

Although all state institutions for the mentally ill and the mentally retarded throughout the United States in the 1940s were far from ideal with respect to the quality of care and treatment offered, not all of them were quite as notorious as the institutions described in the preceding chapters. What distinguished the so-called "better" facilities from those that had become fair game for crusading reporters and state investigatory commissions was a climate in which both creativity and flexibility were allowed to flourish. In such settings, the administrative structure tended to be less rigid and autocratic than that which prevailed in so many state institutions of that period. Superintendents in these facilities were inclined to be receptive to ideas that led to innovative programs or actions that contributed to the welfare of both the patients and the beleaguered staff.

The state institutions that had opted to participate in the Civilian Public Service (CPS) mental hospital program suddenly found themselves with access to a range of labor resources that exceeded their wildest expectations. Included in the CPS units were physicians, educators, social scientists, communications specialists, and others with various degrees of expertise in business, agriculture, and the creative arts. At the time of their induction, approximately one-third of the men in these units were still in the process of pursuing their education at the secondary, undergraduate, and graduate levels.

Needless to say, those men who had completed their medical training were eagerly sought by hospitals with CPS units. As for the remainder of the unit members, they were customarily assigned to duty as ward attendants where the labor shortage was most critical.

Because of the severe budgetary constraints and critical labor shortages faced by all mental hospitals at that time, new ways of dealing with existing problems faced almost insurmountable difficulties in getting off the ground. But some hospital administrations did find opportunities to take advantage of the many talents represented among the conscientious objectors (COs). Those that seized these opportunities reaped rewards, which in many instances lasted long beyond the time when the CPS units were disbanded at the war's end. The purpose of this chapter is to put the spotlight on a few of those institutions that took full advantage of the range of skills that came along with these units.

COs Become an Integral Part of the Duke University Hospital Work Force

In a 1985 article published in the *North Carolina Medical Journal,* Louis E. Swanson and James F. Gifford, Jr., offered a fascinating retrospective of the activities of the CPS unit established at the Duke University Medical Center.[1] Unlike most of the other CPS units that had been authorized by Selective Service for sponsorship by one of the three major peace churches, this unit functioned under the wing of the Commission on World Peace of the Methodist Church. Next to the Mennonites, the Brethren, and the Quakers, more Methodists were represented among COs who had been accepted for the CPS program than any other religious affiliation. The Duke unit began functioning in December 1942. In their account of the history of this unit, Swanson and Gifford noted:

> The opening of this unit led to an experiment, unplanned by the organizers of the unit, in the utilization of highly educated laypersons for clinical duties and responsibilities well beyond the minimum requirements of the attendant's job. The 68 men who rotated through this unit made a major contribution to keeping Duke Hospital running during the war. It also contributed to a constructive national critique of health care for the mentally ill, and prepared a number of these men for health-related careers. Twenty years after deactivation of this unit in 1946, appreciation of their achievement helped prepare acceptance at Duke of the design of a new answer to clinical manpower shortages—"the physician's assistant."

From among the first 30 COs selected for the Duke unit, one-third were assigned to the inpatient psychiatric ward at Duke Hospital; one-third were assigned to Highland Hospital, an affiliated psychiatric hospital at Asheville, North Carolina; and the remaining one-third served as orderlies in the operating rooms in the department of surgery at the Duke Medical Center. The work week for all three groups was 48 hours, including six hours of instruction. In addition, the COs were given six additional hours of training in the evenings. As was the pattern for all CPS mental hospital units, the men received a monthly allowance of $15 in addition to room and board. At the same time that the CPS unit was in place at Duke, a group of German prisoners of war who worked in a mental hospital 15 miles northeast of Durham were receiving a monthly stipend of $21 plus room and board.

In describing the specific assignments for which the COs were responsible at the Duke CPS units, Swanson and Gifford reported:[1]

> On the psychiatric ward at Duke Hospital, patients were admitted for intensive treatment, pointed toward recovery and release. The

average stay for patients was 30 to 40 days. The men fed, clothed, and bathed patients and participated in recreational activities. They administered wet sheet packs to excited patients and nursed others through shock treatments. They took temperature, pulse and respiration, and charted patient behavior. Margaret Pinkerton, Dean of the School of Nursing at Duke, noted, "The efforts of the COs led to splendid results in carrying out occupational therapy measures planned by the doctors. . . . In the past these achievements had not been realized because of the inferior help."

At Highland Hospital the work situation was quite different. Therapy programs here were long term. More than one-half of the employees had been at some time psychiatric patients at the hospital. Some still were ill. Exercise and physical exhaustion were used to maintain the physical condition of the patients and to relieve nervous tension. Both insulin shock and electro-shock therapy were administered more frequently than at the Duke unit. Dr. Robert Carroll, who was in charge of the activities of the CPS unit at Highland, had noted that the male department of the hospital might have closed but for coming of the CPS unit.

By the end of the first year, the excellent performance of the COs in their day-to-day routines and the high percentage of college graduates among them led Dr. Robert Lyman, Chairman of the Neuropsychiatric Department at Duke Hospital, to consider what more these men could do for these patients. "My major interest in the CPS unit," he wrote, "has long since moved from the realm of the once-needed hospital routine to that of possibilities of personal and group development, which have been started but by no means fully attained as yet. Encouraging the men to pursue their personal and professional development might save time for physicians on wards and in labs. The point has been reached where I would enjoy being challenged to prove that we can fulfill some of these possibilities, creating values which were not even recognized to lie within the scope of the project at first."

The values realized were remarkedly varied. One man with previous experience in personnel work was assigned to type patients' social histories for psychiatric residents on a part-time basis. Soon, he was doing this full-time, thus relieving the residents for more important duties.

A background in art and photography led another of the CPS

> men to a full-time assignment, preparing charts, drawings, and photographs all related to research articles as well as exhibits. Following his discharge from the unit at the end of the war, he pursued a life-long career at Duke as a medical illustrator.
>
> Two COs with engineering backgrounds were assigned to the EEG [electroencephalogram] lab to help keep the only EEG machine in the region in operating condition. In the process, they made several modifications of the machine that improved its performance capabilities. Other unit members maintained colonies of experimental research animals, became laboratory technicians and assistants, developed courses of physical therapy to assist patients preparing for discharge from the hospitals, and participated in research on insulin therapy, blood banks, motion sickness, and recreational therapy for children. . . . These contributions, and the savings in manpower they represented, greatly benefited the Duke Hospital. . . . After the war, at least five men who had been part of the CPS unit enrolled in medical schools and, in time, became physicians.
>
> . . . By the 1960s, Duke Hospital again faced a shortage of clinically trained staff. The chairman of the Department of Medicine raised the possibility of multiplying the hands of physicians in both hospitals . . . by training bright high school graduates and ex-military corpsmen for routine clinical tasks. This represented a considerable departure from previous medical manpower policy. . . . He brought his idea to the assistant superintendent of Duke Hospital, who happened to have been a member of the CPS unit at the Highland Hospital. Following his discharge from the CPS program, he had gone on to a career in hospital administration. His presence at that meeting and recollections of the CPS experience affirmed the plausibility of the chairman's proposal, and although the connection may have been indirect, the contributions of the COs in meeting labor shortages at Duke during World War II are reflected in the role of the present-day "physician's assistant."

An apt addendum to the above reference to the beginning of a new job classification known as "physician's assistant" was published in *The New York Times* in 1991.[2] Under a banner headline, "That Person in the White Smock Is Not a Doctor," there was a half-page feature on the role of physician's assistants. In part it observed:

> . . . Ever since the first class of physician assistants graduated from Duke University in 1967, the field has constantly grown. There are now 22,000 P.A.s nationwide, about twice the number a decade ago. . . .
>
> . . . "The physicians' assistants are crucial to running our department and we wouldn't know what to do without them," said Dr. Malcolm S. Beinfield, a senior surgeon at Norwalk Hospital who is an assistant professor at the Yale University School of Medicine. "Some have been with us 15 years and are as good at doing procedures as any doctor in the country."

The Role of Women in CPS Mental Hospital Units

The wives of the COs were an integral part of most CPS mental hospital units. They were customarily involved in all aspects of the unit's life. More often than not, they had to put up with the same "slings and arrows" that their husbands initially faced from co-workers or persons in the community who were hostile to their pacifist positions. In time, most of these ill feelings became muted or disappeared entirely. For some, it was a truly difficult experience. But the wives had one thing going for them. They were not subject to the whims and regulations of Selective Service. They were free agents and could come and go as they pleased. They were entitled to the same employment conditions as regular employees of the hospital. And they often brought with them an array of special skills, ranging from medicine, the behavioral sciences, and nursing to teaching and secretarial services. However, because the most serious staff shortages were on the wards, they were usually assigned to attendant duty.

Looking back from a perspective of nearly 45 years, John Burrowes, who served as a member of the Concord State Hospital CPS unit at New Hampshire, made these observations:[3]

> I think it is all too easy to discount the role of COs' wives in this enterprise. A great many of the men who worked in the hospitals went there because they could be with their wives. . . .
>
> Many of the wives occupied significant positions in the hospital.

They often had more influence on policy than we did. I can think of several wives who were very important in the morale and general management of the group. Without them, we would not have succeeded very well because we were working a long-enough week so that we had very little energy left over.

We worked hard, but our biggest function was in adding both intelligence and sane balance to a world that was often out of proportion. In my case it was important when I was working a 78-hour week that there was an additional force, not only of my wife but of the several wives who were also concerned about our situation.

The wives who lived in the town of Concord made healthy contact with the people in the community. The wives who were nurses and filled other positions did a fine job of relating to the rest of the staff. They made us look like human beings. My wife and I started a cooperative house in Concord which was particularly useful to those wives who became pregnant and were unable to work at the time. Bob Carey helped us get it started. We made very good lifelong friends with a local editor, a former Governor's wife, the head of the New Hampshire Office of Price Administration, the head of a local school, and the director of the League of New Hampshire Arts and Crafts. All of these contacts were the result of our living in the local community. . . . Most of all, I feel that these women were often the clearest minds concerned with the work we were doing.

Eleanor Roosevelt Visits CPS Unit at Hudson River State Hospital

Shortly after the Mennonite-sponsored CPS unit arrived at Hudson River State Hospital in Poughkeepsie, New York, in the spring of 1945, many of the COs began expressing concern about the abusive treatment that they observed being meted out to patients by certain members of the regular attendant staff. Patients were being slapped and violently mistreated in an effort to control their behavior.

Initially, the COs tried to remedy the situation on the wards where this violence appeared to be a typical response to uncooperative patients. Dr. John Ross, the superintendent of the facility, had been aware that such mistreatment of patients was a common practice at the hospital, but he had been unable to identify those responsible for such abuses. Because of information provided by members of the CPS unit, he was finally able to ascertain the identities of four employees who had been brutalizing patients.

Those COs who had brought this matter to the attention of Dr. Ross sought to make their position clear. They remarked that their feelings against the use of violence in settling international conflicts applied with equal validity to dealing with recalcitrant patients on a hospital ward. The COs expressed the hope that Dr. Ross would give the employees responsible for the abuse another chance. But Dr. Ross demurred, and the four employees were dismissed.

As was typical in so many communities where CPS mental hospital units served during the war era, local and county as well as state chapters of the American Legion quickly jumped to the defense of hospital employees accused of mistreating patients. The American Legion defended hospital employees exclusively in those situations where allegations of patient abuse had been made by men in the CPS units or at institutions where Selective Service had authorized the placement of such units.

The county chapter of the American Legion echoed the charge in the *Poughkeepsie New Yorker* that COs in service at the Hudson River State Hospital were being "coddled" by the administration.[4] They complained that the members of the CPS unit only worked on the day shift. They went on to assert "that the men in the unit do not wear distinctive uniforms, that they apparently come and go at will from the hospital grounds, that they are permitted to use the recreation halls after 9 P.M. (which privilege is not granted to other attendants)." They also alleged that the COs "have been allowed to play tennis on the superintendent's private tennis court."

The newspaper account went on to express the outrage of the American Legion chapter at the dismissal of the four hospital attendants accused of brutalizing patients without having been given a fair hearing. In response to this development, officers of the chapter reported that they were going to request their local legislators to "ask for a thorough investigation by the state of the manner in which conscientious objectors are being treated at the Hudson River State Hospital."

Soon thereafter an editorial appeared in the *Poughkeepsie New Yorker* requesting that a fair trial be granted to the four employees accused of patient abuse and that a full investigation be conducted into the presence of the CPS unit at the hospital. It should be noted that according to regulations governing the dismissal of hospital employees, the hospital director had full authority to dismiss employees about whom there had been allegations of improper conduct toward patients.

About the same time that the incident was receiving coverage and editorial commentary in the pages of the local newspaper, Eleanor Roosevelt, who lived nearby, had been invited to meet with the 29 members of the CPS unit at Hudson River State Hospital, along with a number of young women students from several Mennonite colleges. These women had taken summer positions at the hospital to help relieve the staff shortage then prevailing at the institution. In her United Features syndicated newspaper column, "My Day," Mrs. Roosevelt reported on her visit with the CPS unit:[5]

> The superintendent of the hospital told me that they [the COs] had undoubtedly raised the standards of care for the patients, and they had been of tremendous help in disclosing certain practices which had existed there and about which he had never been able to get any real evidence. He said if they could stay longer, they would probably improve the standards even more.
>
> Though it is beginning to be a little less difficult to find people for the work which has to be done, it is true we have never given enough thought to finding the right type of persons for positions in these institutions. The salaries are very low. . . . Every employee in a mental hospital should have some special training, either before he is employed or immediately following his employment. But we often employ people with no training and no background, simply because no one is available at the salary offered. . . .

In response to Mrs. Roosevelt's comments in her column, the editors of the *Poughkeepsie New Yorker* responded with the following editorial:[6]

> . . . Since everyone expects CO employment at the hospital will be of short duration, the future of the hospital without their services also becomes a matter of public concern since, apparently, the state has been unable to duplicate the various duties they perform.
>
> Nor can it be said the public acknowledgment of their services will make tenure of the COs at the hospital any more pleasant. To be dedicated to disclose "certain practices which existed there," and to produce "evidence" which never before had been procurable, is not an enviable assignment.
>
> We can only hope that in consideration for the COs, hospital employees and, above all, the patients themselves, that services rendered thus far by these temporary employees have corrected to a large degree the conditions which Dr. Ross . . . had been unable to remedy.

The engagement of Eleanor Roosevelt in the controversy at the Hudson River State Hospital was a major factor in leading her to become one of the highly influential public citizens who became sponsors of the National Mental Health Foundation. This is the organization that those who had served in the CPS mental hospital program established in the post–World War II era in an effort to fulfill their aims of reforming the care provided for the mentally ill. A fuller account of the foundation and its activities is offered in Chapter 8.

It is especially noteworthy to report at this point that the May 1946 *Life Magazine* article by Albert Q. Maisel (see Chapter 2) that offered an exposé of the horrendous conditions then prevailing in many of the nation's mental hospitals might not have appeared in print had it not been for the good offices of Mrs. Roosevelt. Her endorsement of the National Mental Health Foundation and its cause provided easy assess to high-level editors at both *Life* and *Reader's Digest,* which published a condensed version of that article in July 1946. As noted in Chapter 8, Mrs. Roosevelt's active support of the National Mental Health Foundation inspired many of the nation's prominent citizens to join with her in espousing the organization's objectives.

Establishment of CPS Unit at Connecticut State Hospital Ushers in New Era of Reaching Out to the Community

The preceding chapters have provided descriptions of what life was like in some of the nation's mental hospitals during the time when CPS units first began to make their appearance. Although the Connecticut State Hospital was in some respects similar to many of the institutions already described, it was one of the better facilities of its day. It had no wards running rampant with naked patients. The maximum number of patients on any ward was between 50 and 60 individuals. It would be appropriate to describe the overall setting and ambience of this institution as tolerable for its time.

A few weeks after the author of this book arrived at the Connecticut State Hospital with the first group of volunteers from the Quaker-sponsored CPS forestry camp in New Hampshire's White Mountains, he drafted one of a series of round-robin letters to his friends back home, describing the new world into which he had been thrust.

Letter written by Alex Sareyan, April 1, 1943, Connecticut State Hospital at Middletown.

> . . . Three weeks ago, the long arm of Selective Service gave me the green light to move on to a new front . . . approximately 225 miles due south of the White Mountains. At the moment I am sitting in my room in the Attendants' home of the Connecticut State Hospital at Middletown, Connecticut. One eye keeps peeking at the clock. In 20 minutes I am scheduled to report for a nine-hour tour of duty on Ward 17 where some 60 mentally ill male patients are in residence. There is a good likelihood that I will be the lone attendant on the ward for most of the day as the charge attendant is on vacation.
>
> First a paragraph or two to set the scene. Middletown (pop. 25,000) snuggles alongside the Connecticut River, about 27 miles northeast of New Haven and approximately 15 miles due south of

Hartford. The hospital with its many buildings covers a tract of land larger than many towns and villages. The hospital sprawls along a crest overlooking both the city and the river. At the moment, about 3,000 patients are living out their days in this institution.

A hospital population of this size normally requires a staff of about 850 employees, including doctors, nurses, attendants, therapists, office personnel, kitchen crews, farm hands, maintenance crews, security and grounds personnel, etc. As of the date of our unit's arrival, there were barely 400 employees on staff. The attendant shortage has been so acute that at times one attendant has had to assume responsibility for as many as four wards with a total of 160 or more patients. Under normal conditions a minimum of 12 attendants would be required to staff these wards.

The terrific dislocation in the normal staff-to-patient ratio has not been without consequence. Occupational therapy has taken on the status reserved only for a few patients. For nearly a year the practice of taking patients from their wards to the hospital grounds for exercise has been discontinued. When the men in our unit arrived, this custom was resumed, though on a very infrequent schedule. The institution has a superb facility for hydrotherapy, a treatment procedure which has proved to be very effective for many patients. Unfortunately, it has had to be mothballed for lack of staff.

In the reception service where new patients report on admission and are kept under observation for a 30-day period, prior to ward assignment, many special services are available such as electroshock therapy. But once the 30-day period is up and the patient is transferred to one of the wards, individual attention becomes a rarity.

Except for a few hundred patients who are assigned to work responsibilities in such facilities of the institution as the kitchen, cafeteria, laundry, farm, dairy, and other essential services, the daily routine of the average patient is a pretty dismal affair. A few of the less disturbed patients read or play cards. Many spend the long days just pacing back and forth in their ward or rocking endlessly in a chair.

But a surprisingly large number of patients do indicate by their actions and responses that they are not completely "out of this world." Some even appear to be so normal in their behavior that it is hard to understand what they are doing in a mental hospital.

On Sundays, those patients able to and desirous of attending religious services are afforded an opportunity to do so. Once a week, these same patients along with most of the worker-patients are permitted to attend a weekly movie in the hospital auditorium. Occasionally, a local service group from the community will offer a musical program, and these too are well attended by patients.

If I were to list the duties of an attendant, I'm afraid it would make for dull reading. Perhaps another way of doing this is to share with you a typical nine-hour tour of duty. Today was my day off so let me tell you about what happened yesterday. At 5:30 A.M. the alarm jarred me from my fitful slumbers . . . the first few nights after my arrival I hardly slept at all. Within 45 minutes from the alarm I was on my way to breakfast in the attendants' alcove just off the south end of the huge patients' cafeteria. Cereal, fried eggs that might have been more palatable an hour earlier, toast for which the same could be said, and coffee whose chief virtue had nothing to do with its flavor completed the menu.

At precisely seven o'clock I unlocked and locked my way through a series of steel doors until I arrived on Ward 17. The night attendant was eager to see me as it meant his tour of duty was over. Most of the patients were quietly sitting or standing in the corridor, waiting for the breakfast line-up. I had become accustomed to the oppressively foul odor which permeated the ward at this time of day. I hurriedly glanced into each of the rooms to be certain that the beds were properly arranged for airing.

Next on the list came the porch doors which had to be unlocked. Mr. Whalen (all names used in identifying patients are fanciful concoctions), an old duffer who had been following me all the while, asked for a light. (Patients are not allowed to have matches.) As I struck the match, I noticed that his cigarette was a "Middletown special" . . . that is, it was pipe tobacco that had been rolled in toilet tissue.

Just then, my attention was diverted to Charley Reed, a tall elderly gent who had been a guest of the hospital since 1912. One of the other patients whose patience had been severely taxed by the old chap's behavior had decorated him with a bleeding nose. I was not at all surprised because when Reed goes off on a toot, he really takes off. He's harmless enough unless someone happens to accidentally step into the range of his flailing arms, usually accompanied by such outbursts as "That boy there, take him out and stone him to death! Show him no mercy! No goddam mercy. None, none whatsoever!"

By the time the fracas was over, the supervisor appeared on the scene for his first inspection of the day. After a perfunctory glance around, he made his entry in the day book and strode out of the ward and on to the next. His departure was the signal for leaving the ward for breakfast.

In a place such as this, even a novice soon discovers how to spot characteristics which indicate the degree to which a patient has deteriorated. Complete disregard for personal appearance is one such criterion. A patient's table manners are equally revealing. So please join with me as we enter the dining area to observe a typical meal for the patients.

In the center of the dining area, which incidentally covers about as much space as a typical football-size arena, are the serving counters. Women patients are served from one side and the men patients from the opposite side. There are accommodations for 750 sittings at a time, with the sexes segregated on either side of the counters. As a rule breakfast consists of hot cereal, bread, oleo, and coffee. Noon menus feature such dishes as stews, fish, potatoes, meat loaf on occasion, and puddings. Soups, macaroni, bread and coffee generally find their way to the supper tables. There is plenty of food, and seconds are generally available. The average daily meal expenditure per patient runs to about 18 cents.

Now back to breakfast duty. I followed the stragglers from the ward to the cafeteria. Once they were all in, it was my job along with the other attendants on duty to maintain order. Every now and then, someone would try to snatch food from another's tray. I spotted a young Jewish lad from my ward, who usually ate little or nothing, leave the line. When I urged him to go up to the counter, he retorted, "You can't force me to eat this dirty brown bread." (As a matter of fact, the bread is good and it is the only food he does eat.) After urging him to stay in line, I had to leave him. At this point, the violence-prone patients had arrived, and it was part of my job to help feed those who were in restraints.

As I finished feeding my last patient in a straitjacket, I spied a tall, lean, shifty-eyed man pick up his tray and start for the counter where dirty dishes were returned. I ran up to him and escorted him to the area. I knew from experience, that if given the opportunity, he would dive into the swill bucket under the counter and stuff his pockets with garbage. His tray hadn't been down for a second before his left hand disappeared into the hole which contained the garbage receptacle. I didn't smack him or shove him to the floor as other attendants often did, but I did grab him and force him to loosen his grip on what he had retrieved, and pushed him with my five feet, two inch stature toward the exit.

As I recall meal duty, I must admit that it had its own unique compensations. Often, it would resemble a three-ring circus with clowns operating in all three simultaneously. One particular patient, whose arms were almost always in a perpetual state of motion, would upon completing his meal, stand up and pour over his head whatever liquids remained in his tray such as coffee, tea, soup, etc. He would then vigorously massage the liquids into his scalp.

Upon returning to the ward after breakfast, I checked all the rooms again to make sure that the beds were in order before the doctor made his scheduled rounds for the day. Six of the patients were already at their housecleaning chores. I managed to talk several other patients out of their lethargy into wall-washing and chair-cleaning assignments.

Some patients won't do a lick of work, no matter. If they can't be verbally cajoled, they are left to their own devices. One of the attendant's duties is to try and keep as many patients as possible occupied in some meaningful activity. As a reward for participating the charge attendant customarily doles out small handfuls of tobacco to those in this group.

I spent the rest of the morning folding clothes and distributing them to the individual patients' lockers. One of the patients had a visitor during this period and I devoted 15 minutes to making him presentable and then escorted him to the reception area.

Immediately following lunch, it was time for the weekly bath session. Most of the patients took their shower without pause. Some, however, balked but eventually though reluctantly crawled out of their clothes and into the showers, that is all except one. Polite requests fell upon deaf ears. Reasons and arguments were of no avail. Finally I turned to one of the other attendants who had just arrived, for aid. The air was soon filled with a few choice cuss words, and the battle was over.

> During the balance of the afternoon until four when my duty day officially ended, I intercepted a fight between two patients; dished out some brotherly advice to a young lad; engaged two patients in conversation (only six of the patients on the ward are capable of carrying on an intelligent one); showed an old, one-eyed patient and a five-time escapee how to play solitaire; helped two young patients learn how to make a bed; convinced a patient that the floor was not a spittoon; and played rummy with a long-time resident of the ward. About this time it was four o'clock, my relief had arrived, and so ended my day on Ward 17.

The 85-man American Friends Service Committee-sponsored CPS unit at the Connecticut State Hospital at Middletown was in many respects similar in makeup to the other seven mental hospital units under the committee's auspices at that time. As was the case with all such units, about one-fourth of the men were accompanied by their wives. The women were eagerly welcomed as so many of the hospitals had even more serious staff shortages on the female wards than on the male wards. The presence of the women also provided a morale booster not otherwise available in the base camps from which the COs had been recruited for the hospital units.

On the surface, the Connecticut State Hospital did not reflect the horrendous conditions then characteristic of some of the institutions described earlier in this book. At the Connecticut State Hospital there were no wards teaming with hundreds of naked patients, walking or aimlessly standing in barren dayrooms. But superior as the Connecticut State Hospital was to notorious institutions such as the Philadelphia State Hospital and those at Cleveland and Williamsburg, an undeniable atmosphere of fear hung heavy in many of its wards. Patients were aware that unless they toed the line, punishment was very often a consequence.

The Connecticut State Hospital had another redeeming feature. The administration alertly took advantage of the unique skills that many of the COs had brought with them to the hospital. This chapter focuses on one particular program that emerged as a result of a fortuitous working relationship that developed between the superintendent and the CPS unit's assistant director. This relationship led to the development of a new service that played a major role in the creation of a new and constructive public image for the hospital. In the postwar era, the Connecticut State Hospital served as a model for the state's four other mental health facilities and, as will be described later, its new service contributed to a nationwide effort to gain more responsive public concern for the mentally ill.

The CPS unit at the Connecticut State Hospital was established in March 1943 with the arrival of 15 COs who had been selected from volunteers then assigned to a CPS base camp at West Campton, New Hampshire, under the technical direction of the U.S. Forestry Service. Shortly after their arrival at the Connecticut State Hospital, members of the unit gathered for an organizational meeting. As was the custom with such units serving under auspices of the American Friends Service Committee, one of their group was elected to serve as assistant director for the team. In accord with Selective Service regulations, the director of the hospital, Dr. Roy Leak, was also the designated director of the unit.

The assistant director's primary activities were to maintain personnel records for each of the unit's members and to prepare monthly reports from these data for Selective Service. But his subsidiary responsibilities went far beyond recordkeeping and filing reports. In most situations the assistant director was also initially assigned to duty in one of the institution's services. This duty was usually on a part-time basis so that he could have adequate time for processing the paperwork required by Selective Service. The assistant director also served as counselor to members of the unit and was the channel through which their concerns and gripes got passed on to the superintendent of the hospital, to the sponsoring peace church, or to Selective Service.

In the effort to help boost morale in their respective CPS units, all three peace churches scheduled visits to the units by persons of national repute who also shared the pacifist beliefs held by the COs. It was the assistant director's responsibility to serve as host to these visiting dignitaries and arrange for them to meet with members of the unit. As the size of the units increased to as many as 75 or more men, an educational director was chosen from among the unit members to assume responsibilities for hosting these gatherings. He also facilitated educational and cultural pursuits for the men during their nonduty hours. Customarily, he was granted some relief from his regular hospital duties to fulfill his duties.

The skills and tact that both the assistant director and the educational director brought to their respective tasks greatly influenced the kind of relations that developed among members of the unit, the hospital administration, and the regular employees. In many settings in which CPS units were located, feelings toward the COs ranged from bare tolerance to outright hostility. Where there was skillful leadership within the CPS units, the intensity of these feelings generally subsided within a reasonable period of time.

Dr. Leak arranged to have the assistant director carry on his administrative responsibilities for the CPS unit in a conference room adjacent to his own office. This gave the unit's assistant director a degree of access to the superintendent that went far beyond that enjoyed by the institution's administrative and supervisory staff. Hardly a day went by that the assistant director was not able to get Dr. Leak's attention. Thus, the concerns of those in the CPS unit could be communicated via an almost constantly open channel to the most influential person in the hospital: the superintendent. In most state hospitals in the 1940s, superintendents more often than not ran their institutions as personal fiefdoms in which they reigned as "benevolent despots." Some were more benevolent than others. But one fact was inescapable. The superintendent was in firm control of the destinies of both the patients and the employees.

Within several weeks after arrival of the COs at the hospital, Dr. Leak discovered that the assistant director of the CPS unit had been a journalism and public relations major at the University of Pennsylvania. For some time Dr. Leak had been trying to establish a house organ that would provide a channel of communication between the administration and the employees and patients. After describing his objectives to the assistant director, Dr. Leak arranged to release him from a portion of his clerical and part-time ward duties and gave him a free hand in developing the institution's first in-house newsletter.

Shortly thereafter, the new house organ made its initial appearance as *The Scribe,* a name that had been suggested by one of the

The Scribe

patients in a hospitalwide competition. Although most of the patients at the hospital had readily accepted the COs, this was not the case with a considerable number of the regular employees. Because of this state of affairs, it was important during the introductory period that *The Scribe* not appear to give any impression that its pages were "tainted" by the fact that its editor was a member of the CPS unit. For this reason, the first several issues were released without attribution to an editor. No one was fooled by this management ploy. But it did foster acceptance by the hospital community.

The Scribe offered the administration frequent opportunities to convey messages as well as greetings to both patients and employees. It featured news items of interest to both groups, and both groups were invited to make editorial contributions. In the belief that patients were individuals in the full sense of that term, when contributions from them were accepted for publication, they were given full credit.

Approximately 1,000 copies of *The Scribe* were printed each month so that both patients and employees had full access to the periodical. Each issue was avidly read. Within six months of publication of the first issue, an editorial board made up of 10 regular employees was established. As the work load for producing the monthly issues of *The Scribe* increased, editorial responsibility for it was transferred to other individuals in the CPS unit. It is noteworthy that 20 years after the last man was discharged from the CPS unit, *The Scribe* was still being published in virtually the same format that had prevailed during the CPS era.

In the late summer of 1944, a new set of circumstances at the Connecticut State Hospital permitted the development of a program never before attempted on a full-time basis in a U.S. public mental hospital. Earlier in that year, Dr. Leak retired after a long tenure as its chief administrator, and he was replaced by Dr. Edgar Yerbury. The new superintendent's style of leadership was much less autocratic than that of his predecessor. He was open to new approaches to dealing with the many-faceted problems associated with running a state institution of the size and scope of the Middletown facility. The CPS unit by this time had reached its full authorized strength of 85 men, and it had been augmented by at least 20 of the men's wives who had joined the hospital staff.

The catchment area from which the Connecticut State Hospital drew patients was the central region of the state. It ran from the Massachusetts border on the north to the Long Island Sound on the south. The two largest cities in the state, New Haven and Hartford, were within this region. The state's most influential newspapers and radio stations were also located in this region. Public taxes supported the institution, which were augmented by modest revenues collected from patients' relatives. If possible, families of patients were expected to reimburse the hospital on a sliding scale up to a maximum of $5 per week. However, patients of families unable to meet this requirement were readily accepted.

Unfortunately, at this time the public perceptions of mental hospitals and mentally ill people were almost universally based on fear and ignorance. Mental patients at that time were commonly referred to as "inmates," a term more appropriate for those committed to penal institutions. In the minds of many, persons committed to mental hospitals were thought to be maniacs who needed to be kept in restraints to prevent them from doing harm to themselves and others. On the outside, little was known about what went on in mental hospitals. More appalling than that, few people seemed to care. To a certain extent, the stigma attached to the mentally ill and the institutions to which they had been committed also affected those who toiled as employees in these institutions.

During this period, attendants in mental hospitals were expected to serve a minimum of 54 hours and as many as 80 hours per week for as little as $2 to $3 per day, including room and board. And the room and board were nothing to brag about. It was almost as if state mental hospitals of that era were situated in some proverbial "Siberia." And there was no one out there, day after day, trying to correct the public's misperceptions. Nor was there a consistent voice telling the public what these institutions needed to meet the care and treatment needs of their patients.

At one of their regular meetings, the assistant director broached to Dr. Yerbury the idea of establishing a public relations department. This was to be a full-time assignment. Among the objectives for this proposed program were the following:

1. To explain mental illness to the general public and, in so doing, to offset the widely held misconceptions and social stigma related to it
2. To report and explain activities of the hospital to the surrounding community as well as to the state at large
3. To keep the public informed when the hospital was unable to render the proper level of care and treatment to its patients because of insufficient funds or lack of trained personnel
4. To gain the respect and confidence of both the public and the media through frank and straightforward accounts of all newsworthy developments at the hospital, whether favorable or not
5. To promote harmony and open lines of communication among administration, employees, and patients

It didn't take Dr. Yerbury long to reach the conclusion that such a program was long overdue. Under normal conditions, it could easily have taken months, if not years, to get official sanction to initiate such a major departure from normal operating procedures. But these were not normal times. No new job classification had to be sanctioned by the state personnel office. No new funds had to be budgeted for staffing such a program. All the superintendent had to do was reassign the assistant director directly to his office with a new set of responsibilities. As with all other men in the CPS unit, the new public relations director would continue to work a 54-hour week at a monthly allowance of $15 plus room and board.

During the period that the Connecticut State Hospital public relations office was established, no such similar program was functioning in any of the nation's state mental hospitals. Of equal if not greater significance, no such full-time informational office had been placed in service in any of the nation's state agencies overseeing mental health services in their respective jurisdictions. Furthermore, no such department was operative at the federal agency charged with oversight of mental health services.

About 18 months after the Connecticut State Hospital public relations office had been established, a unique editorial appeared in the pages of *The Hartford Courant,* one of the state's leading newspapers.[7] Although the editorial had been inspired by a press release from the hospital concerning a new foster care program being initiated by the hospital, it was titled "Public Relations." In part, it read as follows:

> Under ordinary circumstances the label "public relations" appended to a news release sets up involuntary resistance in the mind of an editor. He immediately looks for the angle. A news release from the Connecticut State Hospital's public relations office is something else again, because if any group of institutions desperately need good public relations counsel, it is those housing the mentally ill. They had their beginnings in the poorhouse and they have never yet been able to shed completely their humble origins. Usually they are treated like poor relations when it comes time to fix appropriations. Almost invariably they are overcrowded and understaffed. When they make the front page, it is likely to spell trouble for them because they usually become news only when an act of violence or other trouble occurs.
>
> It is therefore pleasant to realize that Dr. Edgar Yerbury, superintendent of the Connecticut State Hospital, realizes that a man-sized public relations effort must be done if the mental hospital is to receive the same attention, confidence, and respect that are accorded hospitals treating physical ailments.
>
> . . . It is good to know that the Connecticut State Hospital has recognized the value of good public relations. It is to be hoped that it will be developed on the sound basis of accomplishments, rather than being like so many public relations programs, a compound of sound and fury signifying nothing.

Soon after the public relations office was established, invitations were sent to newspapers in the hospital's region inviting their representatives to a press conference at the hospital. Because the previous administration had had a closed-door policy to the press, it was important to regain the newspapers' confidence. The basic purpose of this first session was to introduce Dr. Yerbury to the print media and give him an opportunity to get to know those responsible for covering news developments in the area. At the press conference, several reporters were briefed on conditions at the hospital and then were given complete latitude to visit any parts of the facility they wished to see. At the end of the meeting, they were encouraged to call the public relations office whenever they wanted to pursue any specific matters with the superintendent.

The hospital's new public relations officer also visited the editors of all the major newspapers in the hospital's region to explore opportunities for placing feature stories on various aspects of the institution's life and its concerns in their Sunday supplements. He was warmly welcomed and urged to submit any suggestions he believed to be newsworthy. Both *The Hartford Courant* and *The New Haven Register* ran several feature stories from time to time written by the public relations officer. In all cases, the stories, usually accompanied by relevant photos, were printed word for word as submitted.

One of these features was a double-page picture spread in *The Hartford Courant*'s Sunday Magazine for February 24, 1946.[8] It included 12 photos that had been selected to give a revealing glimpse of the hospital in action. A number of patients appeared in these pictures, which had been taken by one of the paper's photographers. The story's basic purpose was to take the reader inside the walls of the hospital. Other than captions for the pictures, the only accompanying text was the following copy:

> More hospital beds are set aside for the care of the mentally ill in this country than for any other type of patient. Yet the story of mental illness, which reaches into the lives of so many, is known to so few. So few indeed, that the nearly 600,000 persons now being cared for in such communities as Connecticut State Hospital at Middletown have so disappeared from the public conscience that they might as well as be living in another world. In the last 20 years, medical science has developed many new techniques in hastening the recovery and rehabilitation of our mentally ill. At present about half of all patients admitted to our state hospitals are able to return home, improved or recovered. Despite severe handicaps, our state hospitals are trying to do what they can to rehabilitate our mentally ill.

One of the hospital's major concerns during this period was finding suitable foster homes for 250 of its patients whose progress was such that they were suitable for placement into transitional housing. Most of these patients had no relatives who could provide the supervision they required to facilitate their transition from the hospital to the community. The foster home concept had been tried and proven to be effective in a demonstration program conducted in New York State in the previous decade.

A press release was drafted that described the need for recruiting foster homes to accommodate those patients who might benefit from such transitional housing. The press release also pointed out that if the effort turned out to be successful, it would relieve the serious overcrowding that then prevailed at the Connecticut State Hospital.

The New Haven Register ran the story as a feature in its Sunday supplement early in 1946.[9] The text furnished by the hospital was used word for word. *The Hartford Times* published an editorial supporting Dr. Yerbury's plea for foster homes, which concluded with this observation:[10]

> The outcome of Dr. Yerbury's idea should be no less successful in Connecticut than it has been elsewhere. It is a welcome advance in the technique of caring for the mentally ill and promising their return to normal life.

One of the Connecticut State Hospital's most frustrating concerns in the summer of 1945 was that two of its newest and most modern buildings had to be closed because of severe labor shortages. Even with the presence of the CPS unit, the hospital still had 375 vacancies among its nursing and maintenance personnel. The closed buildings resulted in severe overcrowding on many of the institution's wards. On some wards, so many beds had to be placed side by side that there was little or no room to walk between the beds. A release accompanied by photos was dispatched to the network of newspapers in the region. As a result, these crowded conditions were widely publicized.

Many of the press releases emanating from the hospital focused on the patients themselves. These stories were written to illustrate to the public that the hospital's patients were human beings whose needs and desires were in many respects similar to their own.

Christmas was an especially poignant time for patients at the hospital. About half the patients had friends and relatives who frequently remembered them, especially at holiday periods. Unfortunately, about 1,500 of the patients had been at the hospital for 10 or more years without ever having been visited by a relative or friend. They were truly the forgotten ones.

About a month before Christmas 1943, the following appeal was sent to all the newspapers in the hospital's region, including the following statement by the hospital director:

> . . . A recent study of the records of the Connecticut State Hospital revealed that nearly half of its 3,000 patients have had no visits from friends or relatives during the past year. Many of them have not seen a visitor for as many as 10 or more years. . . .
>
> For most of these forgotten people, and they are people—the approach of the Christmas season no longer evokes eager anticipation but rather a reminiscent mood revealing poignant memories of Christmas days once enjoyed amid family circles. The exhilaration has gone. Only the nostalgia remains.
>
> To help these forgotten people to recapture the joy of Christmas season . . . we are hoping to provide them with individual gifts and are making plans to give all our patients a varied program of holiday festivities. These plans will succeed—only if the people of Connecticut do not forget these patients when making up their Christmas list.
>
> . . . Packages should be marked "Christmas Gift" and may be sent directly to the hospital. . . . Will you share in this endeavor to keep alive the Spirit of Christmas for those who once may have been your neighbors?

In response to that appeal, which was carried not only on the front page of *The Middletown Press* but also by several other newspapers, over 4,000 gifts inundated the hospital. With the aid of volunteers and staff, all the gifts were packaged and delivered to the wards where they brightened the day for those who once had been the "forgotten ones."

Approximately 600 patients regularly attended Catholic and Protestant services scheduled each Sunday in the auditorium. Those unable to attend were provided an opportunity to hear these services over the hospital's public address system, which reached all the wards throughout the institution.

On weekday mornings, many patients were also accustomed to gathering around the public address system on their individual wards to listen to a 15-minute devotional program emanating from a New Haven radio station. When this program suddenly went off the air, the patients were so disappointed that, at the suggestion of the public relations office, arrangements were made with a radio station in Hartford to record a series of brief devotional programs involving local clergymen. A total of 24 nonsectarian programs, consisting of readings from the Bible, devotional messages, and sacred music, were produced. Once a week, several patients from the regular choir appeared on the program with a

Patients awaiting start of chapel service on a Sunday afternoon in the auditorium of the Connecticut State Hospital at Middletown.

Entertainments
ENTERTAINMENTS GIVEN BY OUTSIDE ORGANIZATIONS AND OTHER SPECIALLY ARRANGED SHOWS AND SPORT EVENTS SUCH AS BALL GAMES ARE ENTHUSIASTICALLY ATTENDED BY LARGE GROUPS · · ·
MOVIE PROGRAMS FROM THE MAJOR HOLLYWOOD STUDIOS ARE SHOWN IN THE HOSPITAL AUDITORIUM EVERY FRIDAY AFTERNOON AND EVENING · ABOUT 800 PATIENTS USUALLY ATTEND THESE PERFORMANCES · · · ·
MOVIE PROGRAMS
RADIO PROGRAMS
RADIO PROGRAMS ARE PICKED-UP FROM THE MAJOR NETWORKS EVERY AFTERNOON AND EVENING AND ARE RELAYED TO ALL THE WARDS · ESPECIALLY POPULAR AMONG THE PATIENTS ARE THE NEWS BROADCASTS · · · · · · ·
IN PROPER BALANCE - RELIGIOUS AND CULTURAL AND RECREATIONAL INTERESTS PLAY AN IMPORTANT PART IN THE SHAPING OF NORMAL AND HEALTHY PERSONALITIES
IF PROPERLY USED - THEY ARE "JUST WHAT THE DOCTOR ORDERED" TO HELP PREVENT US FROM BOGGING DOWN IN THE RUT OF WARPED ONE-TRACKED PERSONALITIES - AS HAS BEEN THE CASE WITH SO MANY PATIENTS - WHO ARE ADMITTED EACH DAY TO MENTAL HOSPITALS
PATIENTS are PEOPLE
MANY PATIENTS ENJOY AND PARTICIPATE IN LEISURE TIME PURSUITS FOUND IN THE NORMAL COMMUNITY
THESE LEISURE-TIME PURSUITS ARE AN INTEGRAL PART OF TREATMENT AT THE CONNECTICUT STATE HOSPITAL -- THEY SERVE TO BRIDGE THE GAP BETWEEN THE UNREAL WORLD OF A PERSON WHO IS MENTALLY ILL AND THE SECURITY THAT PREVAILS IN A GOOD HOME LOCATED IN A NORMAL SOCIETY ·
SERVICES ARE ATTENDED BY MORE THAN 600 PATIENTS EACH SUNDAY · FOR THOSE UNABLE TO ATTEND - THE PROGRAMS ARE BROADCAST OVER THE PUBLIC ADDRESS SYSTEM · ON THREE MORNINGS A WEEK SPECIALLY TRANSCRIBED DEVOTIONAL SERVICES (NON-SECTARIAN) ARE ALSO BROADCAST TO ALL THE WARDS · ·
RELIGIOUS SERVICES
READING
READING IS A FAVORITE PASTIME OF LARGE NUMBERS OF PATIENTS · BOOKS FROM A WELL-EQUIPPED LIBRARY ARE AVAILABLE TO ALL PATIENTS · MANY PATIENTS RECEIVE HOMETOWN NEWSPAPERS · ALSO EVERY MONTH 125 COPIES OF 16 MAGAZINES ARE DISTRIBUTED THROUGHOUT THE WARDS · · ·
SOCIAL DANCES ARE ENJOYED BY NEARLY 200 PATIENTS ONE EVENING A WEEK · THE MUSIC IS FURNISHED BY AN ORCHESTRA COMPOSED OF EMPLOYEES · A POPULAR FEATURE OF THESE SOCIALS IS FOLK DANCING · · · · · ·

number of especially rehearsed hymns.

Other targets of the hospital's public relations efforts were the visitors who streamed into the institution on the two regular visiting days each week. They were considered to be especially vulnerable to educational messages designed to give them greater sensitivity to and awareness of the illness that had prompted the commitment of their relatives and friends to the institution. Among the members of the CPS unit there was a very talented artist who had the gift of translating difficult concepts into attractive and eye-catching presentations. With the permission of the superintendent, this person, William Steinel, was given released time to prepare a number of exhibits that were then prominently displayed in various waiting areas of the hospital. Many of Steinel's creations later appeared in print media and were given wide circulation. On page 112 is an example of one of his creations.

As was previously noted, one of the major objectives of the public relations office was to educate the local community about the true nature of mental illness and in so doing help to eradicate prevailing misconceptions and ignorance about the nature of this disease. To that end, the public relations office arranged to acquire two exceptionally fine documentary films concerning the handling of psychiatric casualties among British and American servicemen for separate public showings at the hospital. The community response to both presentations was so overwhelming that several presentations of each had to be arranged to accommodate all who wished to see them.

The first of these documentaries was a British film, *Psychiatry in Action*. It was a dramatic documentary that showed how psychiatric techniques were used to treat British servicemen who had become mentally ill as a result of their war exposure.

The American film, also produced at about the same time, was titled *Let There Be Light*. It was made at a Long Island state hospital that had been taken over by the U.S. Army as a treatment facility for its servicemen who had become psychiatric casualties. The film offered a very enlightening and dramatic account of the treatment and recovery of several servicemen who had succumbed to a variety of serious mental illnesses. The film was directed by John Huston,

Some people still believe . . .

But science tells us . . .

mental illness is a disgrace and cannot be prevented or cured

Just as with physical ills, mental illness needs early medical treatment and is not a disgrace

mental illness comes suddenly and without warning

Mental illness develops gradually and shows warning signs

mental illness is inherited

Only a few types of mental illness may be due to inherited tendencies; most are the result of other factors who was later to achieve distinction in the American film industry.

Let There Be Light was of special interest to the Connecticut State Hospital community because Dr. Ben Simon, the medical director of the Long Island facility and the physician featured in the story, had been the clinical director at the Connecticut State Hospital before his enlistment in the Army Medical Corps at the beginning of the war. This film was acclaimed at the time as one of the most inspiring and informative documentaries of its kind.

In recognition of radio's unique role as a vehicle for molding and shaping public attitudes and opinions, the public relations office reviewed several ways to use this medium as one of the components of its outreach effort. Finally, it settled on producing two half-hour dramas suitable for radio presentation. These programs were concerned with community perceptions about mental illness and the mentally ill. (Television was not considered to be an appropriate medium as it was still in the experimental stages of development.)

Making effective use of radio to achieve educational objectives required a degree of creativity and expertise for which the office had no budget. Fortunately, one of the men in the CPS unit, Jack Neher, had been exposed to the medium of radio while working at the NBC studios in New York City before his induction. Neher was approached with the hope that it might be possible to develop two half-hour radio dramas drawn from case material taken from the hospital's files. One of these dramas concerned a young mother who had suffered a case of postpartum depression so severe that she had to be hospitalized. The other concerned a young woman who had been institutionalized after the traumatic shock of being jilted by her fiancé on the eve of her wedding day.

Neher agreed to participate in the project, and soon the two radio dramas had been scripted. But another step had to be taken before these plays could be translated into suitable radio dramas. Serendipitously, the Yale Drama School was only a short distance from the hospital. An appointment was arranged with one of the professors there, after which she agreed to recruit volunteers for the project from among her students. Finally, a studio was needed to record the programs with appropriate music and sound effects. The program director at Station WELI in New Haven welcomed the opportunity to grant use of his facility for this purpose. Subsequently, both programs were completed and scheduled for broadcast in both New Haven and Hartford.

Two years later, these same two programs were incorporated into a series of eight radio dramas on mental illness produced at the NBC studios in New York for nationwide distribution. They turned out to be the first dramatic programs on a variety of mental illness–related themes to be broadcast throughout the United States and Canada. A fuller account of this project, as well as two additional series of mental health–related radio programs, can be found in Chapter 8.

Even though the war ended in August 1945, it was another 15 months before all the CPS units were completely discharged. Based on a point system established by Selective Service, men in these units became eligible for release as they met the requirements set by that agency. In many of the CPS mental hospital units, the departure of the COs and their wives precipitated outpourings of appreciation from many of the staff and the patients. Most of these expressions of appreciation were verbal, but many took the form of open letters. Others took a more literary turn. Here are two examples, both from grateful patients at the Connecticut State Hospital who had been touched by the presence of the COs in their midst.

The first of these expressions of gratitude, penned by a woman patient, was titled "In Appreciation of the CO." It appeared in the hospital's house organ, *The Scribe*.

> With the arrival of the CO element at the Connecticut State Hospital, patients and personnel were aware of a flow of Christian culture which immediately dominated every department.
>
> Feminine members, the very essence of loveliness, were assigned to the various wards as day or night attendants. I shall always remember the feeling of utter security with which I fell asleep as a certain little CO, carefully shading her night light with her hand, walked softly past my bed. Who knows but what sound sleep, induced by such a serene little soul, has done much to restore the world to reason.
>
> The young CO attendants working among the men have distinguished themselves along many lines. I have never seen men

> more tender than CO attendants when assisting so-called "tough" patients. If this attitude were practiced universally, peace would prevail. . . .
>
> Within a few weeks, the COs are to be replaced by returning former members of the staff, who while in the U.S. armed forces, risked all in the defense of freedom. In this particular instance, each element assists the other in the defense of unfortunate human beings who might otherwise be forgotten.
>
> . . . While serving here the COs have made a definite contribution to peace. Musicians among them have given freely of their time and talent with the result that music appreciation is now part of the daily program.
>
> . . . Articles of exceptional merit, contributed by personnel and patients, appear regularly in *The Scribe,* edited by CO employees. . . .
>
> To those who are returning to their posts here, as well as to those who are being relieved of their responsibilities here, we say, with deepest gratitude, "Blessed are the peacemakers."

The second item was a poem written by a patient terribly crippled by arthritis, who for many years had been completely forgotten by family and friends. As one of the newly discharged CPS men who had been regularly assigned to this patient's ward was bidding him farewell, the patient handed the CPS man a sheet of paper on which he had written:

> My heart has a tiny window
> Through which your love song flew
> And no matter what I sing
> The melody is you.
> My heart has a shining window
> Which frames a lovely view
> And no matter where I look
> My eyes see only you.

Chapter 6

Perceptions and Misperceptions

Although endless columns of newspaper space were devoted to all varieties of perceptions and misperceptions about conscientious objectors (COs) during the war, other channels of communication were also used to vent feelings about the presence of Civilian Public Service (CPS) units in communities where they were located. In one New England town, a barber shop proprietor gave voice to his feelings about COs on a poster prominently displayed in the front window. This poster is shown on the right.

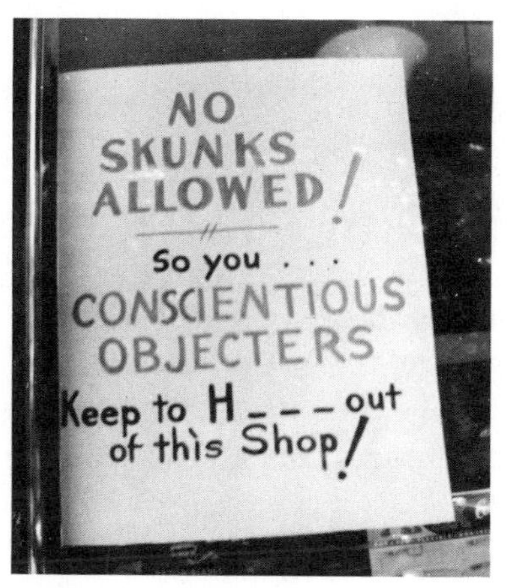

Despite the fact that the climate of public opinion toward COs in World War II appeared to be more tolerant than it had been during World War I, CPS units experienced various degrees of hostility. This was particularly true for those units assigned to public mental hospitals and training schools for the retarded, especially when they first arrived on the scene. The men in these units were much more visible to the public than were their fellow COs serving in isolated settings under the jurisdiction of the National Park Service, the Forestry Service, the Soil Conservation Service, and other similar agencies.

In most of the mental hospital units, regular employees' hostile feelings toward the COs faded to a large extent once they had an opportunity to become better acquainted with the men. However, a small but highly vocal minority persisted in their objection to the presence of the CPS units in their midst. For many of these individuals, the "Letters to the Editor" columns of their local newspapers offered the ideal forum for expressing their negative feelings toward the COs. From time to time, these hostile letters would be countered with responses from persons who were inclined to be tolerant and supportive of the accomplishments of those in the CPS units. Although the letters reprinted in this chapter were drawn from relatively few communities, they were typical of observations that appeared in the news media in virtually every locality in which a CPS unit was stationed.

Newspaper Reactions to the COs

A barrage of pro and con letters appeared in local newspapers in the communities of Norwich and Mansfield, Connecticut. The former was the site of a CPS state hospital unit, and the latter had a similar group assigned to a state training school for the retarded. The flood of anti-CO sentiment in these communities was touched off by an article in the January 1, 1944, issue of the *Norwich Bulletin* in which a trustee of the Mansfield State Training School, the Reverend Charles Hutchinson, Jr., was reported to have stated that it was doubtful that the institution could have continued to function without the presence of the COs. The article indicated that he had published an article a few months earlier in *The Christian Century* in which he stated that the CPS unit "has proved to be a priceless asset." In that article he also had praised the presence at the institution of 11 wives of the men in the CPS unit, who had been hired to fill several vital positions at the facility.

Within days of the publication of that article in the *Norwich Bulletin,* the "Letters to the Editor" column became the focal point for a stream of sharply critical responses from employees of the school, parents of men who had been drafted into the armed services, and citizens from a wide range of backgrounds. The letters ranged the gamut from patriotic outbursts to flagrantly distorted facts on how the men in the CPS unit were being pampered by the school's administration.

Typical of some of these outbursts were the following:

> . . . We buy war bonds to our full capacity. How many bonds have these COs bought? The answer is zero. . . .[1]

> . . . The Reverend Mr. Hutchinson stated that these COs saved our skin at Mansfield. It would be too bad to close a school of this kind, . . . but I think it would be a whole lot worse for all of us to have Hitler come over here and tear our flag down and take over our country. . . .[2]

> . . . Who told trustee Hutchinson that the COs were a priceless asset? . . . The only other employees sharing that opinion are 27 COs themselves. . . .[3]

Other letters directed their jabs at the school's administration for giving the COs gasoline without ration coupons so they could make home visits and giving them preference over the regular employees in housing arrangements.

A spate of angry letters in reference to the CPS unit at Norwich State Hospital also made it to the columns of the *Norwich Bulletin*. They complained about the privileges that they asserted were being granted to members of the unit. Among the charges were that the COs were being allowed vacations, had the freedom to travel at will, and held dances and parties in their rooms, disturbing the regular employees at all hours of the night. The allegation was made that regular employees were restricted to one-half slice of bread at mealtimes and to reduced portions of some foods, whereas the COs could "proudly walk up to the counter and get all they wanted."

But there were rebuttals to these charges. A few were from members of the CPS unit, who tried to present a more accurate picture of their situation. Still others were made by members of the regular hospital community. One of these rebuttals offered the following impression about the CPS unit:[4]

> . . . This is an unbiased point of view on the employee situation at Norwich State Hospital. . . . I believe that the COs are more suited

> to working with patients than the old-time attendants because they use little or no profanity, nor do they shout at the patients or employ unnecessarily brutal methods. Formerly the commands "shut up" and "sit down" were part of the daily routine. The COs rarely or never use such language. . . . This letter is not from a CO but from one who works with and among them on the infirmary wards here. . . .

In response to the flood of letters regarding the presence of the CPS units, particularly the one at Norwich State Hospital, the local chapter of the American Legion launched a formal investigation. On April 20, 1945, the *Norwich Bulletin* published the findings of this study. The report described the provisions that had been established by Congress to deal with COs and the limitations placed on their day-to-day activities by Selective Service. It went on to note that men assigned to CPS units had gone through a procedure in which they had been required to demonstrate the sincerity of their objections to military service. It referred to the fact that Norwich State Hospital had been forced to operate under circumstances of severe staff shortages. It was then when COs became available as a source of labor for the severely understaffed hospital that they were brought in to help meet this crisis. Even so, the institution was still understaffed.

The American Legion commission observed that "the COs are not pampered, but take a lot of abuse from the regular employees." They asserted that "there is no truth to the allegations that the COs are given special preference with respect to living quarters . . . the wives of COs suffer much abuse and are denied many of the perks and privileges of civilian employees at the institution." This response to the presence of COs at Norwich was in sharp contrast to the universally negative reactions that emanated from related veterans' groups in other areas where CPS units were in residence.

Throughout the war, opinions pro and con about the presence of CPS units in local communities and about COs in general were frequently aired in the editorial columns of the nation's press. The National Service Board for Religious Objectors, through its official newsletter, *The Reporter,* tried to keep abreast of these opinions. Almost every issue of this semimonthly bulletin contained excerpts from newspaper commentaries about COs. A typical item appeared in the latter months of 1943 in the *Providence Rhode Island Bulletin*:[5]

> . . . Mennonite conscientious objectors may be a headache to their draft boards, but they have certainly proved to be a boon for the state of Rhode Island. The 50 Mennonites who have been working at the State Hospital for Mental Diseases since last February . . . have practically saved this institution according to its superintendent, Dr. John Ross. He observed, "I don't know what we would have done without them. I only wish we could get a lot more of them."

On the other hand, the following news dispatch that appeared in the Tacoma, Washington, *News Tribune* in mid-1943 illustrated an opposite reaction to the arrival of a CPS unit at a state hospital:[6]

> . . . Employment of conscientious objectors in state institutions was condemned Sunday in a resolution unanimously passed by delegates attending a one-day convention of the Federation of Washington State Employee Unions. . . .

A short time later, however, the Seattle, Washington, *Times* published a news story in which a spokesperson for the state institutions was quoted as saying that the COs would not have been accepted if a terrific labor shortage had not existed. He went on to note that these men were doing an excellent job on the wards, and that it was better to have them meeting a critical labor need in the hospitals than spending their days cutting roads through forests. Soon after, in a feature story in the same paper concerning the introduction of CPS units into the state's institutions, the president of the state employees' union was quoted as follows:[7]

> . . . For one thing, our members don't like to work with COs. Their presence inhibits our ability to negotiate salaries high enough to attract a sufficient number of qualified employees. . . .

This complaint that the presence of COs in hospital settings negatively affects a local union's negotiating stance was common to all institutions where CPS units had been assigned. It was a source of irritation to most of the men in CPS hospital units that their presence could be construed as a deterrent in the struggle of institutional employees for improved working conditions and enhanced salary benefits. But Selective Service was adamant that the men in the CPS units were to be limited to a monthly allowance of $15 plus room and board. The COs in these units were well aware of the awkward position in which they had been placed.

In many hospital units, the COs actively campaigned for higher salary scales and improved working conditions for the institution's regular employees. In several instances, they were joined in these efforts by regular employees. An example of one such campaign took place at Concord State Hospital in New Hampshire. On October 15, 1945, *The Daily Monitor and New Hampshire Patriot* ran the following banner headline on its front page:

Conscientious Objectors Ask State Hospital for 100% Pay Boost and 40-Hour Week

---

The ensuing story reported that these demands had been submitted to Dr. Charles H. Dollof, the hospital's superintendent. Also requested were improved living conditions, better food, and installation of recreational facilities for the institution's lower-paid personnel. Dr. Dollof was reported to have confirmed that attendants were required to work 10 hours a day, five and one-half days per week. In return, salaries ranged from $45 to $50 per month for employees living on the premises and from $90 to $100 per month for those who lived off the grounds.

The demands reported in the newspaper, which had been signed by several members of the regular staff, also called for the elimination of split shifts, improved health insurance benefits, and providing instruction to all attendant personnel.

In a subsequent letter to the newspaper, the unit's assistant director, Ross Sanderson, emphasized that the COs were not seeking pay increases and other benefits for themselves because conditions for their employment were governed by Selective Service. Although complaints about salaries and working conditions had been a sore point with employees long before the arrival of the CPS unit, it was the leadership of the COs that finally articulated the need for more equitable working conditions. Similar initiatives surfaced at the instigation of CPS units at the Connecticut State Hospital and the Eastern State Hospital at Richmond, Virginia, among others.

Two kinds of reactions toward COs were frequently observed in the nation's press. On the one hand, some emanated from outright hatemongers. Others expressed support and understanding for what COs were trying to do in a period that was stressful for all. Here are a few examples from the former group:

From the "Letters to the Editor" column in *The Philadelphia Inquirer,* spring 1945:[8]

> . . . Some things are being implied in the many letters in defense of the conscientious objectors that in my opinion are just about the lowest type of ordinary barnyard lies. . . .

From Hi Waters's column, Martin's Ferry, Ohio, *Times,* winter 1945:[9]

> . . . They have proposed a monument to the conscientious objector. . . . It is a statue with a movable arm: every time a soldier passes it in the public square, the arm flies up and hides its face. . . .

Other items reflected the opposite point of view. In the spring of 1945, the Hackensack, New Jersey, *Bergen Record* reported that in response to an appeal sent by the Episcopal Church for contributions to help support Episcopalian COs and their dependents, the church had received the following letter from an overseas soldier:[10]

> You may wonder why a combat soldier would be willing to give to such a cause. I too would have been an objector if I had been brave enough to stand up to the jeers of people for the rest of my life. Instead, I chose the easy way. . . . I wish I had the faith that these men have.

An editorial in the Memphis, Tennessee, *Commercial Appeal* from the spring of 1945 also defends the COs:[11]

> ... In New Haven, Connecticut, a CO who had volunteered as a "guinea pig" in a dangerous medical research project died this week, a victim of infantile paralysis. ... He is just as dead as if he had stopped a bullet in Okinawa. ... COs have performed menial tasks ... suffered indignities and insult for a principle dearer than life and honor. ... If the human race had been made up of conscientious objectors, there would have been no violent deaths on Anzio and Okinawa. ...

Comments of Hospital Administrators Who Requested CPS Units

Finally, another group of individuals had something to say about COs in this era. They were the hospital administrators who had requested the assignment of CPS units to their facilities during a period that had been a managerial nightmare for many of them. A few of the superintendents in the 61 institutions in which CPS units served found it difficult to say anything commendatory about the work accomplishments of the men in these groups. One or two even requested the withdrawal of the units in response to pressures from labor unions and the community, and for other reasons. But the overwhelming majority of these officials were grateful and publicly stated their appreciation. For the most part, their appraisals were forwarded in letters to the offices of the National Service Board for Religious Objectors and separately to Selective Service Headquarters. Excerpts from a few of these letters appear below:

> ... The members of the CPS unit ... demonstrated a keenness of observation and ability to understand the patient as a human being with an illness.
>
> Because of their stability, dependability, and cooperation, men in the CPS unit helped to keep this hospital operating at its usual high level of service to the community. ...

> ... Members of the CPS unit ... placed a bond of comradeship on the shoulders of the depressed and discouraged; toward the old and feeble, they were kind; and they kindled a light of hope in the eyes of those for whom the world was difficult. ...

> The recent closing of the CPS unit at this hospital has left us with a deep obligation to these men and their wives who joined them here . . . their quick adjustment to an entirely new situation is an example that we hope will set a standard of service in the future.

> During the entire time this CPS unit has been at this institution, I have never had a complaint from the relative of a patient, or any employee regarding the behavior of any member of the unit. . . .

> . . . The CPS unit here (a Veterans Administration Hospital) has performed a most valuable function to this hospital, and undoubtedly has saved many veterans' lives. . . .

> . . . The men in the CPS unit set a very good example to a number of old-line attendants whose approach to patients was more like that of a guard rather then a helper. . . .

Among those whose comments appeared above were the following: M. A. Tarumianz, M.D., Superintendent, Delaware State Hospital; Stella Ackley, Associate Director of Nursing, Colorado Psychopathic Hospital; O. R. Yoder, M.D., Superintendent, Ypsilanti State Hospital; R. L. Hill, M.D., Superintendent, Wernersville State Hospital; R. A. Morter, M.D., Superintendent, Kalamazoo State Hospital; H. E. Foster, M.D., Manager, Lyons, N.J., VA Hospital; and J. F. Bateman, M.D., Superintendent, Columbus State Hospital.

Finally, this is what the commissioner of the Ohio Department of Mental Diseases, Frank Tallman, M.D., had to say as the CPS units within his state were being withdrawn after the war:

> . . . We would be very pleased indeed if we could look forward to the permanent employment of a large number of the 160 men who served in the CPS units in our six state facilities.

It is apt to conclude this chapter with excerpts from two other publications. One of these was a guest editorial that appeared in the Albert Lea, Minnesota, *Evening Tribune* in the late summer of 1944.[12] It was written by John F. D. Meighen, a Department of Justice hearing officer who had specialized in cases relating to COs. In his commentary, Meighen observed:

> . . . When the war is over, the COs will be allowed back to their families and home communities. They should not be ostracized because of honest religious belief. Hitlers may logically torment behind barbed wire in concentration camps those who hold minority religious views, but Freeborn County and Minnesota should not follow that example.
>
> . . . The Quaker has had no small part in forming the American way of life. The Mennonite passed through fire in his journey to America. A conscience that is strong enough to endure adverse public opinion demands respect.

In the other instance, a reporter assigned to *The Lakewood Log*, a Washington State weekly, had his curiosity provoked by the presence of a CPS unit at Western State Hospital. In his news story, the reporter noted that ever since Lew Ayres, the well-known film star of that era, had been taking the rap for his stand as a CO, he had been wondering what other COs were like: "Were they on the order of morons? Were they faking? Why should a minority group hold out against world opinion in fighting our aggressors?"[13]

Through the courtesy of the superintendent at Western State Hospital, he was given the opportunity to meet some of the COs assigned to that institution. After he had learned firsthand who the COs were and what they stood for, he came to the following conclusions:

> . . . No matter how we may disagree with the beliefs of these conscientious objectors, they certainly have a form of intense courage in the face of public contempt.
>
> . . . Religious beliefs are a basic reason of most objectors to military service. . . . I gleaned from my talks with these genuine objectors that what they hope and work for is a millennium of enduring peace among nations and a universal recognition of the realization of how little past wars have been successful in achieving that goal.

Chapter 7

THE TURNING POINT

> Some countries shoot their conscientious objectors. But thanks to the undeniable contributions of the Quakers, Brethren, and the Mennonites . . . we have generally made more intelligent provision for them.
>
> Out of the Civilian Public Service of conscientious objectors in World War II has come another and quite unexpected contribution. One of the services to which they were assigned was that of attendant in mental hospitals.
>
> They were scandalized at the ignorance, brutality, and the sprees of some of the old-time attendants. They set about seriously to raising the standards of care.
>
> From an editorial that appeared in the March 8, 1946, edition of the *Des Moines Register*

It was bound to happen. And it did. Four men in the Civilian Public Service (CPS) unit at the Philadelphia State Hospital (also known as Byberry), utterly frustrated by the bedlam-like atmosphere at that institution, decided to set up a clearinghouse through which their fellow conscientious objectors (COs) in similar institutions throughout the country might share ideas that they had found to be effective in dealing with their patients. They also believed that such a clearinghouse could perform a highly useful function in collecting information about innovative state hospital programs, as well as reliable accounts of conditions in the various institutions in which CPS units were serving.

Early in 1944, one of the group, Leonard Cornell, a Harvard-trained lawyer who had also served a stint with the FBI before his induction into CPS, approached Dr. Charles A. Zeller, Byberry's superintendent, for permission to initiate such an exchange service. In his presentation to Dr. Zeller, Cornell stated that his group hoped that one of the immediate benefits to emerge from this service would be a monthly periodical that would offer practical and medically sound information to attendants about how to care for patients. He also mentioned that gathering and sharing information about the difficulties the institutions were having in providing proper levels of care and treatment for their patients might well stimulate public concern and support for the hospitals.

Dr. Zeller's response was enthusiastic, but he cautioned Cornell that the new program should avoid name-calling in its public disclosures. Rather, it should primarily emphasize the conditions responsible for the sad state of affairs in the mental hospitals. If this condition was acceptable, Dr. Zeller agreed to solicit the support of other hospital directors in establishing this clearinghouse. The American Friends Service Committee, sponsor of the CPS unit at Byberry, gave its blessing to the idea and made a modest contribution to fund the start-up expenses. Dr. Zeller made space available for the new enterprise, but with the proviso that Cornell and his associates would have to pursue the program on their own time.

By April of the same year, Cornell, along with his three associates—Harold Barton, a mining engineer from Oregon, Willard Hetzel, who had a background in legal training, and Philip Steer, a psychology major and writer—formally announced the inauguration of the Mental Hygiene Program of CPS. They stated that this new program was "designed so that we as a united group may leave behind us when we return to private pursuits, a concrete and enduring contribution to the care of mental patients."

In June 1944, under Phil Steer's leadership, one of the first major accomplishments to emerge from the fledgling Mental Hygiene Program was *The Attendant*. This was the first in a series of monthly periodicals designed to offer information and advice to attendants in mental hospitals. Dr. Earl Bond, a past president of the American Psychiatric Association and one of the Mental Hygiene Program's principal consultants, took on the role of professional adviser to the new publication. After the release of several issues of the magazine, other highly respected mental health professionals joined Dr. Bond as members of the advisory board. They included Dr. Samuel Hamilton, U.S. Public Health Service; Dr. James Lewald, Superintendent, District Training School at Laurel, Maryland; Dr. George S. Stevenson, Executive Director, National Committee for Mental Hygiene; and Dr. Charles A. Zeller, Superintendent, Philadelphia State Hospital.

Articles for the magazine were solicited not only from COs based in both state mental hospitals and state training schools for the retarded, but also from members of the regular institutional staffs in these facilities. Each issue usually featured a single theme. But space was also allotted for at least two or three other topics of special interest. Each issue ran from eight to 12 pages. The text was written to catch the reader's attention. One of the early issues carried an article by Floyd Greenleaf, who at the time was a member of the CPS unit at Byberry. It was titled "Patient Restraint and Attendant Protection," which was a highly charged topic of the day. This issue received so much attention that it had to be reprinted many times to accommodate the demand for it. Pages 3 and 4 of this article are reprinted on page 133.

After the release of the above issue, many letters were sent to the editor protesting that the "full Nelson" technique for restraining patients as illustrated in the lead article could be highly dangerous to the patient undergoing restraint. Alternative suggestions that were more effective and less threatening to the patient's well-being were offered in subsequent issues. Despite the criticisms provoked by this article, it was in steady demand as a training aid for many years in mental hospitals in the United States and Canada.

The scope and range of the issues brought to light in *The Attendant* over its first two years may be glimpsed by reviewing its tables of contents. They included themes such as the following:

- The Use of Force
- Attendant-Patient Relationships
- Patients' Leisure-Time Activities

THE ATTENDANT

THIS ISSUE:
Symposium — The Use of Force
Number Ninety-three
Here's How

VOL. I, No. 2
JULY, 1944

ATTENDANT CARE OF ORGANIC MENTAL DISORDERS

By Ruth L. Dingman, R.N.

This is the first of a series of three articles by Miss Dingman. In later issues she will discuss attendant care of functional mental disorders and attendant care of the mentally deficient.

Miss Dingman is the director of Women's Service in Mental Hospitals and of the Attendant Training Program for the American Friends Service Committee. She was formerly supervisor of the Psychiatric Service of the Louisville (Ky.) General Hospital, and Director of Nursing Education at the Hartford (Conn.) Retreat.

●

The organic mental disorders are those in which there is actual structural damage to the brain tissue. Approximately forty-five per cent of the patients in state hospitals fall into this group. In approaching some of the attendant problems in the care of these disorders, let us first consider what qualities we would want to find in the attendant:

He should be healthy—physically, mentally and emotionally. He should be a person with many interests and activities outside his work.

He should know and be able to recognize the characteristics of the various disorders.

He should have patience and self-control, and be ready to recognize unpleasant behavior as a symptom of a condition to be treated rather than just perversity of human nature.

He should be alert in observation and have skill in reporting and recording his observations.

Gentleness, firmness, sympathy and reassurance—these are the most important therapeutic weapons.

Now let us turn to the patient himself and his care.

Symptomatic Care

There is a general deterioration in personal habits of patients with organic disorders. They are untidy and may soil and wet. Under these conditions the care of the skin takes on special importance. Sweet or mineral oil is used if the skin is especially dry. If the patient is confined to bed, the attendant will need to give special attention to the prevention of bedsores and hypostatic pneumonia.

Care of nails must not be overlooked. If the fingernails are allowed to grow long, the patient may injure himself by scratching and picking; if he is resistive or combative, the attendant may be injured.

Through supervision the attendant can teach the patient to care for his mouth and teeth routinely morning and night. This is of especial importance in patients who are dehydrated or who hold saliva and food in their mouths.

In the matter of food the attendant is frequently faced with unpleasant situations. These patients are sometimes messy and untidy; they hoard food and even may hide it to be soon forgotten and left to putrify. To meet this situation the attendant should try to establish better habits, keeping in mind the likes and dislikes of the patient as well as racial and religious customs.

Refusal to eat is frequently a problem. If all other procedures fail, tube feeding

(Continued on page 7)

- Morale and the Attendant
- Mechanical Restraint in the Hospital
- A Century of Progress in Mental Deficiency
- Attendant Care of Organic Mental Disorders
- The Care of Bed Patients

Here are just a few of the kinds of constructive suggestions that appeared in an extensive report about the use of force in one issue of the magazine:[1]

> One useful technique is to show the patient that you recognize him as an individual. . . . A name is a very real part of the self and differentiates one from the group. If a fight starts at the other end of the dayroom, and I can call to the patients by name, I may be able to prevent injuries.

PATIENT RESTRAINT . . .

(*Continued from page* 1)

ONE ATTENDANT

Arm Hold

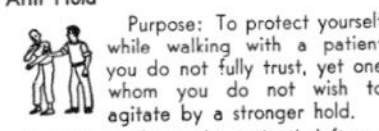

Purpose: To protect yourself while walking with a patient you do not fully trust, yet one whom you do not wish to agitate by a stronger hold.

Technique: Grasp the patient's left arm just above the elbow. If the patient attempts to strike with his right arm, push his left arm up toward his face. He will be unable to reach you with his right arm; the force of his swing will push you out of reach of his fist. You may pull the patient toward you in such a manner that his back will be presented, and then be in position to secure a half nelson and arm lock, or a full nelson.

Elbow-Wrist Hold

Purpose: To permit you to walk a mildly resistive patient in a desired direction.

Technique: Approach the patient from the left side. Grasp the patient's left wrist with your left hand; grasp his left elbow with your right hand. Raise the elbow and lower the wrist, forming a right angle at the bend of the patient's elbow. Pressure may be applied by drawing back on the wrist and pushing forward on the elbow. This hold is not too effective on a large and active patient.

Half Nelson and Arm Lock

Purpose: To restrain and move a patient.

Technique: Approach the patient from the rear. Slip your right hand under his right arm and up and around the back of his neck; at the same time, grasp his left wrist with your left hand. Draw his left wrist to the rear and up the spinal column until you have an arm lock. This hold will usually permit you to move and direct the patient at will.

Bar Hold

Purpose: To restrain a comparatively mild patient.

Technique: Approach the patient from the rear. Grasp his left arm with your left hand; simultaneously slip your right arm over his right arm and across his back and grasp his upper left arm with your right hand. Your right shoulder should be close to the patient's right arm. Pressure may be applied by pulling with your right hand on the left arm and by pushing with your right shoulder on the patient's right arm. This hold may be maintained with one arm, leaving the other arm free to open doors. If the patient attempts to reach back with his hands, turn slightly to the left, place your hip against his buttocks and arch backward. This hold is not too effective with patients who are considerably taller than the attendant.

Full Nelson

Purpose: To restrain a strong and dangerous patient.

Technique: Approach the patient from the rear. Simultaneously slip both of your arms under the patient's armpits; place both of your hands on the back of the patient's neck. Interlace your fingers in a grip on the back of the neck and the hold is complete.

Head Hold

Purpose: To hold a patient's head securely on a bed. This hold is valuable in tube-feeding. Also, it is difficult for a patient to strike effectively or to struggle when his head is held down.

Technique: Stand at the head of the bed, facing the foot. Fold a hand towel flat about four inches wide. Grasp the ends of the towel and place it on the patient's forehead. Pull each end of the towel toward the ears. The patient will

3

now be able to move his head only slightly from side to side.

MORE THAN ONE ATTENDANT

General Suggestions

(1) Decide what each attendant is going to do before you approach the patient.

(2) Once you grasp the patient, hang on! Your failure may result in injury to your partner.

(3) If the patient is strong and very resistive, try to get him off his feet.

(4) When you have the patient on the floor, try to turn him face down in order to protect yourselves from kicks, bites and fists.

(5) With the patient on the floor, lie across his chest or back with your legs spread apart to make turning over difficult. When the patient is face down, try to secure an arm lock. In this position, the patient will soon exhaust himself if he continues to struggle.

Problem A

Patient has his back to the wall and is prepared to stand off all comers.

Technique: Two attendants should approach simultaneously from opposite sides. When the patient's attention is focused on one attendant, the other may step in, grasp the patient's arm just above the elbow, and pull him away from the wall. If possible, the attendant then secures a full nelson or other hold while the second attendant either grabs the patient's feet from under him or secures the free arm according to the type of hold his partner has been able to secure. If a third attendant is present, two attendants' may secure the patient's arms while the third pulls his feet from under him, approaching from the rear if possible.

Problem B

Patient is in an open space; he is disturbed and assaultive.

Technique: One attendant distracts the

4

patient while the other approaches from the rear and secures a restraining hold.

Problem C

Patient is assaultive and has a weapon.

Technique: Never try to get a weapon away from a patient alone! With the help of at least one other attendant, try to foul the weapon with a sheet, blanket or towel. Try to get behind the patient to secure a restraining hold. Sometimes it is advisable to throw a blanket or sheet completely over the patient, fouling his weapon and temporarily blinding him. If the weapon is extremely dangerous, secure plenty of help and try to back the patient into a corner, protecting yourselves with mattresses held in front of you.

Bed Hold

Purpose: To restrain a patient in bed when two attendants are present, but one has to leave.

Technique: The two attendants place the patient on his back in the bed. One attendant stands on the left side of the patient, near the head of the bed, facing the foot. He slips his right arm over the patient's left arm, under the back, and grasps the patient's right wrist. The wrist is drawn toward the attendant until the attendant's right wrist rests upon the patient's left arm just above the bend of the patient's elbow. The attendant places his left foot on the under rail of the bed, bringing his left knee and leg into a position which blocks the patient's left arm. The hold is now completed. The patient's right arm is secured in an arm lock. His left arm will be able to bend at the elbow a bit, but will be blocked by the attendant's right hand and the patient's right hand. The attendant's left leg and knee will brace his right arm as well as prevent the patient from falling out of bed. The second attendant may leave at this point. This hold leaves one hand free which you may use to keep the patient's head down.

Floyd Greenleaf, "Patient Restraint and Attendant Protection," *The Attendant*, Volume 1, Number 5, October 1944.

Another symposium participant offered the following observation:

> One day I wanted a patient to do some work. I called to him by name and remarked, "Mr. Edwards, would you please do this for me?" He turned around, smiled and thanked me. He hadn't heard anyone address him by name in some time.

One symposium participant noted:

> By being straightforward and honest with a man who has been in restraints for a long time, I've been able to achieve results which no amount of bullying . . . could have accomplished.

Within the first few months of the appearance of *The Attendant,* letters of appreciation poured into the cramped quarters where Cornell and his three associates had been given space to carry on their Mental Hygiene Program activities. Those responding included hospital superintendents, nursing supervisors, and attendants themselves—not only from those institutions to which CPS units had been assigned but from virtually every mental hospital in the country. All expressed their gratitude that a critically needed training aid was available for the first time. Eleanor Roosevelt, who had made it her business to see for herself what life was like in the nation's mental hospitals during that period and who had seen a copy of the new magazine, responded with this comment to the Mental Hygiene Program staff: "I know of your work and think it is good."[2]

By the end of its first year of publication, *The Attendant* had been introduced to every mental hospital and training school in the United States, as well as to several institutions in Canada, Mexico, and England. Many of these hospitals arranged to order 100 or more subscriptions for members of their nursing and attendant staffs.

In the meantime, Harold Barton of the Mental Hygiene Program team was laying the groundwork for launching the program's educational phase. This phase had three aims:[3]

1. Facilitate the adaptation of COs who had volunteered for service in state mental hospitals and state training schools to their new environments. This was to be accomplished by sharing with them

practical guidelines for relating in a positive manner to their patients, in what was for all of them a strange and new world.
2. Assist in developing a sound educational framework for all persons engaged in attendant duties in a mental health facility.
3. Enlighten the general public about its responsibilities in meeting the needs of its mentally ill and mentally retarded citizens and, in the process of so doing, aid people in better understanding how to promote their own mental well-being.

One of the first steps Barton took was to send a questionnaire to each of the men in the various CPS units. The questionnaire solicited data relating to all aspects of life in the institutions where they were serving. There were queries about the status of the facility's physical plant; the quality of its medical, nursing, and attendant staffs; the range of therapies available to its patients; the food service; recreational facilities for both staff and patients; employment practices; and a host of other related concerns. Barton also invited eyewitness accounts of patient abuse, staff incompetence, and other facts that shed light on an institution's lack of sensitivity to both patients and employees. To ensure that the information he was gathering could be substantiated, Barton admonished his respondents that their reports must be absolutely accurate and unassailable.

Before long, the Mental Hygiene Program had assembled reports from more than 1,400 men. This body of information later became an important resource for several journalists who used it to illustrate their exposés of the inhumane conditions in so many of the nation's mental hospitals of that era. Without this file, Frank Wright, author of *Out of Sight, Out of Mind* (excerpts from which appeared in Chapter 2), could never have told the devastating story of what it was like to be a mental patient in a public mental hospital in the 1940s. Albert Maisel drew on this same body of information for his 1946 *Life Magazine* exposé of U.S. mental hospitals (an excerpt from which also appears in Chapter 2). Albert Deutsch, the highly respected New York journalist, used this information as background material for the many syndicated newspaper features that he wrote on the sorry state of this nation's mental hospitals in the mid- to late 1940s.

In developing their strategy for informing the American public about conditions in public mental hospitals, the four organizers of the Mental Hygiene Program reaffirmed their commitment to Dr. Zeller that it would be in their best interests to gain the support of the superintendents and work with them rather than against them. Their objective was to concentrate on the evils that were being imposed on patients rather than pointing accusing fingers at particular individuals. Even more important, they wanted to offer constructive suggestions for overcoming the shortcomings of the system and for raising the levels of care and treatment in the state institutions for mentally ill and retarded people.

In the summer of 1944, a deep crisis touched the Mental Hygiene Program. Marvin Weisbord, in his narrative history *Some Form of Peace—True Stories of the American Friends Service Committee at Home and Abroad,* provided this account of what happened:[4]

> Over a period of months, Barton collected the most complete file of data on United States mental hospital conditions ever assembled. It was based on reports from 1,400 men in 60 hospitals. The composite portrait of medieval plants, undermanned staffs, low budgets, and vicious practices that emerged made Byberry look almost like a rest home. So devastating were the contents of his Pandora's Box that Barton, a demon of energy and dedication, began to despair of the project.
>
> "CPS attendants everywhere," he wrote to the American Friends Service Committee, "experienced a tragic deadening of sensibilities from the filth and brutality, staff pressures against change, lack of training, and public apathy." He feared that the Mental Hygiene Program could never relieve such a deteriorated situation. "We soon realized," he said, "that our hands were tied on the wards. We really were contributing to what was largely a dead-end program of custodial care . . . not to the improved health and adjustment to society of the patients. Once we left, the patients would be back where they started." Even trained attendants could not solve the dilemma of hospitals where cure and discharge were last on the list of priorities. To clean up dirty wards and build better buildings were not enough either.
>
> At one point, . . . Barton came to the verge of quitting. To Hetzel, he confided he had made a decision: the job was hopeless. His

> bag was packed, and when a replacement could be found on the violent ward, he was going home to await arrest. His conscience would be better served by jail than by this futility and compromise.
>
> Hetzel too had his doubts. . . .The MHP [Mental Hygiene Program], carried on in free time with little expectation of success, was a fine idea, but it, CPS, the war, were all one big hoax, Hetzel concluded in a moment of abject frustration. In December, when his year was up, he had decided he would have to defy the system too, and, if necessary, accept prison.

Cornell asked the two men to reconsider. Instead of quitting now, he said, maybe they ought to raise their sights. . . . The war wasn't over yet; more than a thousand CPS men in hospitals still looked to them for guidance. Perhaps, Cornell went on, letting his imagination play, Selective Service would detach them from hospital duty to work full-time with the Mental Hygiene Program. Surely four men could be spared if lasting changes in mental hospitals could be achieved.

> Hetzel and Barton were skeptical. "Leonard, it's fantastic," Hetzel remembers saying. "I don't think Selective Service will go for this. They closed down our unit in Cleveland because they didn't want us in the public eye. Go ahead and try, but you're not going to get anywhere." Barton felt the same way but agreed to delay his departure to give Cornell's new scheme a chance.
>
> The American Friends Service Committee . . . immediately liked the idea. Cornell was dispatched to Washington to talk it over with Paul Comly French, head of the National Service Board for Religious Objectors, through which the CPS program was being coordinated with Selective Service. . . . French urged Colonel Lewis F. Kosch, an official of that agency, to consider the plan.
>
> Kosch, to French's delight, already had seen copies of *The Attendant* and had found hospital officials . . . "extremely enthusiastic about the work you are doing." In this spirit, the Colonel agreed to detached service for the four men, if reputable medical men served as advisers, with veto powers over ideas for publications.

After many conferences, the details were worked out, the medical advisory board was set in place, and the Mental Hygiene Program's operations were shifted to the oversight of the National Service Board for Religious Objectors, under whose auspices it continued to function until the war's end. All three major peace churches sponsoring the CPS program shared in providing operating expenses for the revitalized Mental Hygiene Program.

Despite their independent status, Cornell, Barton, Hetzel, and Steer decided it would be desirable for them to continue using Byberry as the base of operations of the Mental Hygiene Program. To accommodate their expanded space needs, Dr. Zeller arranged to turn over to them a vacant, one-room building on the hospital grounds. He also assigned two male worker-patients to aid them with clerical and typing chores. Initially, these two were given spending allowances, but when in a few months they had demonstrated their ability to perform the work assignments, the Mental Hygiene Program arranged for them to be formally discharged as patients and placed on salary status.

Dr. George Stevenson, Executive Director of the National Committee for Mental Hygiene, was invited to serve as one of the chief advisers to the Mental Hygiene Program. This organization had been established in 1909 by Clifford Beers in collaboration with a group of mental health professionals and public-spirited citizens who had been stirred into action by Beers's moving account of his own experiences as a mental patient in the classic, *A Mind That Found Itself.* Although the National Committee for Mental Hygiene's support base was meager, it was able to develop a network of local and state affiliates throughout the country.

At the time of Dr. Stevenson's association with the Mental Hygiene Program, his organization's primary activities were stimulating medical research into the causes of mental illness and pressuring both state and federal programs into providing more adequate funding in support of mental health services. Although Dr. Stevenson did not hold the pacifist point of view, he believed that the mental health movement had much to gain from the COs who had volunteered for service in the nation's mental hospitals. He had this to say about the Mental Hygiene Program:[5]

> The MHP can be an invaluable aid in meeting this [war-time] emergency, but promises even greater benefits through the fact that hundreds of men, after the war, will through firsthand experience be acquainted with the problems and the needs of mental hospitals.
>
> The CO is bound at the present time to suffer from the attitude accompanying a united forceful effort to win the war. I think of this group of a few thousand men as an army of vigilantes who in this society of ours carry the function of preserving and securing peace. The loss of a few thousand men from the armed forces is a small price for a country to pay to have within it an intelligent group, directed, year in and year out, toward those elements that tend to preserve international good-will and directed against those elements that will destroy it.
>
> If we can add to this value that is potentially a nucleus of informed citizenry directed against violence in the handling of the mentally ill and aimed at the reduction of conflict in the minds of the mentally disturbed, the price paid will be even more justified.

The legal aspect of the Mental Hygiene Program grew out of the fact that many men in the CPS units were beginning to sense that state laws governing the commitment of mental patients to state institutions were based on long-outmoded concepts of mental illness. They had been enacted at a time when the popular perception of a mentally ill person was based on the adage, "once insane, always insane." To a large extent, the commitment laws and other legislation pertinent to the conduct of mental hospitals neither facilitated the welfare of patients nor protected their human rights.

Typical of the obstructive nature of many state laws at the time was the requirement that mentally ill persons seeking treatment in a hospital must first be provided with a trial by jury. The purpose of this common provision was to prevent the "railroading" of sane persons into mental institutions. Its instigation was attributed to a Mrs. E. Packard, who in 1860 had been placed in a mental hospital against her will, as she claimed, by a malicious husband. When she was discharged, she took it on herself to travel from state to state lobbying for laws that made jury trials mandatory before commitment.[6]

Inasmuch as every citizen of the United States is guaranteed the right to trial by jury under the federal constitution, the forced imposition of this cumbersome, often-embarrassing procedure exposed many persons suffering with mental illness to unnecessary humiliation. This legal procedure also imparted a taint of criminality to an individual whose offense against society was no more heinous than that of someone who had fallen victim to a disease such as tuberculosis. Mentally ill persons whose only entry to a mental hospital was by way of the legal system often found themselves confined in criminal custody pending outcome of their trials. In these situations, they were often at the mercy of unsympathetic jailers.

In many states, legislation relating to the administration of public facilities for the mentally ill and the retarded gave those responsible for them so much latitude that ample opportunity developed for abuses to flourish. In many instances, patients in these institutions, under the guise of being engaged in occupational therapy, were in reality being exploited in a peonage system that required them to work as many as 80–90 hours per week without reimbursement for their services.

In an effort to overcome the above conditions and others that undermined the therapeutic climate of state mental hospitals, the Mental Hygiene Program's legal division embarked on an intensive survey of laws governing these facilities on a state-by-state basis. Willard Hetzel, who before his induction into CPS had acquired a legal background, took on the responsibility of directing this phase of the agency's operations. William Draper Lewis, former dean of the University of Pennsylvania Law School and, at that time, director of the American Law Institute, gladly agreed to serve in an advisory capacity for this project. Another objective of Hetzel's division was to draft a model set of regulations pertaining to the commitment and care of patients in state mental hospitals. As was the case with all other activities of the Mental Hygiene Program, the new legal concerns of the agency were also subject to review by its five psychiatric consultants: Dr. Bond, Dr. Hamilton, Dr. Stevenson, Dr. Zeller, and Dr. Lewald.

The first state briefs pertaining to the mentally ill to be completed were those for the state of Kansas. With the aid of volunteers from the CPS units, many of whom had had some legal training or had demonstrated special skills in engaging in this type of research, briefs of mental health legislation on the books of several other states were soon completed. In mid-1945, the American Bar Association awarded a contract to the Mental Hygiene Program to facilitate completion of this assignment.

Although the development of a model mental hygiene law loomed as a long-term project, a first draft was soon completed. Considerable interest in this preliminary version was expressed by state mental hygiene societies, as well as by the American Bar Association. Even in this early stage, the model law incorporated many features that attracted widespread interest. These included provision for psychiatric examinations as a prerequisite for commitment, development of local mental hygiene clinics to encourage availability of community-based mental health services, prohibition of penal custody before hospitalization, and more adequate provisions for discharge and rehabilitation of patients.

As the end of 1945 approached and the prospects for discharge of the men in the CPS units began to brighten, the four leaders of the Mental Hygiene Program began searching for some practical ways to sustain and carry forward the mental health crusade that they had initiated. By this time, Selective Service had authorized the Mental Hygiene Program to expand its staff by an additional 12 men. Wives of some of the men and volunteers from the American Friends Service Committee had also joined forces with the program to facilitate handling its expanded volume of correspondence and reports.

After a series of conferences with their advisers, the program leaders decided that the Mental Hygiene Program should be transformed into a national organization under lay leadership. Among some of the professionals, there were misgivings that such an approach would not be in the best interests of the mentally ill. But others demurred. Dr. Earl Bond called the Mental Hygiene Program "the chance that comes once in a lifetime to raise the work standards of attendants in mental hospitals."[7] He also expressed the opinion that those in this program had demonstrated their skills in communicating mental health issues in an effective and responsible manner to the general public. Other professionals supported Dr. Bond's assessment. From that point forward, the vision of a national lay movement to replace the Mental Hygiene Program in the postwar era became a realistic goal.

To share their hopes and expectations for the postwar phase of the Mental Hygiene Program's operations, its four leaders drafted a statement in August 1945 to be sent to all 61 CPS units then in active service. It read as follows:

> This is a confidential report. We want to describe to you as clearly as we can the strategy underlying our activities and our plan for future action. We have hesitated to circulate this information in the formative period of our program lest we inadvertently arouse distrust or misunderstanding among regular staff members in the institutions you are serving, and alienate those persons who are as anxious as we to accomplish the goals ahead. Now that . . . our objectives have been demonstrated by concrete projects, we can risk the chance of being misunderstood without fearing that the whole program will be jeopardized. Here is our proposal.
>
> Rather than attempt exposés of individual institutions . . . we plan to disclose . . . the inherent weaknesses of all the facilities we are now serving. This disclosure will be made as soon as sufficient material is organized in such a manner that it will give an accurate representation of the conditions prevailing in these institutions, but not until after the war has been concluded. If we were to present any material to the public now, it could be misunderstood, or used to divert attention against us as COs rather than upon the institutional problems for which we are seeking relief and understanding. Some reactionaries might also rally to the overworked cliché, "this is the war—what else can you expect in times like these?"—when in reality the conditions which we wish to bring to light have become ingrained in the system. Realistically, at present we are unable to enlist the full support of the press, religious agencies, as well as veterans' organizations. . . .
>
> For now, we must gather as much in the way of firsthand information on institutional practices and needs to properly document our story when the time is at hand for its release. From each of you we need eye-witness accounts that will document the many ways in which these hospitals are being short-changed in the delivery of services for their proper care and treatment of patients. We are also eager to obtain information that will bring to light

examples of institutional practices that are contributing in a positive way to the welfare of the patients in their care.

When the above information has been assembled and organized, it is our intent to present it to the public in such a manner as to protect the confidentiality of the institutions involved, as well as names of individuals related to these facilities. . . . We want to tell the story of America's mental institutions as we have observed them, in as colorful and appealing a way as we can. In this context, we want to explain the underlying problems which are hampering their abilities to serve as hospitals in the true sense of that term. And we also plan to offer our recommendations for bringing about changes in public attitudes and commitments needed to effect these changes.

The presentation of the above report to the nation would be accompanied by press releases and supported by reviews and commentaries from persons prominent in medicine, social welfare, religion, public affairs, and others in the public limelight. We would also solicit supporting statements for the work from members of our advisory board, attesting to the authenticity of the report's disclosures and recommendations.

It would be our hope that the report's publication might coincide as an integral feature of a newly established "National Mental Health Week," which also could serve as a springboard for a countrywide fund appeal. Release of the report also could serve to announce the formation of a new national citizens' organization as a successor to the Mental Hygiene Program. In many ways, this event might herald a new day for the mentally ill in much the same way the publication of Clifford Beers's classic, *A Mind That Found Itself* some 40 years earlier had led the way to the establishment of the National Committee for Mental Hygiene.

Once a permanent organization is in place with sufficient funds to facilitate the implementation of its goals we can proceed to move forward in improving conditions for the mentally ill. Among our more immediate goals would be the following:

> Encourage college students to consider pursuing careers in the mental health professions such as psychiatry, psychology, social work, nursing, and occupational and recreational therapy.

Encourage students interested in pursuing careers in the social service arena to devote summer vacation periods to working in mental hospitals as attendants. Such experience would be highly useful to them as part of their basic training and provide a highly useful function for the institutions and their patients.

Develop plans that would enhance the skills of those attendants in mental hospitals in a manner that would enhance their work performance as well as their self-image as care-providers. Out of this thrust it would be hoped that a new professional status would emerge for hospital attendants.

This then, is our plan of action—and we have been given much encouragement to pursue it vigorously by our many friends from outside the CPS ranks. At present, there is no single national organization capable of speaking effectively on behalf of the disenfranchised mentally ill in our public institutions. You can help us in reaching this objective by sharing with us accounts of your own experiences that will enable us to tell the story of the CPS experience of our nation's mental health facilities in a manner that will arouse the public's concern and stimulate it to action. Demobilization is almost at hand. Please don't delay in letting us hear from you.

Obediently yours for the MHP,

Len, Will, Hal, and Phil

The responses poured in to the Mental Hygiene Program from virtually all 61 CPS units based in mental hospitals and state training schools for the retarded. They were to the point. They were graphic. And they made it possible to launch a truly nationwide public education campaign in the spring and early summer of 1946. By this time, the CPS program had been almost completely dismantled. In place of the Mental Hygiene Program, a new nationwide lay mental health organization, the National Mental Health Foundation, had emerged. Its arrival had been heralded with two major media events: the publication in May of that year of Albert Q. Maisel's shocking exposé of U.S. mental hospitals in *Life Magazine,* followed two months later by a condensed version of Maisel's article in *Reader's Digest*.

By the early months of 1945, word of the CPS Mental Hygiene Program had begun to reach many persons of high repute throughout the country. Their expressions of support were a tremendous morale booster for the leaders of this "shoestring"-financed but highly dedicated band of COs. Among the group of these supporters was Pearl Buck, who remarked:[8]

> I have known of the work of the conscientious objectors in mental institutions and have watched it with great interest and approval. . . . Anything which the conscientious objectors can do to set higher standards of care and kindness for the unfortunate patients is one of the greatest contributions that could possibly be made to mankind. . . . I hope that the work that the conscientious objectors are doing can be made known to the public. They deserve all praise.

Chapter 8

PLAN FOR ACTION BECOMES A REALITY

> . . . I share your concern for the ever-increasing number of mental patients needing hospital care. I am deeply concerned, too, as to how we can prevent this toll of mental illness. To make a dent in this problem, we need the concerted effort of all of us. The most striking need, of course, is for personnel of all sorts—aides, nurses, and psychiatrists, for our hospital patients.
>
> The effort of your organization in seeking to improve the quality of psychiatric aides and attendants throughout the country will be a stimulation, I hope, to many groups to work for the same and related purposes. . . .
>
> Again, I want to commend you for your own fine work and urge you and the National Mental Health Foundation to carry forward the splendid program you have started so vigorously.
>
> President Harry S. Truman
> Letter to the Honorable Owen J. Roberts
> Chairman, National Mental Health Foundation
> July 26, 1946

If ever there was a red-letter day for the four conscientious objectors (COs) whose vision in the summer of 1944 led them to create the Mental Hygiene Program of the Civilian Public Service (CPS) program, it had to be May 6, 1946. On that date the American public was first introduced to the National

Mental Health Foundation (NMHF), successor to the Mental Hygiene Program of CPS. In addition, it was on that date that *Life Magazine* hit the newsstands with its historic exposé of conditions in U.S. mental hospitals, based largely on reports that had been collected by NMHF's predecessor organization.

Also on May 6, 1946, the Associated Press and the United Press fed the nation's newspapers with the story that former Supreme Court Justice Owen J. Roberts had agreed to serve as national chairman of NMHF, joined by a panel of 38 distinguished public citizens as sponsors. This story was picked up by *The Philadelphia Inquirer, The New York Herald Tribune, The New York Sun, The Baltimore Sun, The New York Times, The Philadelphia Evening Bulletin, The Philadelphia Record, The New York Post,* and *PM.*

The connection between the new NMHF and the work done by the COs in the CPS units was directly acknowledged in an article published in *The Philadelphia Inquirer:*[1]

> The organization, dedicated to the conservation of mental health and to the highest obtainable standards of treatment for the mentally ill, is an outgrowth of a wartime program of service to mental institutions under the auspices of several church agencies, notably the American Friends Service Committee, the Brethren Service Committee, and the Mennonite Central Committee.

Early in 1946, as plans began to emerge for transforming the Mental Hygiene Program of CPS into a nationwide citizens' mental health movement, its base of operations was shifted from the Philadelphia State Hospital to the city proper. For a brief period it moved into an unoccupied Friends' Meeting House in West Philadelphia. Then through the good offices of the American Friends Service Committee, larger and more useful space was made available to the new organization in a vacant school building at 15th and Race Streets.

In the months preceding the media blitz that erupted on and after May 6th, the executive staff, aided by Justice Roberts and several of NMHF's influential sponsors, had recruited a panel of persons held in high public esteem to its board of directors, professional advisory board, and an augmented board of sponsors. (See page 179 for a complete listing of those who joined NMHF in these three categories.)

On the day after it ran a news story on the formation of NMHF, *The Philadelphia Evening Bulletin* published an editorial titled "Help for Mental Cases."[2] It emphasized the importance of public opinion in effecting change in the nation's mental hospitals:

> The National Mental Health Foundation can perform a service of inestimable value by arousing public opinion to the need for more humane treatment of the mentally ill. The duty of the public is not performed when it locks them up and feeds them. They are entitled to the best facilities for cure that money can buy.
>
> Public opinion, based on reliable information sponsored by such a body as the new Foundation, can influence legislative action. There may be in this new movement the dawn of a brighter day for neglected patients in some of the country's mental hospitals.

In the months preceding the public announcement of NMHF's formation, its executive staff had assembled a team of eight men who had been released from their responsibilities in the CPS mental hospital program. These individuals had a broad range of skills that the new organization desperately needed to implement its objectives. Because of its then-limited financial resources, the maximum salary NMHF could offer members of its senior staff was $200 per month.

Within a short time, separate divisions were in place for activities such as education, publishing, legal affairs, marketing and public relations, fund-raising, and financial management. During this same period, a young New York psychiatrist, Dr. Dallas Pratt, was introduced to Leonard Cornell, the new agency's executive director, through the good offices of the American Friends Service Committee. At their meeting, Dr. Pratt became deeply impressed with the objectives of NMHF. Soon after this meeting he volunteered to serve as a consultant to the new organization two days per week. His offer was readily accepted. In the next several years, Dr. Pratt's sage advice and counsel contributed enormously to NMHF's growth and credibility.

In her widely read *Mental Health in the United States: A Fifty-Year History,* Nina Ridenour, Ph.D., a former staff member of the National Committee for Mental Hygiene and its successor, the National Mental Health Association, credits NMHF with stimulating the publication of a flood of media exposés on the deplorable state of affairs in the nation's mental hospitals. She made this observation:[3]

> These articles, appearing in two of the nation's most widely read publications, *Life Magazine* and the *Reader's Digest,* triggered a barrage of similar exposés in other magazines and the daily press. . . .
>
> Press exposés are an old story to mental institutions. One recalls Nellie Bly, the *New York World*'s extraordinary "girl correspondent" who in 1887 had herself committed to the New York City Lunatic Asylum and later wrote a lurid series, revealing asylum horrors. Nor was Nellie's escapade either the first or last such affair. Many reporters before her and since have made their way into mental hospitals, either as patients or employees, and it is part of the tragedy that conditions in mental hospitals have invariably been such as to provide "good copy."
>
> . . . Such exposés in the past . . . rarely brought about lasting reforms. All too often they resulted, not in inspiring people to constructive action, but in frightening and alienating them and in further demoralizing overburdened public officials . . . most of whom were struggling to do the best they could with insufficient funds and against public indifference.
>
> A distinguishing mark of the flood of exposés in the 1940s was that, whether initiated by journalists or by organized mental health and other civic groups (the COs directly stimulated several), they were carried through with the cooperation of hospital staffs, medical leaders in the community, and public officials. One newspaper after another all over the country produced thoughtful, carefully planned series . . . describing conditions in its own state and making recommendations for reform.

Dr. Ridenour alludes to Walter Lerch's series in *The Cleveland Press* and Albert Deutsch's "Shame of the States" series, which appeared in New York in 1945 in *PM* and continued in the following year in another New York newspaper, *The Star.* Deutsch's series on the shocking conditions on the psychiatric wards in Veterans Administration hospitals instigated a congressional investigation and eventually led to reforms in the Veterans Administration hospital system. Similar critical newspaper accounts of inhumane conditions in mental hospitals were published in Oklahoma, Kansas, California, Maryland, Minnesota, Iowa, and Texas. These articles were written by reporters who had been inspired by the flood of such stories that began appearing in the spring of 1946.

Throughout NMHF's history, its staff made assiduous efforts to cultivate relations with key science writers affiliated with the leading newspapers of the day and the major wire services. Besides those mentioned previously, these contacts included well-known reporters such as Lucy Freeman of *The New York Times,* Earl Ubel of *The New York Herald Tribune,* Alton Blakeslee of the Associated Press, and Delos Smith of the United Press. Relationships with these and other journalists covering health and mental health issues throughout the country enabled NMHF's public relations staff to enjoy ready access to many of the nation's respected newspapers and periodicals.

The Barry Bingham Campaign

Perhaps the most important coup achieved by NMHF in its campaign to give the public a new point of view about the mentally ill happened in the spring of 1949. At that time, the U.S. Junior Chamber of Commerce had decided to have all its chapters join in sponsoring a first-ever National Mental Health Week during the last week of April.

To take advantage of the momentum that would be generated from this event, NMHF asked one of its sponsors, Barry Bingham, then president of *The Louisville Courier-Journal* and also president of the American Newspaper Publishers Association, to address an appeal to his fellow newspaper publishers. NMHF's purpose was to enlist the aid of this group in eliminating widely held public misperceptions about mental illness. This goal had to be achieved for NMHF to be successful in developing a solid support base of people with a new and enlightened attitude toward the mentally ill and their needs.

The Courier-Journal

LOUISVILLE, KY.

March 2, 1949

Barry Bingham, Editor

Dear Editor:

Would you be willing to help in the cure of sick people by the simple power of words? This letter is to suggest how you can do just that. I have been asked to write it by the National Mental Health Foundation. It is a request for help from you -- not for money, but a still more vital contribution to public understanding of the problems of mental illness.

With the widespread attention now being given to the care of patients in mental hospitals and with the approaching National Mental Health Week to be sponsored by the Junior Chamber of Commerce beginning April 24, your newspaper will have occasion to write numerous stories on the subject of America's number one health problem -- MENTAL HEALTH. Newspapers sometimes inadvertently use certain archaic expressions which have a tendency to perpetuate the false stigma so generally prevalent concerning mental illness. The widespread ignorance regarding the nature of mental illness has been one of the chief barriers in conquering this disease. It has retarded the use of cures now definitely known and established.

Medical science has proved that mental illness is no disgrace, and that like any other physical ailment it may be cured if treated with prompt and skillful attention Over 600,000 Americans are now in mental hospitals. Because of the false stigma surrounding their illness they are, almost without exception, receiving pitifully inadequate care and treatment. Yet one in ten of us in America will suffer some form of mental illness in our lifetime, one in twenty will require mental hospital treatment.

As you well know, words and ideas for which they currently stand influence our point of view. For example, the use of such a term as "inmate" in referring to the mentally ill suggests an element of crime and retribution. Yet, medical science asserts that the mentally ill are just as sick and just as innocent of crime as patients in a T.B. sanitarium.

You can perform a great service in promoting the cause of mental health by helping to take the stigma out of mental illness. You can do this by discarding from the vocabulary of your paper any possible archaic and stigmatized expressions, and substituting others. Three that I would especially like to urge are PATIENT in place of INMATE; MENTAL ILLNESS in place of INSANITY or LUNACY; MENTAL HOSPITAL instead of INSANE ASYLUM.

Please let me know if you are willing to join with other newspapers in this campaign against a common enemy.

Sincerely yours,

Barry Bingham

Barry Bingham
President

It was a tall order, considering the size of the population that had to be reached. Realistically, there was no way that an organization with NMHF's limited resources could make a meaningful attempt to reach out to such a huge audience on its own.

Then someone came up with a simple and creative solution. "Why don't we invite Mr. Bingham to consider sending a letter to the editor of each and every newspaper in the country in which he would appeal for their support in creating a new and more wholesome image for the mentally ill?" After the idea was presented to Mr. Bingham, along with the draft of a sample letter, he readily consented to join in the campaign. Early in March of that same year, the letter was dispatched by his office to every newspaper editor in the country. It is shown on page 152, exactly as it left his office:[4]

In response to his appeal for a more enlightened approach on the part of the nation's press in covering stories related to mental illness and the mentally ill, Mr. Bingham received nearly 1,000 replies, the overwhelming majority of which supported his position. In hundreds of instances, the editors' responses were accompanied by editorials that had been written in support of his appeal for eradicating stigmatizing language in referring to mental disorders and those afflicted with these illnesses. Many replies were accompanied by directives to editorial departments requiring the adoption of more scientifically acceptable terms in place of the stigmatizing verbiage then more commonly used. One of these editorials—published in *The Augusta [Ga.] Herald*—and a directive issued by the Style Book Committee of *The Cincinnati Enquirer* are reproduced on pages 154 and 155.

In retrospect, the Barry Bingham campaign played a major role in changing the way that the public perceived mental illness and the mentally ill in the months and years that followed. The network of local and state mental hygiene societies that had been trying to lead the struggle for better conditions in state institutions had only been able to muster relatively small numbers of the public to join in their crusade. When the newspapers, at the urging of their esteemed colleague Barry Bingham, began to espouse a deeper and more compassionate consideration of the nation's mentally ill, it became easier for the mental hygiene societies to enlarge their ranks. Legislators began taking more notice of the demands of the organized mental health movement for more adequate funds to support existing mental health services.

When the National Institute of Mental Health was established in 1946 by Congress, it was awarded a budget of $3 million for its initial year of operation. In response to professional and public pressures, by 1956 the agency's annual operating budget had increased to $18 million; by 1962 it had increased to $107 million. By the mid-1970s the institute's annual budget had mushroomed to several hundred million dollars.[5]

In the same period that the National Institute of Mental Health was created, state budgets for mental health services also increased dramatically. It would be unfair to claim that the NMHF-sponsored Barry Bingham appeal to newspaper editors was solely responsible for bringing about this historic change. But there is no question that the Bingham campaign did play an important part in encouraging a gentler and more compassionate viewpoint toward mental illness and mentally ill people. That effort also contributed to a kindlier attitude on the part of legislative bodies in considering programs to raise existing standards of care and treatment in mental hospitals and in fostering the development of innovative methods for dealing with psychiatric disorders.

6—THE AUGUSTA (GA.) HERALD—Wednesday, Mar. 16, 1949

MENTALLY ILL STIGMATIZED BY ARCHAIC LAWS, IGNORANCE

THROUGHOUT the ages of man a stigma has been attached to the unhappy individuals who have been so unfortunate as to be afflicted with mental illness.

This stigma was born in the fallacy of early man that a "crazy" person had been taken over by an evil spirit and was to be avoided. All types of torture were practiced for ages in attempts to drive out the demon.

On down to the present day the mental anguish caused the victims and the families of such are little less painful than the physical suffering imposed in the early days.

In an attempt to remove this curse that damns the mentally ill, The National Mental Health Foundation has instituted a program designed through publicity and other means to bring about a better public understanding of the problems of mental illness.

The foundation, recognizing that widespread ignorance regarding the nature of mental illness, has been one of the chief barriers in conquering this disease, is seeking to dispel this misinformation with the true facts. This ignorance, it states, has retarded the use of cures now definitely known and established.

Mental illness is no disgrace, and like any other physical ailment may be cured if treated with prompt and skilful attention. Over 600,000 Americans are now in mental hospitals, and Georgia has more than her share of this number. Because of the false stigma surrounding their illness they are receiving pitifully inadequate care and treatment.

Mental illness is no more a crime than T.B., yet the terms we apply to the insane and the way we handle them brands them as such.

In Georgia we treat the mentally ill almost as if we were living in the days of Bedlam. Our law, based on the Old English code, calls for the arrest of the insane on a warrant. They are taken into custody by armed officers and must be brought to trial, just like a criminal, before a jury.

These jurors, laymen just as in the case of other court trials, know no more about psychiatry and are no more qualified to judge a person's sanity than they would be to decide whether he had leprosy.

Perhaps this is a contributing factor to the great number of mentally ill in our state. Our treatment of these unfortunates has placed a stigma on their condition that is as great and perhaps greater than in any other state in the union.

People almost had rather die than to admit a member of their family is deranged. As a consequence conditions which could be remedied early in cases are allowed to progress until a mind is hopelessly gone.

This is something our lawmakers should look into at the earliest possible date. Let's change the law and make it humane and while we are doing that we should change our personal attitude and help others do likewise.

The mentally sick are ill with a special type of ailment. They are not criminals and we should not treat them as such. Above all, we should never refer to them, in speaking or in writing, by any term which, by any chance, would tend to place any stigma upon them.

The Cincinnati Enquirer
One of the World's Greatest Newspapers

OFFICE OF
MANAGING EDITOR

March 4, 1949

Mr. Barry Bingham
The Courier-Journal
Louisville, Kentucky

Dear Mr. Bingham:

The Enquirer is happy to go along with you on your suggestions as to the use of "mental" rather than "insane."

Enclosed is proof of our Style Book Committee's directive, effective immediately.

Sincerely yours,

Everett M. Boyd

EMB*ew
Enc.

STYLE RULE OF THE WEEK.

To remove the stigma from mental illness, use PATIENT in place of inmate; MENTAL ILLNESS in place of insanity or lunacy; MENTAL HOSPITAL instead of insane asylum. This does not apply to Hospital For Criminal Insane, where the element of crime is present.

ENQUIRER STYLE BOOK COMMITTEE.
March 3, 1949.

One final observation deserves to be made about the Barry Bingham campaign. It was one of the most cost-effective public relations efforts ever undertaken by NMHF in the pursuit of its objectives. The entire out-of-pocket expenses to develop and mount this nationwide campaign amounted to less than a few hundred dollars.

The Attendant Becomes *The Psychiatric Aide*

The development and publication of *The Attendant* shortly after the CPS Mental Hygiene Program was initiated in the summer of 1944 was acclaimed as a major contribution in upgrading the quality of care by mental hospital attendants. Hospital superintendents as well as nursing supervisors heralded its appearance as a long-overdue training aid. One of NMHF's primary concerns was that attendants deserved a title that reflected more accurately the true nature of their responsibilities; hence, it decided to rename this monthly magazine *The Psychiatric Aide.* The cover and a feature page from this magazine are reproduced on page 157.

Many of the original features of *The Attendant* were retained in *The Psychiatric Aide,* but they were given more sprightly presentations. A monthly cartoon feature was introduced, illustrating constructive ways of handling difficult situations with patients. The new magazine also began to solicit articles from an ever-widening circle of mental hospital personnel. As the CPS units began disappearing from the hospital scene with the close of the war, more and more of the editorial contributions came from hospital workers, many of whom had initially been antagonistic to the arrival of COs in their midst.

The new periodical continued to find an ever-increasing audience through the late 1940s and well into the 1950s. During Governor Luther Youngdahl's tenure as chief executive in Minnesota, when he was leading a crusade to upgrade his state's seven mental hospitals, arrangements were made to acquire enough copies of the magazine so that each employee in these hospitals could have one.

THE PSYCHIATRIC AIDE

Article of the Month:
A WORLD IN SLOW MOTION

February 1951, Vol. 8, No. 2

—George Thorman and Simon Frankel.

ONE METHOD OF TEACHING AIDES TO BE MORE HUMANE

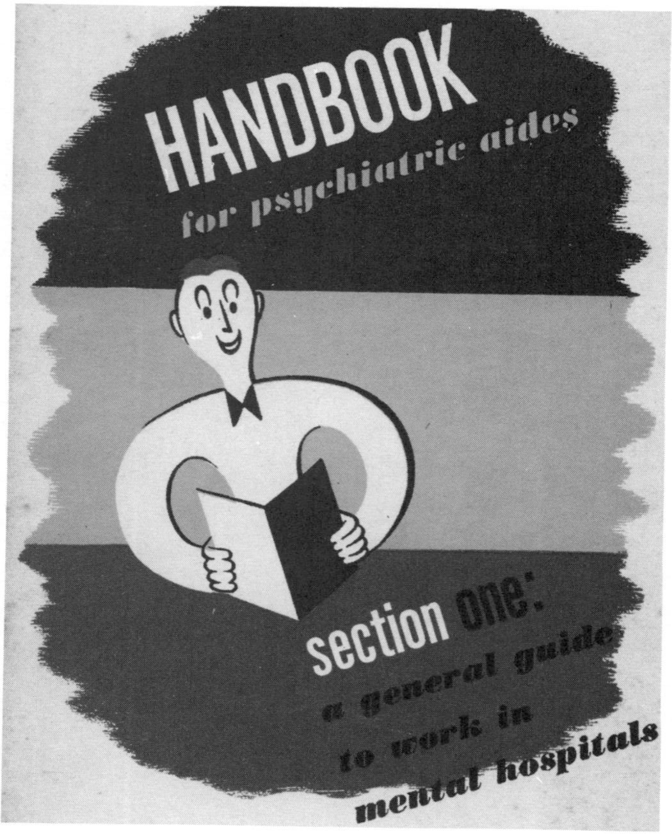

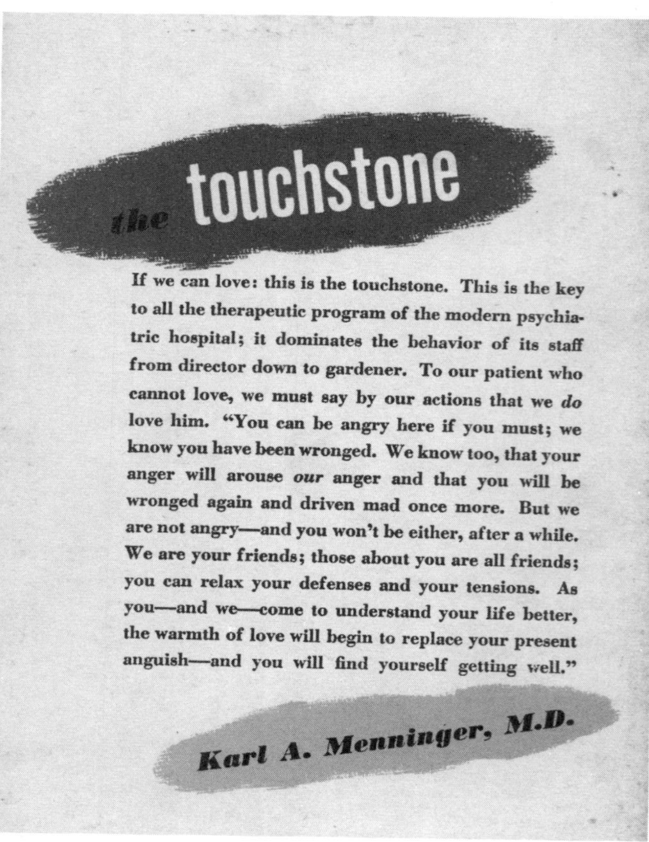

the touchstone

If we can love: this is the touchstone. This is the key to all the therapeutic program of the modern psychiatric hospital; it dominates the behavior of its staff from director down to gardener. To our patient who cannot love, we must say by our actions that we *do* love him. "You can be angry here if you must; we know you have been wronged. We know too, that your anger will arouse *our* anger and that you will be wronged again and driven mad once more. But we are not angry—and you won't be either, after a while. We are your friends; those about you are all friends; you can relax your defenses and your tensions. As you—and we—come to understand your life better, the warmth of love will begin to replace your present anguish—and you will find yourself getting well."

Karl A. Menninger, M.D.

One of the most useful publications to emanate from NMHF during this period was the *Handbook for Psychiatric Aides: A General Guide to Work in Mental Hospitals.* It was one of the first training manuals of its kind. Using easy-to-understand language, it offered mental hospital personnel assigned to ward duty highly practical information about how to deal with the day-to-day problems they faced on the wards. Frank L. Wright, Jr., author of *Out of Sight, Out of Mind* (see Chapter 2), edited this publication in close collaboration with a panel of professional advisers. The manual was immediately and enthusiastically received throughout the several hundred mental hospitals in both the United States and Canada. By the end of 1949, nearly 20,000 copies had been acquired by these institutions.

In February 1950, a second manual in this series was released: *Handbook for Psychiatric Aides: Care of the Overactive and Disturbed Patient.* Paul Harris III, a member of the staff, was the editor responsible for its development. A highly respected group of advisers made important contributions to its contents. It, too, was well received as a training aid in mental hospitals and continued to be in print through the 1950s.

"The Psychiatric Aide of the Year" Award

In an attempt to gain public recognition for the important services rendered by mental hospital attendants, NMHF launched a nation-wide search for The Psychiatric Aide of the Year in the fall of 1947. The objective of this campaign was to encourage each of the nation's mental hospitals to select from among their attendant personnel the one individual whose performance in the previous year had been so exemplary as to deserve the hospital's designation as the "Aide of the Year." Participating institutions were requested to involve the entire hospital community, including patients wherever possible, in the selection process.

An advisory board was appointed by NMHF to review all the nominations and to determine the most deserving candidate from among those entered. A cash award of $500 would be given to the one chosen as the The Psychiatric Aide of the Year. In addition, the individuals designated for the award by their respective institutions were given certificates recognizing their selection by their peers. In almost every state where hospitals participated in the award program, those selected for this honor were invited to their state capitols, where their achievements were publicly acknowledged in ceremonies conducted at joint sessions of their state legislatures. At many of these affairs the governor of the state participated in the presentation of the individual citations. These ceremonial occasions were widely publicized and served to aid in bringing about a new respect for the entire profession of mental hospital attendants.

Launching of this program was initially made possible by a grant from one of NMHF's early benefactors, Mary Griggs Burke. In the years that followed, the Catherwood-Kirkbride Fund for Research in Psychiatry funded the awards feature of the program. In each of the next several years, an increasing number of hospitals participated in this event. During the first three years of the award program, those who were selected for top honors received national recognition in the nation's weekly news magazines. In the award's third year, Fox Movietone Newsreel had a sequence in one of its regular newsreels featuring Olivia deHavilland, who had recently completed a starring role in *The Snakepit,* making the presentation to that year's top award winner. The newsreels in that period were the equivalent of abbreviated versions of the nightly news programs on TV in the 1980s and 1990s. This particular sequence was shown on the screens of thousands of movie theaters throughout the country.

When in 1950 NMHF merged with the National Committee for Mental Hygiene and the American Psychiatric Foundation to become the National Association for Mental Health, the award program for psychiatric aides was sustained for several additional years and then passed along as a continuing project to that agency's local and state affiliates. Some 40 years after this award program was introduced, it is still very much alive in many parts of the country.

The Texas Mental Health Association has continuously sponsored this event since it was first initiated. In the May–June 1990 issue of *Impact,* the bimonthly magazine of the Texas Department of Mental Health and Retardation, nine psychiatric aides were featured as winners of that year's awards.

The award program for outstanding attendants is another illustration of the creative manner in which NMHF used its resources to bring about positive and long-lasting attitudinal changes toward a group of mental hospital employees who for so long had been held in such low public esteem. Once this campaign was launched and then nurtured for a period of time, it gathered sufficient momentum to be continued on its own.

NMHF Takes to the Airwaves to Spread Its Message

In the summer of 1946, NMHF's Special Services Division proposed that it produce a series of eight radio dramas on themes related to giving the public new and enlightened insights into the nature of mental illness and the problems faced by the mentally ill and their families. The two radio dramas that had been developed at Connecticut State Hospital by Alex Sareyan and Jack Neher were to be used as models for this new series. To get as much exposure as possible for these programs with the limited financial resources of NMHF, each of the eight programs in this series was plotted to run to 15 minutes—a common format at that time. The programs were to be recorded so that they would be suitable for broadcast under the auspices of local and state health and mental health agencies throughout the country.

Each of the programs was designed so that it had an appropriate and relevant introduction by a well-known celebrity. Individual programs had a story line and also provided the sponsoring agency with an opportunity for a 30-second closing announcement. To ensure that the technical quality of the programs was such that they would be readily accepted for broadcast by local radio stations, the entire series was produced at the facilities of the National Broadcasting Company. The actors playing the roles were all drawn from professional ranks. All other production personnel had extensive credits in producing radio dramas. Special music for all eight programs was written and performed by Rosa Rio, one of the well-known radio organists of the day.

Four of NMHF's sponsors—Eleanor Roosevelt, Helen Hayes, Mary Jane Ward, and the Reverend Dr. Harry Emerson Fosdick—each agreed to introduce two of the programs in the series. Because of the public service nature of the programs, services of all the professionals involved in their production were secured at minimum scale. The studio facilities were also provided at special rates.

However, NMHF had to pay for the first two programs in advance: a total of $1,600. This was a big outlay for the organization at that time. To get the series into production, the initial costs were underwritten by a friend of the organization.

Only the first two programs in the series went into production immediately. The intention was that these programs would then be auditioned for prospective sponsors. Once the programs were completed, one of the members of the Special Services Division left on a field trip, covering 16 states where he had arranged to introduce the programs to state and voluntary mental health agencies.

The auditions were an instant hit. It was the first time in anyone's memory that a dramatic radio series on mental health concerns had become available for local sponsorship. Acquisition of the rights to broadcast the series was widely requested in response to this visit, and the financial success of the series was ensured. In Canada, the Department of National Health and Welfare acquired rights to the series for the entire country for broadcast on the CBC network. When the series was subsequently aired in Canada, it was personally introduced on the air by the governor-general. The first eight programs had been given the overall title, *For These We Speak.*

Shortly after the first two programs in the series were aired late in 1946 in New York City on Station WINS in prime time, *Variety* ran the following review:[6]

> . . . This series is designed to shed some light on psychiatric problems and upset some of the popular prejudices toward mental cases that have been a hangover from the Middle Ages.
>
> . . . Opening session, entitled "Aunt Millie and the Family Skeleton," was themed to the idea that mental illness is no disgrace. Story, which revolved around a small-town family which was

> forced to commit one of its members to a state institution for the mentally ill, pointed up the irrationality of the embarrassment flowing from such a necessity. Thesping and scripting were high caliber and show, despite its frank public service pitch, should garner a considerable amount of dialer interest.
>
> In a brief intro to the story, Mrs. Franklin Roosevelt also stressed the falsity of the ancient notions still current about insanity.

By midsummer of 1947, a demand had swelled for another series of similar radio dramas. At this point, television had not yet become a fixture in the overwhelming majority of American homes. The two staff members who had been responsible for the first radio series planned and completed a 13-episode series, *The Tenth Man*. Dr. Dallas Pratt, NMHF's staff consultant who had served as an adviser for the production of the initial radio series, also played a key role in the development and production of this new series.

The title for the new series was based on the fact that one person in 10 will, at some time, require care and treatment for a psychiatric illness. The radio plays were designed to stimulate the public to take an active interest in learning about community mental health facilities. They were also intended to inform the public about the many facets of mental illness, as well as to provide insights into dealing with the kinds of pressures that could lead to serious emotional problems if not handled properly. The actor Ralph Bellamy narrated this series and made brief appearances in all 13 programs. All the programs were produced at facilities of the National Broadcasting Company with the same mix of professional talent that was used in the first series. Below is a brief description of each of the plays in this series:

- *Punishment Without Crime*. This episode dramatizes the inhumane and barbarous commitment procedures now existing (1948) in many states, which force mentally ill individuals to be lodged in jail pending a trial by jury before hospitalization.
- *The Silent Men*. Laura Kennedy reluctantly joins a volunteer unit that services a local mental hospital. She not only has a fear of the patients, but also doubts that her piano playing for a group of

depressed patients has any value. Her playing moves a depressed patient to express his gratitude, and she learns her fears were groundless.

- *The Old Folks at Home.* Illustrates the need and function of social groups for older people in community settings as a means of sustaining their mental health.
- *Which World for Susan?* Adolescence is a very unhappy time for Susan. She is inhibited from socially interacting with her classmates in light of her mother's fears she will get into "bad company." As a result Susan is a petulant, aloof girl who takes refuge in a dream world. The intervention of a caring teacher helps bring the girl out of her shell.
- *Love Without Words.* The purpose of this vignette is to illustrate the function of a marriage counselor in helping a couple resolve their differences.
- *On Wings of Clay.* This drama demonstrates the contribution of a trained occupational therapist in the recovery of mentally ill patients.
- *Out of the Shadow.* The destructive impact of social stigma that follows recovered mentally ill patients into their communities after discharge is the focus of this play.
- *Figs From Thistles.* This dramatization reveals that given the proper understanding, a mentally retarded individual can make a suitable adjustment to both family and community life.
- *Doctor Troubleshooter.* How a psychiatrically trained physician can facilitate the mental health of employees in an industrial setting is the focus of this presentation.
- *The Tie That Binds.* The problems faced by a mother who has made a complete recovery from an episode of mental illness, only to be treated as an invalid by her family, are highlighted in this play.
- *Out of Sight, Out of Mind.* The need for more adequate funding for state hospitals so that they can offer a higher level of medical care and treatment for their patients is highlighted in this dramatization.
- *The Lady and the Lawmakers.* This play develops the theme that public pressure, properly organized, can bring about desired

action for improved mental health facilities. It offers an additional perspective to the previous program.

* *The Child Is Father of the Man*. This play reveals how a young mother's too-strict adherence to the textbook in bringing up her child results in an anxiety state that in turn produces a loathing for food and a speech defect in her child. The play does not disparage the work of experts in child psychology but tries to free the parent from "the tyranny of the norm."

When word was released that *The Tenth Man* was available for distribution in the fall of 1947, it was immediately picked up for local sponsorship by governmental and voluntary agencies throughout the country. A conservative estimate made two years later indicated that the programs in this series had been aired on nearly 1,000 radio stations in more than 40 states, as well as in all the Canadian provinces. An equally impressive fact was that approximately 40% of the programs in both this series and the preceding series had been scheduled during prime time—the period that attracts the largest listening audience.

In *The New York World-Telegram* for October 30, 1947, Harriet Van Horne, that paper's radio commentator, reviewed two of the episodes from *The Tenth Man*. This review is reprinted on page 166.

In 1949, a third series of 10 radio dramas, *Hi Neighbor,* was produced with the popular actor Eddie Albert as narrator for the series. These programs were recorded at the Columbia Broadcasting Company studios with the same basic dramatic format that had been characteristic of their two predecessors. Unlike the previous series, this one dealt with the day-to-day emotional problems faced by families. It included themes such as teenage rebellion, marriage and family life education, the importance of birthing mothers having constant access to their infants in the hospital, understanding the needs of preadolescents, how personal involvement of parents in meeting the recreational needs of their children is an important aspect of parenting, and constructive solutions for dealing with normal interfamily problems.

The *Hi Neighbor* radio series proved to be every bit as popular as the earlier ones. All three series garnered many commendations

NEW YORK WORLD-TELEGRAM, THURSDAY, OCTOBER 30, 1947

Radio

'The 10th Man' Spotlights Problem of Mentally Ill

By HARRIET VAN HORNE.

Every tenth man in your community will need, sometime before he dies, a doctor to minister to his sick mind, his ailing emotions.

Harriet Van Horne.

This having been established by psychiatry, it is the better part of valor for all of us to investigate the subject of mental hygiene. Your mind to you may be a kingdom today, a dark cavern tomorrow. For who is to say which of us will be designated "The Tenth Man?"

In co-operation with the National Mental Health Foundation, WNEW is presenting, each Friday night at 10, a program dedicated to Man No. 10. In the simplest and gentlest of terms, it seeks to explain, first: What is mental illness? How should we treat it? And can we prevent it?

Only 15 minutes in length, the productions, nevertheless, have meaning and purpose. Moreover, the talent is first rate. Ralph Bellamy is narrator and the cast includes such sterling radio names as Anne Seymour, Jackson Beck and Hester Sondergaard.

The first program, two weeks ago, opened with a flashback to 1841. The scene was a women's prison and a visitor was being admitted to conduct a Sunday school class. It was her first visit and she was appalled. "You keep the insane *HERE*, in jail?" she asked.

It was a question that launched a 40-year reform campaign. For the woman was Dorothea Dix and we have her to thank for the enlightened notion of separating the mentally ill from criminals.

"That was 100 years ago," said Mr. Bellamy, "but what about the present? Are we still punishing people for being mentally ill? Have we improved as much as we should?"

* * *

There followed the story of Harry Andrews, "The Tenth Man," described as "a composite of many cases." Because 15 minutes allows small scope for plot development, the story, necessarily, bore a strong resemblance to a case history file card. Harry was deranged, disappeared from home shortly after his wife pleaded with the doctor not to "put him away." The sheriff picked up Harry, put him in jail on a charge of drunkenness. And there he languished until a "lunatic commission" met to pass on his mental fitness.

This circumstance is one of the bitterest in a case history. For the commission consisted of the county clerk, the village pharmacist and a general practitioner. They found Harry insane, recommended that he be committed to a state hospital.

Martha, his wife, felt a deep sense of shame. Her family doctor, by explaining the nature of Harry's illness, dispelled this feeling. He couldn't, however, erase the pain she felt at seeing her husband brought to the hospital in a patrol wogan, handcuffed. "He wouldn't have tried to run away," she whispered.

Said the doctor: "We must get rid of our oldfashioned ideas before we can get rid of our old-fashioned laws."

The second script stressed one of the basic concepts of modern psychology—that the child is father to the man. That the emotional stresses of childhood may be at the root of a breakdown in later life. "That's why bringing up children is such an awful responsibility," said Bellamy, "and such an awfully beautiful experience."

In the play that followed we met Stanley, a shy boy who stuttered. Stuttered and refused to eat. His parents devoted each mealtime to saying grimly, "Stanley, eat your potato." It took a child psychologist to show them that Stanley would probably enjoy his potato hugely if his parents simply left him alone. He even got over his stutter.

* * *

from the organizations that sponsored them for broadcast in their communities, as well as from the radio stations that agreed to schedule them. For the sponsoring agencies, the cost of acquiring these programs from NMHF ranged from a low of $10 to as much as $40 per program. The amount of the fee depended on the size of the population to which the programs were delivered. Because of the public service nature of the series, the programs were aired without charge by the radio stations. If the sponsoring agencies had endeavored to replicate the programs independently, their expenses would have run well in excess of $1,500 per program.[7]

Broad Popular Appeal Was Earmark of NMHF Educational Materials

One of the unique contributions made by NMHF was that for the first time the citizens' mental health movement, as well as the governmental agencies engaged in mental health education, had access to a wide range of educational aids. These aids were not only relevant and sound in content, but also eye-catching and attention-grabbing.

NMHF's basic policy was that the most effective way to reach the American public with its various mental health messages was to take advantage of the already-established networks rather than to develop its own direct links with the various audiences to which these messages were targeted. Among others, these networks included the health and behavioral science professions, educational institutions, service organizations, the religious communities, the voluntary and governmental health agencies, and the business world. NMHF staff responsible for executing the organization's marketing strategy planned and implemented a visitation program that reached out to every state in the country. These contacts were not only welcomed by the above groups, but also gave NMHF a unique advantage in developing new materials that were especially responsive to the needs in the field.

NMHF's Education Division developed an impressive array of informational and educational materials. These ranged from single-page flyers and brochures to leaflets, pamphlets, books, posters, and a variety of visual aids (see pages 168–171 for examples). They were distributed to the general public through governmental and voluntary health and mental health organizations in the mid- to late 1940s.

The release of some of these materials resulted in extensive press coverage. This coverage in turn yielded tremendous additional mileage for the educational messages included in these materials. A case in point was the publication of a 72-page booklet, *Some Special Problems of Children*. Initially, the contents had been published by the New York State Association for Mental Health as a series of eight separate leaflets intended to provide parents with helpful guidelines in addressing common behavioral problems of young children. As

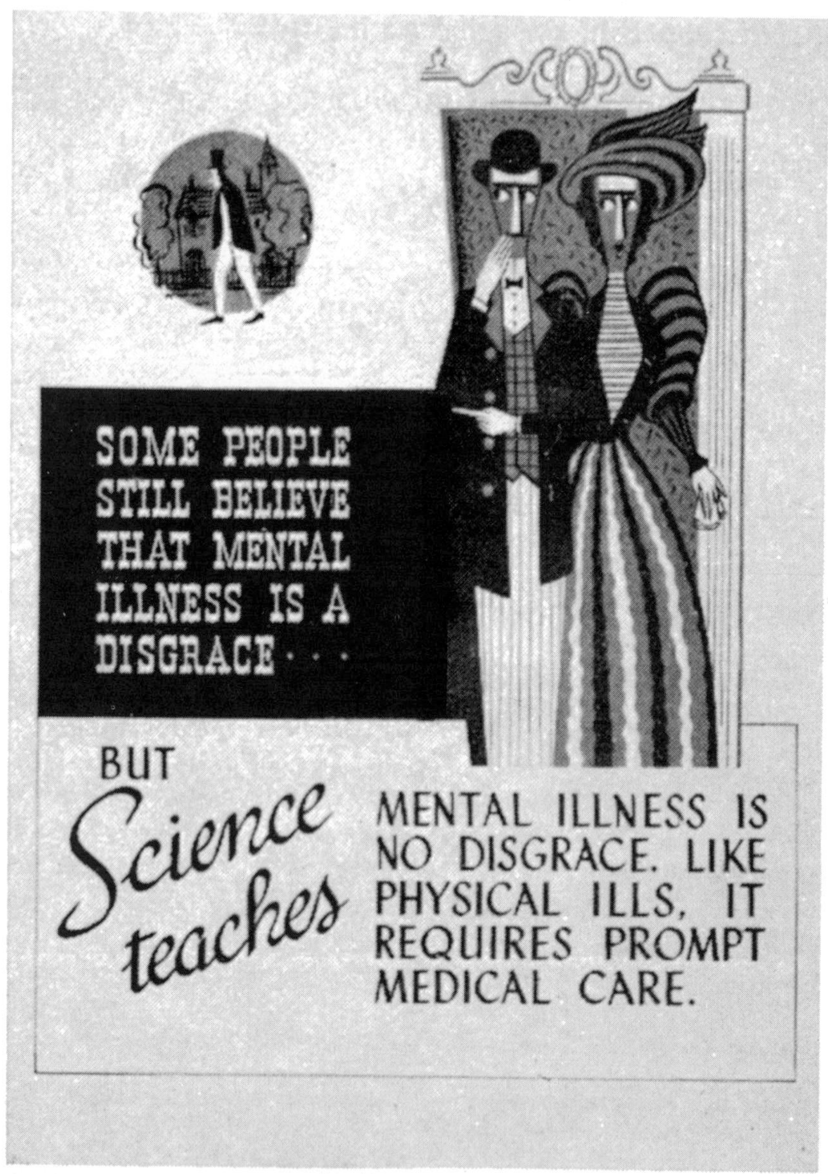

POSTER No. 1-A

This was one of a series of 16- by 20-inch posters intended for display in hospital waiting or reception areas or other appropriate display areas. These were among the first mental health–related posters to be released nationwide.

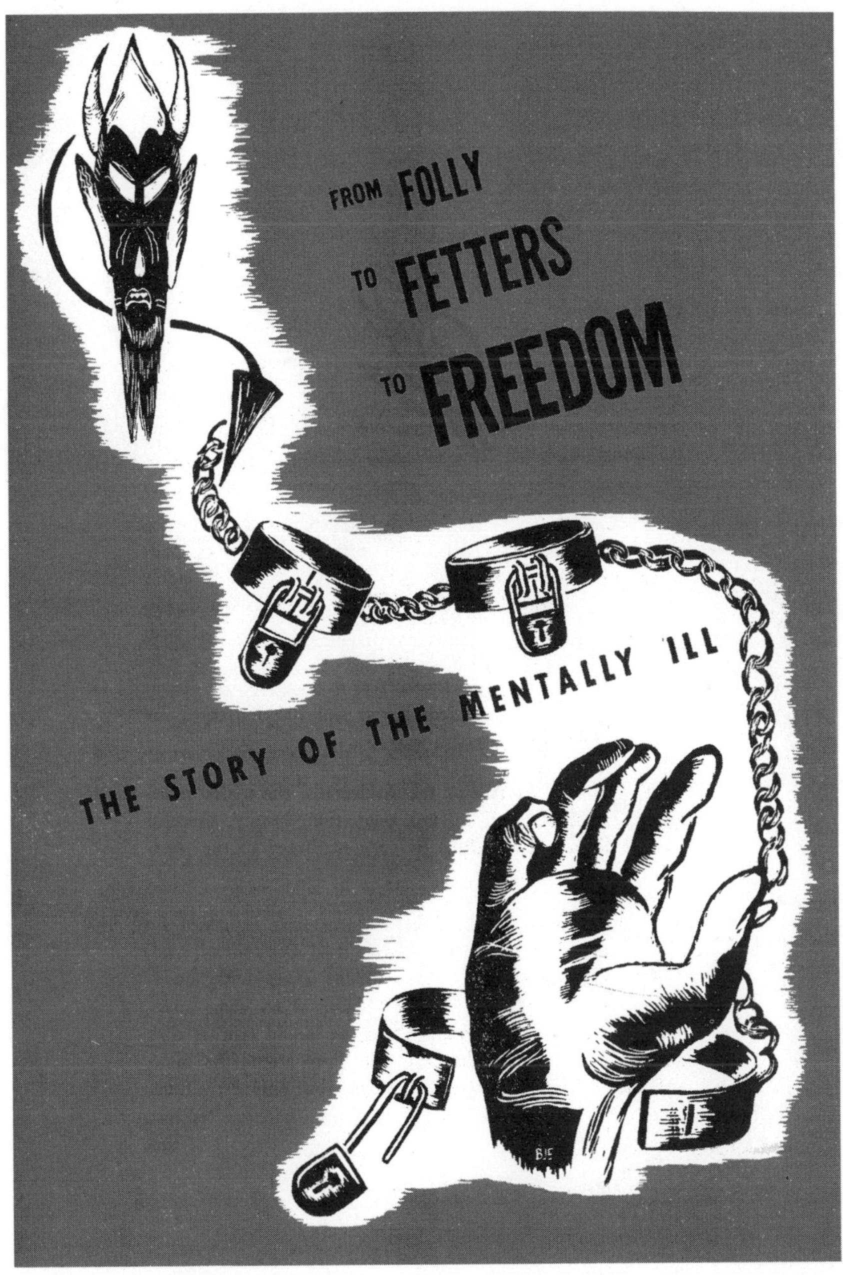

This eight-page leaflet provided a brief history of the care of the mentally ill from 400 B.C. to the present.

This four-page, cartoon-style leaflet was designed to give families and friends visiting patients in properly functioning mental hospitals some insights into how the institutions were organized to serve their patients.

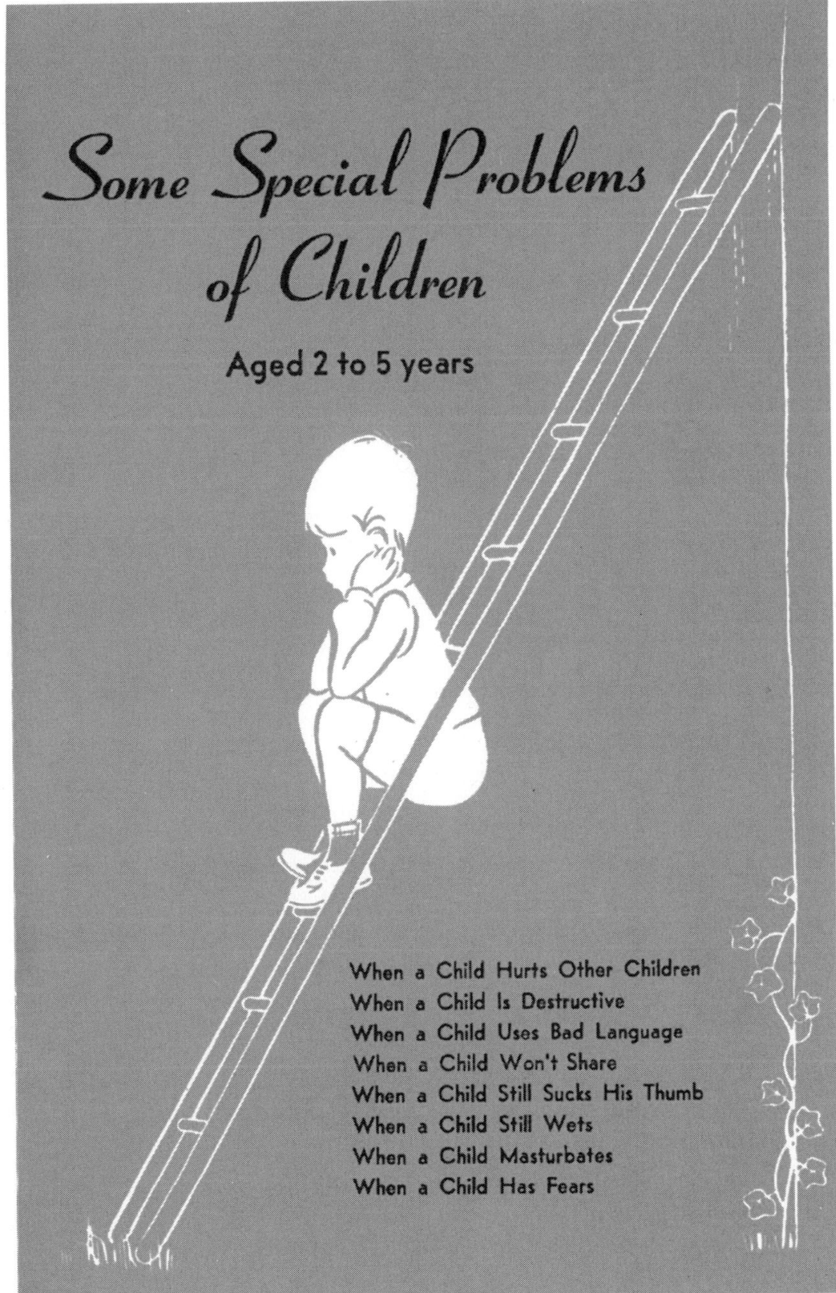

By the mid-1950s, demand for this title had exceeded 1,250,000 copies.

leaflets, they had enjoyed a modest distribution in New York City. Before the 72-page version was off press, NMHF had garnered advance orders for over 250,000 copies from agencies throughout the country. Its release was enhanced by a major feature story based on its contents in the Sunday Magazine Supplement of *The New York Times.* As a result of this story, over 20,000 individual requests for this book flooded NMHF's cramped New York City office. These requests were accompanied by quarters, neatly taped to return addresses. (The mail response was gratifying! But stripping the quarters from under their Scotch tape blankets was something else again.) Before the demand for this publication had run its course, several hundred thousand additional copies had to be printed.

Among other notable publications developed by NMHF were two Public Affairs Committee pamphlets, *Toward Mental Health,* by George Thorman, who had been a member of the staff during its first year, and *Mental Health Is a Family Affair,* coauthored by Jack Neher and Dallas Pratt. Both pamphlets received extensive press coverage after their publication. Thorman's pamphlet was reissued in several revised editions. Sales of the two pamphlets exceeded several hundred thousand copies each, largely as a result of efforts by NMHF's Special Services Division.

Legal Division Pursues Compilation of State Mental Health Laws

From 1946 until NMHF's merger with the National Committee for Mental Hygiene and the American Psychiatric Foundation was consummated in 1950, NMHF's Legal Division was diligently engaged in preparing briefs on legislation pertaining to mental illness in each of the 48 states. This aspect of the agency's program had been initiated under the direction of Willard Hetzel during the Mental Hygiene Program of CPS. By 1949, this division had completed briefs of the legislation on the books of 10 states. Briefs on the mental health legislation in 16 other states had advanced to near completion.

Grants from the Robert Marshall Civil Liberties Trust and the Columbia Foundation enabled NMHF to undertake a study of actual practices compared with statutory provisions regarding commitment and discharge. The objectives of this particular project were described in NMHF's annual report for 1949:

> The major problem with reference to commitment is the need to provide legal protection for the patient and the community without becoming unduly legalistic. . . . Among the practices in question are the too-frequent denial of access to legal counsel, and the denial of opportunities for hearing as to discharge, including ability to use the writ of habeas corpus. . . .
>
> It is hoped that through this study it will be possible to provide statutory provisions which will eliminate temporary detention in jail, jury trial, and other similar antiquated procedures where they exist. It is also hoped that certain general practices may be established which will conform to ideal statutory provisions.

NMHF Takes on Role of Coordinating National Mental Health Week

As reported earlier in this chapter, NMHF played a major supporting role in the U.S. Junior Chamber of Commerce–sponsored National Mental Health Week in 1949. By the following year, however, the country's major mental health agencies had joined forces to take over leadership responsibilities for this event. The National Institute for Mental Health, The American Psychiatric Association, The National Committee for Mental Hygiene, and NMHF, together with state and local citizens' mental health associations, established a coordinating committee to develop and execute a master plan for the event. Alex Sareyan, NMHF's director of Special Services, was designated to chair this committee.

The Junior Chamber of Commerce lent its support to this second observance of National Mental Health Week. The focus for the 1950 week, as agreed on by the steering committee, was "Mental Health Is the Key to Effective Living." Motivating the entire project was the hope that the public would be stimulated to better understand the importance of mental health to their well-being. Several months before the week in April that had been set aside as National Mental Health Week, packets were developed for distribution to local and state mental health agencies that offered a range of program materials and suggestions for implementing observance of the week.

Among the highlights of the 1950 National Mental Health Week were two half-hour radio dramas produced and sponsored by the

PAUL PARKER PHOTO

Representatives of organizations participating in Mental Health Week meet to discuss plans and make reports. Seated, *left to right:* Nina Ridenour, Director of the Educational Division of the National Committee for Mental Hygiene; Alex Sareyan, Director of the Special Services Section of the National Mental Health Foundation; Alberta Altman, Chief of the Publications and Reports Branch of the National Institute of Mental Health; Emily Ann Haynes, assistant to Mrs. Altman. Standing, *left to right:* Lynn Stratton, Public Relations Consultant to the National Committee for Mental Hygiene; William Beaty, Coordinator of Mental Health Week activities for New York State; Merle Morgan, representing the American Psychiatric Association's Committee on Participation With Lay Groups; Lowell Iberg, Associate Executive Director of the State Charities Aid Association.

National Broadcasting Company for scheduling on its national network. The Columbia Broadcasting System produced and ran a one-hour documentary drama in prime time on its national network. It starred Faye Emerson and was based on a statewide citizens' campaign to bring Minnesota's state mental hospitals into an enlightened new era during the administration of Governor Luther Youngdahl. During this same period, Fox Movietone News ran a 30-second mental health message featuring Celeste Holm. Thousands of theaters across the country ran this segment.

The print media were generous in providing editorials and features in support of the campaign. Another very popular and helpful resource used in this period was a series of mental health–oriented half-hour plays developed by the National Committee for Mental Hygiene in collaboration with the American Theatre Wing's Community Plays Division just before its merger with the NMHF and the American Psychiatric Foundation. These plays were designed to be followed by discussion periods presided over by mental health professionals interacting with members of the audience. Public service radio announcements featuring well-known personalities from Broadway and Hollywood were also offered to local mental health organizations for distribution to their radio stations.

The particular significance of the 1950 observance of National Mental Health Week was that it was done under the direction of a coalition of mental health agencies. Since that time, it has been continued as a high-priority public relations opportunity for the organized mental health movement.

Financing the National Mental Health Foundation

Richard Hunter was the executive director of NMHF at the time of the merger that resulted in the creation of the National Association for Mental Health. In a statement prepared for the author of *The Turning Point* in October 1988, he recalled the financing problems faced by NMHF:

It was one thing to crusade for the mentally ill while functioning within the framework of Selective Service. There was no payroll to meet, and there was personnel time available for use in meaningful, constructive ways. Activity cost was at a low level, and the amounts needed could be raised from a few sympathetic sources.

When the CPS program became NMHF, the staff found it essential to have some personal income in order to live in the world to which they had returned. With program expenses, rent, and other costs of doing business, the task of crusading took on new realities.

Despite pitifully small salaries, the professional staff were often obliged to miss occasional paychecks so that the support staff could be paid. That never happened for two pay periods in a row, and eventually all were paid. Nevertheless, life was not easy.

There were four noteworthy sources of funding which contributed to the foundation's viability between its founding in 1946 and its merger in 1950:

> Through aggressive marketing of its educational resources to other agencies it generated a modest but regular revenue base.
>
> Foundation grants enabled the organization to have the momentum it needed to gain a firm foothold in getting its program off the ground. Matching grants in the amount of $25,000 each from the Rockefeller and Carnegie Foundations in early 1947 contributed significantly to this effort.
>
> Formation of a Business and Industry Committee under the leadership of the President of the Curtis Publishing Company facilitated a modest flow of income from major companies throughout the country.
>
> The most significant of the funding resources was the "Truth or Consequences" program developed by Ralph Edwards in the heyday of his radio popularity. In the late 1940s, Edwards had raised a million and a half dollars for the American Heart Association from this program in which listeners were invited to identify a famous couple from a clue provided each week on his national program. Listeners wishing to take part in this contest were asked to mail their guess as to the identity of the mystery couple, along with a contribution for the designated charity.

> In 1948, Ralph Edwards agreed to designate the three mental health agencies then contemplating a merger as the beneficiaries of a similar contest. Unfortunately, fate conspired to make this opportunity much less profitable than had been expected. Most devastating was a ruling handed down by a federal agency overseeing broadcast activities that persons wishing to participate in the contest need not be required to send a contribution along with their entries. This action severely dampened the flow of contributions. Even more disappointing to the prospective donees was the fact that the mystery couple was identified the very first week of the contest when proceeds had been designated for the mental health agencies.
>
> Because of the unexpected turn of events, Ralph Edwards gave the mental health groups another opportunity at the jackpot. But by this time the excitement of the show had ebbed considerably and the contributions that had been raised represented only about 10% of the amount that had been raised for the American Heart Association. Nevertheless, these funds provided the impetus for the merger which was finally consummated in the fall of 1950.

This was hardly an auspicious start for the new National Association for Mental Health. (The name was later changed to the National Mental Health Association.) At least it dispelled any illusions that there might be an easy road ahead for the voluntary mental health movement.

Forty-Five Years Later

From the perspective of 45 years later, it is difficult to comprehend fully the impact of those early years when those in the Mental Hygiene Program of CPS were struggling to awaken the conscience of America to the mental health concerns they had discovered. In retrospect, it is hard to believe that the dreams and visions of so many of those who came out of this experience were to blossom into reality within only a few years after their reentry into normal civilian life.

No, the millennium did not arrive. But there was perceptible and positive change in the making. Conditions in the state institutions for the mentally ill did improve in the postwar era. There was in the land a growing recognition that mental health was an important part of good health in general.

As NMHF prepared to go out into the world to accomplish its stated objectives, it gathered an impressive group of public citizens to facilitate its course of action. They provided NMHF with an aura of credibility without which its task would have been infinitely more difficult. They were there when doors needed to be opened. And many of them continued to play major supporting roles on behalf of the newly emerging National Association for Mental Health.

It all started as a vision in the mind of one member of the CPS unit at the Philadelphia State Hospital, Leonard Cornell, who was soon to be joined by Hal Barton, Phil Steer, and Will Hetzel. From time to time in the brief history of NMHF, its leadership shifted from one person to another. Initially, it was Cornell who served as its chief executive officer. At the end of the first year, the baton shifted to Hal Barton for the next two years, after which he decided to return to Oregon and the mining career he had left at the beginning of the war. It then became Richard Hunter's turn to assume the leadership role and help direct NMHF to its eventual merger with the National Committee for Mental Hygiene and the American Psychiatric Foundation to become the National Association for Mental Health.

On page 179 is a complete list of board members, sponsors, directors, and staff at NMHF at the time that the merger was consummated.

THE NATIONAL MENTAL HEALTH FOUNDATION

1520 Race Street Philadelphia 2, Pa.

HONORARY PRESIDENT

Owen J. Roberts

VICE CHAIRMEN

Alexander J. Cassatt
Mrs. Percy C. Madeira, Jr.
Giles L. Zimmerman

TREASURER

Robert K. Zerbe
c/o Girard Trust Company
Philadelphia 2, Pa.

EXECUTIVE SECRETARY

Richard C. Hunter

BOARD OF DIRECTORS

Frederick H. Allen, M.D.
Roger N. Baldwin
Brandon Barringer
Mrs. Leonard T. Beale
Mrs. Charles G. Berwind
Jacob Billikopf
Mrs. J. L. Blair Buck
Edward G. Budd, Jr.
Alexander J. Cassatt
Mrs. Walter A. Craig
William P. Drake
Paul Comly French
Maurice Heckscher
Mordecai W. Johnson
Arthur Littleton
Mrs. Robert McLean
Mrs. Percy C. Madeira, Jr.
Orie O. Miller
F. Perry Olds
Clarence E. Pickett
Herman I. Pollock
Mrs. R. Stewart Rauch, Jr.
Mary Jane Ward
Mrs. John P. Wheeler
Morris Wolf
Robert K. Zerbe
M. R. Zigler
Giles L. Zimmerman

NATIONAL SPONSORS

Harry Emerson Fosdick, *Chairman*

Leo H. Bartemeier, M.D.
Carl A. L. Binger, M.D.
Barry Bingham
Daniel Blain, M.D.
Pearl Buck
James B. Carey
Helen Gahagan Douglas
Dorothy Canfield Fisher
William Green
Helen Hayes
John Haynes Holmes
Lawrence S. Kubie, M.D.
W. Appleton Lawrence
Henry R. Luce
Ralph McGill
Mrs. Rustin McIntosh
Thomas Mann
Adolf Meyer, M.D.
Arthur Morgan
Felix Morley
Reinhold Niebuhr
J. Robert Oppenheimer
Thomas Parran, M.D.
James G. Patton
Daniel A. Poling
Howard W. Potter, M.D.
Thomas A. C. Rennie, M.D.
Walter P. Reuther
A. Newton Richards
Mrs. Franklin D. Roosevelt
Lessing J. Rosenwald
Arthur H. Ruggles, M.D.
George N. Shuster
Harold E. Stassen
Mrs. Harry S. Truman
Henry P. Van Dusen
Rabbi David H. Wice
Gregory Zilboorg, M.D.

PROFESSIONAL ADVISORS

Lauretta Bender, M.D.
Associate Professor of Psychiatry
New York University

Earl D. Bond, M.D.
Director of Research, Institute of
Pennsylvania Hospital

Robert H. Felix, M.D., Director
National Institute of Mental Health
Washington, D. C.

Earl G. Harrison, Esq.
Former Dean, University of
Pennsylvania Law School

Karl Menninger, M.D.
The Menninger Foundation
Topeka, Kansas

Mrs. Elizabeth Ross
Psychiatric Social Worker
Washington, D. C.

STAFF

Dallas Pratt, M.D., Psychiatrist
Paul Harris, III, Education Associate
Roy C. Simon, Education Associate
Alex Sareyan, Special Services Director
Marjorie K. Bondy, Special Services Associate
Jack Neher, Special Services Associate
Leon Ehrlich, Legal Director
Zelda B. Wolfman, Legal Associate
Clifford Moore, Legal Associate
George S. Vyverberg, Business Manager
Philip Steer, Executive Assistant
Howard M. Curry, Executive Assistant

Chapter 9

MINNESOTA JOINS THE CRUSADE

. . . More than any other voluntary agency of which I know, the National Mental Health Foundation has been responsible for the widespread concern for the mentally ill.

From remarks by the
Honorable Luther W. Youngdahl,
Governor of Minnesota, at a dinner in his honor
given by the National Mental Health Foundation
December 6, 1949, in recognition of his efforts in
improving conditions in that state's mental hospitals.

When the 56th session of the Minnesota legislature adjourned in the late spring of 1949, it was reported that it had done the following:

- Broken the backbone of the vicious caste system and custodial approach that had shackled that state's mentally ill patients to the asylum days of the past.
- Enacted the first law in any state recognizing mental illness as a sickness, and placing on the statute books for this and following sessions an official policy for the state of Minnesota—to provide mental health services consistent with human obligations and professional standards.

The information reported in this chapter was derived in large part from Governor Luther Youngdahl's Records, Minnesota State Archives, Minnesota Historical Society, St. Paul, Minnesota. Permission to use these data has been granted by the Minnesota Historical Society.

It was as if the dreams of the founders of the National Mental Health Foundation (NMHF) had come alive. Governor Luther W. Youngdahl, the spark plug behind the drive that had moved his state's legislature into action, later acknowledged NMHF's role in aiding his state in bringing its concerns for the mentally ill into the twentieth century.[1]

As a prelude to the story of Governor Youngdahl's crusade for the mentally ill in his state, some background information may be useful. From May 1946 until the consummation of its merger with the National Committee for Mental Hygiene and the American Psychiatric Foundation, NMHF had one all-consuming mission—to stir the American public into doing something constructive about the plight of the mentally ill.

One of the most effective strategies used by NMHF to achieve its objectives was to enlist the support and engagement of those who controlled the nation's media—or those whose access to the media was such that they commanded its respect and attention. Among the latter group were the science editors and freelance reporters who had established impeccable reputations for the authenticity of the health information that they provided to the public via various media-oriented channels. Because it gained the confidence of these highly respected journalists, NMHF discovered that its mental health crusade was reaching millions upon millions of people who relied on these writers as one of their primary sources of information on health and mental health concerns.

These writers reached the "movers and shakers" as well as the average person. In the former group was Governor Youngdahl, whose conscience had been deeply touched and who was moved to action. Shortly after he took office in 1947, he made a commitment to marshal public support to reform his state's seven mental hospitals (with their 10,500 patients) into institutions that more accurately reflected the meaning of "hospital" rather than of "asylum," as the term was commonly understood at that time.

By mid-1949, leading U.S. psychiatrists were extolling Governor Youngdahl for making major strides in accomplishing his goals. In December of that same year, NMHF honored Governor Youngdahl at a dinner given in his honor hosted by former U.S. Supreme Court

Justice Owen J. Roberts, the agency's honorary president. How this successful Minnesota crusade was organized and carried out is the primary focus of this chapter.

By the spring of 1948, Governor Youngdahl had created the Governor's Citizens Mental Health Committee to facilitate the establishment of an enlightened mental health program for Minnesota. This committee's immediate objective was to ensure that modern psychiatric treatment and humane care were made available to all patients in Minnesota's seven state mental institutions. But equally important, its long-range purpose was to develop plans for fostering the mental well-being of the state's population through an effective working coalition of governmental and voluntary health agencies, as well as a wide range of citizens' groups.

The public response to the governor's appeal was most encouraging. Members of the committee were appointed by Governor Youngdahl and his staff from the ranks of those prominent in religious groups, veterans affairs, labor unions, the business community, the farming industry, service organizations, education, and the medical and legal professions, among others.

To coordinate and expedite the activities of the Citizens Mental Health Committee, Governor Youngdahl appointed Justin Reese as its executive secretary. At that time, Reese had been serving as executive secretary of the Minnesota Mental Hygiene Society, an affiliate of the National Committee for Mental Hygiene. During the war, Reese, then a conscientious objector (CO), had been a member of the Civilian Public Service unit at Cleveland State Hospital when that institution had become the target of a state investigation (see Chapter 4).

After the war, Reese was hired as a field representative by the National Committee for Mental Hygiene and assigned to Minnesota. Reese had the same zeal and drive that had fueled the efforts of the four men in the Civilian Public Service unit at the Philadelphia State Hospital—efforts that led to the establishment of NMHF. This quality had no doubt drawn him to the attention of Governor Youngdahl.

Throughout his tenure as executive secretary of the Citizens Mental Health Committee, Reese represented the governor in promoting and advancing its objectives. He traveled extensively throughout the state, meeting with individuals and groups of citizens who had committed themselves to the campaign. On frequent occasions, he lobbied state legislators to gain their support. Reese also served as spokesperson for both the governor and the committee in dealings with the media. In this capacity, he arranged for numerous radio appearances throughout the state for the governor and others who had allied themselves with the committee.

By the time 1948 drew to a close, hundreds of local Citizens Mental Health Committees had been activated in support of Youngdahl's mental health crusade. To help gain further momentum for the campaign, the governor was persuaded to proclaim the period from November 29th to December 4th as Mental Health Week. This was one of the first such weeks, if not the first, to be set aside in the United States for the purpose of focusing public attention on mental health concerns. It was not until the following year that the first-ever National Mental Health Week was observed throughout the nation under the auspices of the National Junior Chamber of Commerce.

The Mental Health Week observance proclaimed by the governor precipitated a media blitz throughout Minnesota. The news media and radio stations, in particular, devoted liberal attention to the shortcomings of the state's efforts in meeting the needs of its mentally ill citizens. The governor himself, as well as members of his hand-picked Citizens Mental Health Committee, made numerous radio appearances in support of the drive. The newspapers also provided generous coverage of the campaign with supporting news stories, features, and editorials, all pointing up the critical need for enlisting legislative support for Governor Youngdahl's expanded mental health program.

NMHF contributed immeasurably to the Minnesota crusade by providing access to highly useful resources such as its *The Tenth Man* series of radio dramas, each of which offered the kind of information the public needed to understand the underlying issues of the campaign. Virtually every radio station in the state ran all 13 programs in this series. Posters, leaflets, and pamphlets developed by NMHF were used in large quantities to back up the educational effort.

One of Governor Youngdahl's major objectives in his mental

health crusade was to give public recognition to the important role played by mental hospital attendants in the care of patients. For many decades, those serving in this capacity had been expected to put in exceptionally long hours under very trying circumstances. Their remuneration barely enabled them to eke out a living. For most employed in this capacity, normal family life was rarely—if ever—achieved. There were no meaningful perks related to this occupation. As a consequence, few highly qualified individuals were attracted to this type of work. The Citizens Mental Health Committee drew heavily on the resources developed by NMHF to improve the public's understanding of the importance of attendants in the care of mental patients, including training materials developed by NMHF such as *The Psychiatric Aide* and *The Handbook for Psychiatric Aides*. The committee also took advantage of The Psychiatric Aide of the Year award initiated by NMHF to gain public recognition for the important work performed by mental hospital attendants.

The governor's platform for restructuring Minnesota's mental hospitals called for substantial improvements in pay and working conditions for those employed as attendants, as well as other members of the nursing and medical staffs. A basic element in the master plan also called for changing the designation of those who served as mental hospital attendants to "psychiatric aide." To enhance the self-image of those assigned to this duty, NMHF had long advocated such a change.

A summary of the accomplishments of Governor Youngdahl's mental health crusade was reported in a newsletter published by the Citizens Mental Health Committee in May 1949. Excerpts from this report follow:

> Surveying the gains of the 56th session of the Minnesota Legislature, Governor Youngdahl announced: "The end of the session marks the beginning, not the end, of the citizens' mental health drive. The big job is still ahead . . . consolidating present gains and extending the new programs into the future."
>
> Workers in the citizens' mental health drive in every section of the state, standing by the call to further action, took time to catch their breaths and review accomplishments before starting on the

> second step of the long road ahead.
>
> . . . As a result of these labors, Topeka's famed Dr. Karl Menninger was able to state: "Minnesota comes nearer than any state of the nation to meeting the recommendations of the American Psychiatric Association. . . . It has taken the lead in mental health services due to your extraordinary Governor and the fine mental health program in your state."
>
> When the 56th session of the Minnesota legislature adjourned, it had . . . appropriated $28,000,000 of the $30,000,000 biennial operating budget requested by the Governor.
>
> The appropriations provided for: . . . A Commissioner of Mental Health to administer the new program; . . . 1,200 additional doctors, nurses, psychiatric aides, therapists, social workers, dietitians, and other mental health professionals. The following provisions were also mandated: . . . increased salary levels for all employees; . . . a 40-hour week to be established in all institutions; . . . a single standard of food service for patients and employees; . . . reclassification of the asylum-rooted "attendant" classification to that of "psychiatric aide"; . . . two teaching hospitals for the training of psychiatric residents and other mental health personnel, with the objective of eventually converting every state hospital to the status of a teaching hospital; . . . $100,000 for research; . . . two clinics, to be supplemented by as many outpatient clinics as available hospital personnel will permit; . . . increased funds for supplies, equipment, and clothing for all hospital personnel and patients.

This newsletter also reported that mechanical restraints were no longer being used at one state mental hospital: "One of the most dramatic restraint-elimination projects in mental hospital history has been successfully completed at the Moose Lake State Hospital. The institution, once the scene of one of the highest known restraint rates of the nation, is now operating completely free of restraint."

The magnitude of this accomplishment may best be understood by contrasting it with the situation that existed in mid-1948, when at least 1,000 of the patients in the state's seven mental hospitals (about 10% of the state's total patient population) were kept in straitjackets or other forms of mechanical restraint. By the end of 1949, only 30 patients in these same institutions were reported to be in restraint.

The committee's newsletter also reported that at three of the state's institutions, the summer slack in available hospital staff would be taken up by college students recruited by the Unitarian and American Friends Service committees. Most of the students assigned to two of these hospitals would be functioning as psychiatric aides, whereas those at a third facility would be serving as interns in the social service department.

At the dinner given by NMHF in his honor referred to earlier in this chapter, Governor Youngdahl remarked that changing concepts in the care of mental patients promised more success in the rehabilitation of these patients. One of these changing concepts, he observed, is the new regard for the person who has more contact with the patient than anyone else—the psychiatric aide. In his closing words, he credited NMHF for helping to bring about this change:

> If the Foundation never does any other single thing, this alone will constitute a major milestone in America's care of the mentally ill. This alone will justify the support which it has received from friends of the mentally ill.

Chapter 10

The Mennonite Mental Health Story

> . . . The Mennonite Mental Health Service can take pride in its accomplishments on a national scale. Its few centers have had limited input but their performance has served as a demonstration and model to the entire country and has charted the pathways for a nation to follow in providing psychiatric care where and when people need such help. . . .

> Lucy Ozarin, M.D.
> Coordinator, Rural Mental Health Services
> National Institute of Mental Health
> [Opinion cited in *If We Can Love: The Mennonite Mental Health Story*.
> Edited by Vernon Neufeld.
> Newton, KS, Faith and Life Press, 1983]

In an article published in the January 1982 edition of *The Mennonite Quarterly Review,* Elmer Ediger, Executive Director of the Prairie View Mental Health Center and one of the chief architects of the post–World War II network of community mental health centers developed by the Mennonites, offered this observation on what had provided the impetus for this undertaking:[1] "Through their engagement in the CPS program the 200,000 Mennonite membership in the United States probably encountered the biggest experimental impact of any Christian church group in all history regarding mental illness and treatment." The several Mennonite mental health centers that emerged from this experience, many of which went on to become role models of excellence for other similar facilities throughout the nation, are the primary focus of this chapter.

The tenets of Mennonite faith as laid down by its leaders in the sixteenth and seventeenth centuries required its followers to espouse nonviolence and compassion in relating to their neighbors and even their adversaries. Mennonites have had a long history of practicing pacifism. As these beliefs came into conflict with the demands of authorities in the communities where they resided, notably in Holland, Switzerland, and Germany, large numbers of them fled to other countries, principally to Eastern Europe, Canada, and the United States, where they settled into self-contained communities.

In an article published in the *McCormick Quarterly Review,* William Klassen, a New Testament professor at Associated Mennonite Seminaries at Elkhart, Indiana, tells the story of the first known case in which Mennonites took responsibility for a mentally ill person. During the period when Mennonites had first settled in the Russian Ukraine, it was the prevailing practice of the authorities to imprison mentally ill individuals. The assumption behind this practice was that in the dungeon-like setting among other mentally deranged persons such an individual might be brought back to his or her senses. In one of these villages, there was a man who had been imprisoned time and again because of violent attacks against his wife and children. Klassen relates that the man's relatives, overtaken by compassion, "finally asked permission to take custody of him, guaranteeing that they would take care of him and assume responsibility for his violent outbursts."[2]

Early in the twentieth century, also in the Ukraine, a custodial facility for the mentally ill among the Mennonites was established. It was staffed entirely by members of their church. It continued to function as the Bethania Mental Hospital until 1927, when the building was razed to make way for a dam then under construction on the Dnieper River. In the early 1930s, a similar facility named Bethesda was opened in the Canadian Province of Ontario in the village of Vineland to serve the local Mennonite community. Many of those who had served as nurses and attendants at the Ukrainian institution and who had emigrated to Canada were credited with having played major roles in its establishment.

It wasn't until the Civilian Public Service (CPS) mental hospital program made its appearance in 1942 that the Mennonites made their next major commitment to the care of the mentally ill. By 1946, when the CPS program ended, 1,400 draft-age men had volunteered for service in one of the 28 mental hospital and training school CPS units under the sponsorship of the Mennonite Central Committee. The overwhelming number of men in this program were affiliated with Mennonite churches; however, conscientious objectors (COs) from other church groups were also present in these units. Although they were considered regular employees, some 400 or more wives of the Mennonite men also shared in the mental hospital or training school experience.

From 1945 through the early 1960s, approximately 3,000 or more additional young Mennonites, primarily of college age, became acquainted with mental health care in institutional settings as they participated in the voluntary service units sponsored by the Mennonite Central Committee. Members of voluntary service units were hired by the mental institutions for periods ranging from three to four months to as long as one year to help deal with chronic staffing problems (see Chapter 11).

During the postwar years when plans for the evolving Mennonite mental health centers were moving from concept to reality, the COs, their wives, and the young people in the voluntary service units (approximately 5,000 young Mennonites in all) provided a strong support base as their churches made a firm commitment to introduce a new and enlightened era in the care of mentally ill and mentally retarded people.

As reported earlier, many of the men assigned to the CPS base camps after their induction soon became disenchanted with the "make-work" nature of the chores they were directed to perform in these settings. It was difficult for many of these men to justify repairing a woodland trail in a forest preserve at a time when gas rationing precluded any thought of traveling to such places. And it was equally impossible to accept the long, backbreaking days planting tree seedlings on a hill as work of national importance at a time when so many urgent human needs were crying out for attention. So when Selective Service finally yielded to insistent pressures from the peace church agencies to open up service opportunities in state mental hospitals and training schools for the retarded, men in Mennonite-sponsored CPS base camps responded as eagerly to the new challenge as did their CO brethren in similar units under the auspices of the other two peace churches.

When the first contingent of Mennonite COs arrived at the Lima, Ohio, State Hospital for the Criminally Insane, they discovered that it was common practice for all attendants to carry blackjacks for self-protection. Because their consciences were troubled by this employment behavior, they requested permission to report to their ward assignments without these clubs. The administration had misgivings about agreeing to this condition but gave in with the admonition that the procedure could be dangerous. The new arrangement proved to work out so well that in a short time blackjacks were taken away from all employees. As a result, an entirely new and more acceptable form of attendant-patient relationship developed in the institution.[3]

Commenting on the achievements of men in such CPS units as the Lima institution, William Klassen observed: "What seems clear is that the Mennonites would never have established mental hospitals had they not been spurred on by a corps of dedicated and visionary men who had worked in mental hospitals and become convinced that something could be done for the mentally ill and that the church do something for them."[4]

In discussing the origins of Mennonite postwar programs for the mentally ill, no event was more significant than a conference convened September 10–13, 1944, at the Sideling Hill CPS Camp at Wells Tannery, Pennsylvania. Among the 29 CPS participants, seven subsequently pursued careers as pastors, five became psychologists, administrators, and policy makers in mental health programs, and four eventually assumed roles as university professors in the behavioral sciences.

Discussions at the Sideling Hill conference ranged over a wide variety of issues. Led by resource persons Ralph C. Kauffman, a psychologist affiliated with Bethel College at North Newton, Kansas, and Harold Barton, then a staff member of the CPS Mental Hygiene

Program, meeting participants focused attention on the topic "Improving Our Contribution to the Patients and the Institutions." Dr. Kauffman challenged the men with "the unique opportunity the Mennonite Church has in finding its conscience and attitude toward institutions and patient care, and in particular, the possibility of the church operating mental hospitals guided by religious principles." After an enthusiastic discussion in support of this premise, those present reached consensus on the following recommendations:

1. The Mennonite Central Committee would be urged to solicit commentaries on the role of the church in administering mental hospitals from among its leaders and then arrange to share these recommendations throughout its constituency.
2. Opinions and attitudes toward church involvement in the operation of mental health facilities would be solicited from individual churches.
3. Men serving in the various Mennonite-sponsored CPS mental hospital units would be asked to share their opinions on the desirability of the churches taking a direct role in the establishment of mental hospitals. The men in these units would be encouraged to hold group discussions before arriving at their recommendations. In the context of these sessions, it was also expected that some light might be shed on the number of men in these units who in the postwar era would be willing to seek employment in church-sponsored mental health facilities.

Some six months before World War II finally ended in August 1945, the Mennonite Central Committee published a report on a symposium titled, "Should the Churches Establish and Maintain Hospitals for the Mentally Ill?" Four of the nine contributors to this report were still serving in the Mennonite-sponsored CPS units at that time. One of the participants, Arthur Jost, who was then serving as an assistant director of the CPS unit at the Provo State Hospital in Utah, concluded his presentation with these words: " . . . In a church mental hospital with a highly trained Christian staff there could be set unprecedented standards for mental care—standards which could become goals for state hospitals." This symposium was the precursor of a continuing series of informal and formal discussions under the leadership of the Mennonite Central Committee concerning the desirability of establishing a mental health facility under the auspices of the Mennonite churches.

In mid-1945, the General Conference of the Mennonites of North America endorsed the idea of establishing a mental hospital in cooperation with the Mennonite Central Committee. This action led to the appointment of a three-person committee to make preliminary studies of the feasibility of implementing this recommendation with instructions to report back to the executive committee of the Mennonite Central Committee. Among the members of this trio was Robert Kreider, who had served as director of the Mennonite CPS Hospital Section. In an article that he prepared for publication in the spring of 1945, Kreider identified six basic lessons that had been learned from the Mennonite mental hospital experience:[5]

1. Our men in these units made excellent attendants.
2. We learned that a Christian approach to the care of mental patients is compatible with the most desirable form of psychotherapy.
3. An institution is more than bricks and mortar. The soul of an institution is to be found in the men and women who serve there. . . .
4. . . . A Christian attendant in a secular institution is inhibited in his desire to create a completely Christian environment for the patients.
5. . . . Large state institutions are inhibited by limitations. . . . Conscious of these limitations, we envisage the possibilities of a private church-sponsored hospital.
6. . . . Large public mental hospitals are besieged by administrative problems.

By the fall of 1945 Kreider and his colleagues had consulted with a number of mental hospital administrators on the role of the church in the institutional care of mentally ill people. Data on the prevalence of mental illness and mental retardation within individual congregations had been gathered from Mennonite pastors. Their opinions had been solicited on the desirability of establishing church-sponsored mental health facilities as adjuncts to general hospitals or as independently functioning services. Kreider and his colleagues also sought the viewpoints of medically trained Mennonite professionals. In drawing up their final report, the committee broached the possibility of establishing foster homes for recovering mental patients within the Mennonite community as an alternative to setting up full-service mental hospitals.

In January 1946 at its annual meeting, the Mennonite Central Committee moved to recommend that plans be developed for the establishment of three Mennonite-sponsored mental health facilities: one in the East, one in the Midwest, and one in the Far West of the United States. A planning committee was named to implement the recommendations. Funds for carrying out the committee's plans were authorized to be taken out of unspent reserves that had been allocated for the administration of the CPS program and were no longer needed for that purpose. The minutes of that meeting acknowledged that the participation of the Mennonite Central Committee in the CPS mental hospital experience had contributed significantly to reaching this decision. Many of the older leaders on the committee were especially enthusiastic in their support of this action. As COs during World War I they had suffered abuse and ostracism for their refusal to ac-

Robert Kreider, about 1947. Kreider was one of four conscientious objectors who played a major role in the postwar development of the Mennonite mental health centers.

cept noncombatant roles in the armed services. Without the options for alternative service available to World War II COs, the World War I COs had been confined to military barracks (see Chapter 1).

Another vital force that contributed to transforming the Mennonite mental health initiative from a vision to a reality was the presence at the Mennonite Central Committee's Akron, Pennsylvania, headquarters of a small band of ex-CPS "graduates" who had joined the staff there when their draft obligations were discharged at the close of the war. Many of them had worked in the CPS mental hospital program. This new association offered a fertile climate for these men to brainstorm. As program ideas took shape, their easy access to the elders of the churches enabled them to lobby hard and vigorously on behalf of these projects—in particular those that had been inspired by their CPS experiences. "It was this combination of young and old with the readiness of the church which were crucial in realizing the mental health vision," observed Elmer Ediger in his account of the growth and development of the Mennonite mental health centers.[6]

Elmer Ediger, about 1950. After the war, Ediger took on the leadership of the newly formed Mennonite Mental Health Services program and later became executive director of the Prairie View Mental Health Center, Newton, Kansas.

The Mennonite mental health initiative finally neared reality in September 1946 when the executive committee of the Mennonite Central Committee received a proposal to convert the farm property it owned at Leitersburg, Maryland, into a rest home for Mennonites needing mental health care. This facility had been operated during the war as one of the Mennonite Central Committee's CPS base camps under the technical direction of the Soil Conservation Service. The members of the committee decided to explore this possibility and asked Ediger to prepare a detailed operational plan for a mental hospital at that location.

By the end of October, Ediger had presented a plan to the Mennonite Central Committee outlining the steps leading to the transformation of this property into a hospital. His recommendations were accepted in principle by the executive committee, and Ediger and Arthur Jost were then requested to gather additional data for the new undertaking. The pair turned to mental health professionals and to the National Mental Health Foundation, among others, for guidance. One of their most useful meetings was with the foundation's psychiatric consultant, Dallas Pratt, M.D. Dr. Pratt offered a series of recommendations to the two men that turned out to influence the range of mental health services offered not only at the Leitersburg site but also at most of the other Mennonite Central Committee–sponsored mental health centers that were to emerge in the next several years.

In a subsequent reflection on the import of Dr. Pratt's advice, Ediger observed that "it represented the type of linkage the developing Mennonite mental health program was to have with some of the most progressive forces in the country."[7] Other leaders in the Mennonite Central Committee also acknowledged that Dr. Pratt's suggestions had been particularly influential in determining the future direction of their network of mental health centers toward providing active treatment rather than simply offering custodial care for the patients they served.[8]

Another highly respected mental health authority whose advice was sought by the Mennonite Central Committee concerning their proposed church-sponsored mental hospitals was Robert Felix, M.D. At the time, Dr. Felix was the director of the Mental Hygiene Division of the U.S. Public Health Service, and he was soon to be designated as the first director of the National Institute of Mental Health. Dr. Felix was reported to have reminded the Mennonite Central Committee of the unique strengths possessed by the Mennonites and of their potential for doing in the field of mental health what had been accomplished by the Seventh-Day Adventists in the field of general health.[9]

In December 1946, the Pacific Conference of the Mennonite Brethren advised the Mennonite Central Committee that they were prepared to cooperate in establishing a mental health facility on the West Coast. A month later at its annual meeting, the Mennonite Central Committee formally agreed to underwrite the establishment of the three mental health centers, as had been recommended at its previous annual session. They also decided to set up a standing committee to facilitate the implementation of their objectives. Once again, Elmer Ediger was asked to lead this advisory group.

Before long, this standing committee had been designated as the Mennonite Mental Health Services Committee. During the committee's formative period, other colleagues of Ediger—including Robert Kreider, Arthur Jost, and Delmar Stahly—were asked to join. When pressing commitments to oversee personally the building of the Midwest facility at Newton, Kansas, kept Ediger away from the Mennonite Central Committee's Akron headquarters, the leadership of the Mennonite Mental Health Services Committee was passed on to Stahly, who continued in this role until the mid-1960s.

Delmar L. Stahly, 1953. At the time this photo was taken, Stahly was the director of Mennonite Mental Health Services in Akron, Pennsylvania.

In January 1949, the first of the Mennonite Central Committee–sponsored mental health services opened at the 105-acre farm that it owned at Leitersburg, Maryland. It was renamed Brook Lane

Farm. Admission to the 23-bed facility was initially restricted to those with moderate mental disorders, and the period of treatment was limited to six months for each patient at a per diem rate of $3.50.[10]

The second of the three mental health centers authorized by the Mennonite Central Committee, slated for Reedley, California, received the green light for development in March 1947. A few months later, Arthur Jost was designated to go to California to oversee the development of this new facility. Plans called for building a 30-bed facility with the potential for expansion to 100 beds. With the site selected, a fund-raising goal of $100,000 was approved to finance the new facility. In 1951, the new center, which had been named Kings View Homes, was ready to receive its first patients. Administration of the new facility was turned over to Jost, who continued to serve as its executive officer until his retirement in the late 1980s.[11]

Arthur Jost. Jost, like Delmar Stahly, Elmer Ediger, and Robert Kreider, was a conscientious objector who devoted his postwar career to helping the mentally ill.

Because of the preoccupation of the Mennonite Mental Health Services Committee with getting the first two of its mental hospitals operational, completion of the facility at Newton, Kansas, was delayed. The Newton center, budgeted at a cost of $200,000 and designed to accommodate 40 patients, finally opened its doors in mid-1954. Initially, Myron Ebersole was asked to manage this facility. Subsequently, Elmer Ediger took over this responsibility and managed the center until his untimely death in the early 1980s.

During the first decade, with a network of hard-working persons and committees, the Mennonite Central Committee served exceptionally well in initiating and operating the first three programs. The Mennonite Central Committee philosophy of serving "in the name of Christ" permeated the program and strongly influenced its entire development. The emphasis was on service, volunteerism, frugality, and witness. The leadership was strong, creative, dedicated, and resourceful. With nothing to begin with except a memory of Bethania and the difficult experience of untrained young people in state hospitals, this group of leaders managed to create mental health service programs with ever-increasing credibility and respectability.

A major reason for the success of the Mennonite Central Committee program was the committee's sensitivity and openness to change.* The people in positions of leadership sought the advice of trained and experienced professionals, searched for appropriate and useful models, learned from others' success or failure, and were prepared to adapt if this seemed the best way to go. Originally the thought was to serve Mennonites, that is, "the household of faith." As planning proceeded, it was evident that the services were to be available to anyone.

Earlier, the leaders talked vaguely about serving the mentally ill and mentally retarded. The *mentally ill* at first meant seriously ill, hospitalized persons, such as those seen by CPS men in the state hospitals. Over the first few years the focus shifted from serving chronically ill former hospital patients in a homelike atmosphere for a long period of time to treating acutely ill patients in an active treatment facility for a shorter time. This change in concept undoubtedly occurred because of the numerous contacts with mental health professionals and the influences of the first medical directors of the Mennonite Central Committee's programs, including Helmut Prager, M.D., of Brook Lane Farm and Jackson Dillon, M.D., of the Kings View facility.

In a real sense, this overall movement toward active treatment

---

*Beginning at this point and continuing to the end of the chapter, the text was condensed and paraphrased by Jack Neher from the book *If We Can Love* by Vernon Neufeld. Newton, KS, Faith and Life Press, 1983.

thwarted the original idea that the three homes were to be "experimental," with each providing different mental health services. When Brook Lane set its direction under Prager to treat persons with acute mental illness, the plan was for Kings View to serve chronically ill and elderly disturbed patients. Prairie View, located in an area with three Mennonite colleges and several Mennonite hospitals, was to focus on training and education, among other services. But both Kings View and Prairie View, like Brook Lane, became primarily active treatment hospitals when they opened. This fact disturbed some in the system. As late as 1954, the Mennonite Mental Health Services Committee discussed how Kings View had diverged from its original mission, and there was concern about the needs of chronically ill patients and "our neglect of them." Fear was expressed that "we were following our psychiatrists rather than acting indepen-

Aerial view of the Prairie View Mental Health Center campus, Newton, Kansas.

dently as our constituency would prefer to have us act." In a report to the Mennonite Mental Health Services Committee, Prairie View's advisory committee stressed the seriousness of needs not met, "such as the needs of the aged, the chronic, and the mentally retarded." But little was done immediately to change the situation.

Another result of the shift to active treatment was the need for professional staff. The earlier vision of providing "homes for the mentally ill and/or rest homes" suggested that these homes could be operated largely by untrained staff members, for example, by former CPS men with part-time psychiatric coverage. But active treatment meant psychiatric treatment, and the Mennonite Mental Health Services Committee faced the fact that no Mennonite psychiatrists were available. Consequently, the first psychiatrists and medical directors in each of the first three mental health facilities came from outside the constituency.

Initially, the Mennonite Central Committee had hoped to use mostly volunteers in staffing the new programs, with a few more permanent staff members in key slots. This plan worked for a while. But in addition to the increased need for professional staff, it became more and more difficult to secure and hold other staff members. What should permanent staff be paid? This became a recurring and difficult problem as facilities complained of a critical staff shortage because low salaries were cutting them out of the local labor markets. Ultimately, the general hospital model was adopted, and competitive salaries were offered to attract competent staff.

After the three hospitals were established and operating, those involved realized that the mental health program needed an overall review and evaluation. There were two primary reasons for this. One was that the original master plan of 1947 had been carried out, and in the normal manner of operating, the Mennonite Central Committee felt that it was time to evaluate the programs and decide what to do with them in the future. The other reason was internal. The local programs were experiencing growing pains under the current arrangements with the Mennonite Central Committee, largely around the issue of local initiative and responsibility versus control by those in the Akron headquarters. Accordingly, a committee was appointed to review procedures and propose new relationship patterns.

There followed a period of struggle and pain for all three major participants: the Mennonite Central Committee, the Mennonite Mental Health Services Committee, and the hospitals. It was not easy for the Mennonite Central Committee to transfer greater autonomy to the hospitals. A major reason for this reluctance was that the Mennonite Central Committee felt that control of the local hospitals was essentially in the hands of their medical directors—all nonconstituent psychiatrists. This situation produced ideological tension because the founders had envisioned a Christian institution that was allied with and the servant of the church. Psychiatry, whether Freudian, Adlerian, or whatever, was seen as more humanistic in its approach and outlook. It was felt that to loosen Mennonite Central Committee ties was to loosen ties to the church.

Nevertheless, a number of substantial changes were made. The committee tasked with reviewing and evaluating the mental health program specified that the Mennonite Mental Health Services Committee should determine the broad policies of Mennonite Central Committee Mental Health Services, although it would still be in line of responsibility to the Mennonite Central Committee. The Mennonite Mental Health Services Committee director was to become a "coordinator" and serve as executive officer. Local advisory committees were to be organized as boards of directors, with members still appointed by the Mennonite Central Committee. Local administrators were to be directly responsible to local boards.

Meanwhile, Mennonites in other sections of the country were expressing interest in establishing mental health centers to meet local needs. Conceived in the mid-1950s, Oaklawn Psychiatric Center at Elkhart, Indiana, the fourth of the Mennonite Central Committee–sponsored institutions, began operating in 1963 as a day hospital and outpatient clinic. Kern View Hospital at Bakersfield, California, began as a satellite program of Kings View but was separately incorporated in 1967 as the fifth Mennonite Central Committee mental health center.

In addition, three Mennonite mental health facilities that had been developed independent of the Mennonite Central Committee became affiliated with the Mennonite Mental Health Services Committee. These included Eden Mental Health Centre, Winkler, Manitoba, Canada; Philhaven Hospital, Lebanon, Pennsylvania; and the Penn Foundation for Mental Health, Sellersville, Pennsylvania. Before their affiliation with the Mennonite Mental Health Services Committee, all of these centers had entered into informal relationships with the Mennonite Central Committee.

There are three discernible periods in the unfolding Mennonite mental health story. In each there were adjustments in the roles played by the Mennonite Central Committee, the Mennonite Mental Health Services Committee, and the mental health centers. During the first decade, the Mennonite Central Committee was clearly in charge. With its organization, its staff, its leadership, its vision, and its sense of mission, the Mennonite Central Committee was in the position to act responsibly in getting the programs started. The Mennonite Central Committee carefully nurtured and guided the programs, all the while closely monitoring and controlling them.

But the offspring grew up, and during the second decade the Mennonite Central Committee wisely loosened its control, although not without fear for the welfare of the young programs in a strange and threatening professional world associated with a secular community. The mental health centers struggled for self-identity and independence, for community involvement, and for competence, at times with an almost adolescent sense of rebellion. The Mennonite Central Committee's subsidiary, the Mennonite Mental Health Services Committee, emerged as an intermediary and came to be a buffer and interpreter between the centers and the Mennonite Central Committee and between the centers and the church.

Since the early 1970s, further shifts have occurred. The once-predicted complete separation of the mental health centers from the Mennonite Central Committee and the Mennonite Mental Health Services Committee has not occurred. The centers have matured into responsible institutions; they are no longer anxious to sever connections with their origins, but rather are discovering a new relationship with the church as partners and collaborators. Once individual identity and responsibility were achieved, the centers valued their connection to the church even more. As a collaborative service agency joining together the Mennonite Central Committee and the mental health centers, the Mennonite Mental Health Services Committee was able to expand the ministry of the church into new areas of service and thus find its own unique mission.

The achievements of the Mennonite Mental Health Services Committee have been widely praised by many "outsiders" in the psychiatric field. One of the most interesting assessments was made by Lucy Ozarin, M.D., a former staff member of the National Institute of Mental Health. One of Dr. Ozarin's tasks at that agency was to serve as coordinator of its Rural Mental Health Services. This gave her a unique vantage point to become conversant with the delivery of mental health services by the Mennonite mental health centers (most of which rendered services in rural settings). This is what she observed:[12]

> I do not know why the MMHS [Mennonite Mental Health Services Committee] chose to establish mental hospitals in rural areas. But whether it was planned or by chance, they have rendered a great service to the people of those areas. The facilities have located highly trained and qualified staff in all the mental health disciplines and have been successful in keeping them for a period of years, no doubt because of the high standards of patient care and the professional opportunities offered.
>
> Vernon Neufeld described the early MMHS philosophy in terms of *service, volunteerism, frugality, and witness.* The Judeo-Christian tradition stresses the duty of each person to help a fellow human being. The MMHS seems to have found a way to do so.

Chapter 11

Legacies of the Civilian Public Service Mental Hospital Program

Although the number of men involved is small and a few of them are themselves considered "queer," this kind of approach to their work promises great good for future generations of patients in mental disease hospitals. What is needed more than anything else is a body of intelligent, informed, and courageous citizens who will speak out boldly and clearly on behalf of better care of these patients. After the war, these conscientious objectors may form the nucleus for such groups.

From an editorial that appeared in *The Modern Hospital* (circa spring 1945)

The Civilian Public Service (CPS) mental hospital experience had a profound influence on a substantial number of the men who participated in this program. By their own admission, those who served in mental hospitals during World War II to fulfill their draft obligations had their political and social outlooks considerably expanded as a result. Slightly more than one in three of those who participated in the survey on which *The Turning Point* is largely based (see Appendix A) reported that this experience caused them to redirect their postwar careers into one of the helping professions: medicine, social work, psychology, ministry, nursing, hospital administration, education, and other related fields.

Even more profound was the influence these men exerted in the various social agencies in which they assumed major roles in the postwar period. They had come out of an experience in which they had seen the validity of their pacifist convictions come alive. They had kindled nationwide public concern about developing an enlightened approach to meeting the needs of several hundred thousand mentally ill persons languishing in so-called hospitals. They had been parties to "moving mountains by faith." They knew the impossible could be achieved. They brought this knowledge, fueled by what they'd been through, to their postwar careers.

This chapter focuses on a few of the many health and mental health agencies in which ex-CPS men continued to carry out their commitment to bring a new and expanded awareness of mental health concerns to the American public. Some stayed on in these assignments for several years and then moved on to other careers, whereas others continued to play vital roles in the mental health scene for the remainder of their lives. Some of the more prominent of these programs, such as the development and operation of the Mennonite mental health centers and the National Mental Health Foundation (NMHF), are described in earlier chapters. To describe all such postwar programs involving ex-CPS men is beyond the scope of this work. The vignettes that follow provide a glimpse of how the CPS mental hospital experience has continued to have an impact—from the 1950s to the present day.

The National Association for Mental Health

When the NMHF, the National Committee for Mental Hygiene, and the Psychiatric Foundation merged in the fall of 1950 to form the National Association for Mental Health (NAMH), several key members of the NMHF's staff became part of the new organization's leadership. These included Richard Hunter, Alex Sareyan, Jack Neher, Phil Steer, and Paul Harris. Hunter, who had been NMHF's executive director, assumed a major administrative role in the new agency. Shortly thereafter, he was asked to return to Philadelphia where his services were needed to give new life to the Mental Health Association of Southeastern Pennsylvania, a struggling National Association of Mental Health affiliate. Under Hunter's leadership, it developed into one of the NAMH's strongest and most effective chapters. In the late 1960s, Hunter was recalled to the NAMH's headquarters to take on new responsibilities as part of the executive staff. For a brief period, he was named as the agency's acting executive director while a search for a new leader was in progress. On his retirement from the NAMH, Hunter became involved in the affairs of the World Federation for Mental Health and took charge of its secretariat, and he has been serving ever since as its deputy secretary-general in a volunteer capacity.

When the NAMH became a reality, the new agency took over the programs that the NMHF had developed to facilitate the training of attendants. These included the monthly magazine *The Psychiatric Aide,* the foundation's training manuals for those serving in state hospitals for the mentally ill and in the state training schools for the retarded, and the Psychiatric Aide of the Year program. Phil Steer continued to edit the magazine, and Paul Harris took over responsibility for administering the awards program. By this time, the awards program had been extended to include, in a separate category, those persons serving as aides in state training schools. Both projects were sustained for several years under the aegis of the NAMH, and their influence continued to spread to more and more institutions. Concurrently with the development of these attendant-oriented programs, aides themselves began taking the initiative in establishing their own organizations in an effort to enhance their status as paraprofessionals. In some states (e.g., California) they gave themselves a new designation—psychiatric technician.

One of the most long-lasting legacies of NMHF has been the Psychiatric Aide of the Year program, created in 1947. During the 1940s, no experience was required of those who applied for positions as hospital attendants (see Chapter 8). To make matters worse, virtually no formal training was provided by the institutions that hired them. Yet the attendants were the ones who had the most sustained and frequent relationships with patients. More often than not, the manner in which attendants related to the patients in their charge ran counter to the therapeutic environment that was supposed to prevail in these institutions. At that time, attendants worked unconscionably long hours for pitifully low wages. But despite these circumstances, many hospital attendants gave unstinting care and consideration to their patients. They were the unsung heroes of the day.

The award program, which gained increased momentum under NAMH sponsorship, gave the public a totally new image of what mental hospitals and training schools could become. It served to create a new public image for attendants, and it also gave them a new sense of self-esteem. The NAMH continued to foster this award program for several years after the merger but in time shifted responsibility for continuing the program to local and state affiliates.

One of the greatest challenges faced by the newly organized NAMH was to gain public recognition and support for its three primary objectives:

- Facilitate the best possible care and treatment resources for those suffering with mental illness
- Stimulate research that will lead to the cure and amelioration of mental diseases
- Promote activities that will lead to the prevention of mental and emotional disorders

At the time that the NAMH formulated these goals, it had in place a network of relatively weak local affiliates and state chapters. For the NAMH to attain its objectives, it had to move rapidly to strengthen these groups so that they could become effective in gaining public support and understanding in the fight against America's number-one health problem—mental illness. That was one of the association's earliest priorities.

It was very important that these affiliated groups have quick access to a wide range of eye-catching, popularly slanted educational materials with which to capture public interest. This was an area in which the NMHF had demonstrated its aptitude. Not only had the NMHF responded successfully to this need before the merger, but even more important, the foundation had established an impressive record in marketing the kinds of mental health educational materials it had developed. Alex Sareyan, who while at the foundation had been largely responsible for publicizing and marketing these materials as well as for the foundation's public relations activities, was asked to take on these same activities on behalf of the newly formed NAMH. In this effort, he was joined by Jack Neher, who had played such a vital role in the development of the extensive series of radio dramas for which the NMHF had received so many accolades.

The NAMH's new public relations staff worked in close collaboration with its Educational Division, then under the leadership of Nina Ridenour, Ph.D., one of the nation's highly respected authorities on mental health education. Her section's responsibility was to ensure that the educational materials issued by the NAMH accurately reflected the current state of mental health knowledge. The public relations office played a major role in determining the format of these materials before they were released to their various target audiences.

The public relations office was given the lead role in coordinating the 1951 National Mental Health Week activities. Nearly 5,000 organizations—governmental, voluntary, professional, and a wide variety of service groups—participated actively in sponsoring this event. Every radio station in the country—all 2,265 at that time—was showered with 30-second spot announcements on mental health themes recorded by leading personalities of the day. The print media, including both newspapers and magazines, ran news items and feature stories related to mental health. The major radio networks scheduled dramatic programs on themes related to mental health and mental illness. Local radio stations did their share throughout the campaign by arranging to include well-known mental health authorities on their regularly scheduled talk shows. Both state and private mental health facilities throughout the nation arranged for open houses at their institutions.

One of the most popular pieces of mental health literature ever distributed in the United States was introduced during this period. It was a brief, attractively designed leaflet developed by Dr. Ridenour and her staff in the NAMH's Education Division titled *Mental Health Is . . . 1-2-3*. The objective of this leaflet was to help the public understand the characteristics of mental health.

The public relations office was charged with marketing *Mental Health Is . . . 1-2-3*. Within a few years of its introduction, more than 10 million copies had been procured by state and local agencies in

Mental health is...

These are some of the characteristics of people with good mental health.

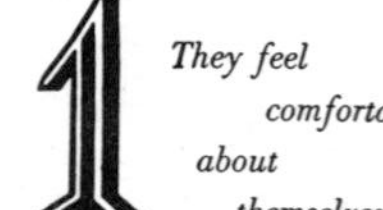

They feel comfortable about themselves.

They are not bowled over by their own emotions—by their fears, anger, love, jealousy, guilt or worries.

They can take life's disappointments in their stride.

They have a tolerant, easy-going attitude towards themselves as well as others; they can laugh at themselves.

They neither under-estimate nor over-estimate their abilities.

They can accept their own shortcomings.

They have self-respect.

They feel able to deal with most situations that come their way.

They get satisfaction from the simple, every-day pleasures.

2 *They feel right about other people.*

They are able to give love and to consider the interests of others.

They have personal relationships that are satisfying and lasting.

They expect to like and trust others, and take it for granted that others will like and trust them.

They respect the many differences they find in people.

They do not push people around, nor do they allow themselves to be pushed around.

They can feel they are part of a group.

They feel a sense of responsibility to their neighbors and fellow men.

3 *They are able to meet the demands of life.*

They do something about their problems as they arise.

They accept their responsibilities.

They shape their environment whenever possible; they adjust to it whenever necessary.

They plan ahead but do not fear the future.

They welcome new experiences and new ideas.

They make use of their natural capacities.

They set realistic goals for themselves.

They are able to think for themselves and make their own decisions.

They put their best effort into what they do, and get satisfaction out of doing it.

support of their mental health education efforts. And many more tens of millions of people were given access to the leaflet's message, because countless newspapers and magazines published the contents of the leaflet.

It is pertinent to note that many of the print and other resources that became integral features of the first National Mental Health Week sponsored by the NAMH were derived from activities that had been initiated by the NMHF. The Psychiatric Aide Award contributed importantly to some of the most widely seen National Mental Health Week events. *The Tenth Man* and *Hi Neighbor* radio series developed by the NMHF were extensively broadcast during this period. Perhaps the most noteworthy contribution of the NMHF to the success of this event was the extensive network of state and voluntary agencies it had established in the years before the merger. Agencies in this network were responsible for key mental health–related programs in every one of the then 48 states.

One final observation: The members of the NAMH's public relations staff who were involved in coordinating this national event were largely drawn from the ex-CPS contingent who had been on the NMHF staff at the time of the merger. They brought to the new agency a range of public relations and marketing skills that proved to be very useful to the NAMH in reaching out to the American public. Their work earned commendations from groups that cosponsored National Mental Health Week in 1951, such as the following from the Alabama Society for Mental Health:

> We want to congratulate the NAMH on the wonderful planning and the excellent and . . . detailed material which arrived so constantly just at the right moment. It was a stunning job. . . .

College Students Take Over Mental Hospital Service as CPS Program Is Phased Out

The CPS mental hospital program ended in the latter days of 1946 as Selective Service closed down the few remaining CPS units. But as described earlier, the momentum for change and reform in the nation's mental hospitals that sprang out of this experience could not be halted.

Under the leadership of the NMHF, the public's conscience had been aroused to do something positive about improving the lot of those who had been hospitalized because of mental illness. In Oklahoma, Mike Gorman, an investigative reporter, had written a series of articles that helped bring that state's mental hospitals into the twentieth century. Minnesota's Governor Luther W. Youngdahl had successfully launched a statewide citizens' crusade to bring about a new and compassionate era for the 10,000 patients then confined in Minnesota's seven state institutions.

Countless other mental health programs sprang out of the CPS experience. Unique among them were the institutional service units. Initially, they emerged on a small scale while the CPS mental hospital units were still functioning. But as the war drew to a close, they mushroomed to involve thousands of college students, beginning in the mid-1940s and continuing for another 20 years.

The precursor to the institutional service units was the Women's Service in Mental Health project initiated by the American Friends Service Committee at the Philadelphia State Hospital in the summer of 1943 with a group of seven young women. Members of this unit had been recruited from nearby colleges to help the hospital cope with a desperately critical staff shortage on its wards for female patients. The institution hired the individuals in this unit at the prevailing salaries for attendant personnel. By early summer of the following year, the Mennonites had recruited two groups of college women to participate in summer relief training units, one at Michigan's Ypsilanti State Hospital and the other at Rhode Island's Howard State Hospital. Soon after, the Brethren followed suit with similar units in Maryland institutions.[1]

As the war drew to a close in mid-1945 and the CPS mental hospital units began to be phased out, all three major peace churches stepped up their recruiting efforts to provide institutional service units for those state hospitals and training schools for the retarded willing to accommodate such units for the summer. In the postwar era, a large number of these units included both men and women. In some instances, students were given the opportunity to offer their services for a full year. By the time this program was in full swing, several denominations had joined the peace churches in sponsoring this service. These included the Disciples of Christ, Methodist, Presbyterian U.S.A., and the Universalist Church of America.

In the years immediately after the war, state hospitals and training schools continued to suffer staff shortages. These staff problems were exacerbated during the summer because of employee vacations. The availability of the college students as summer replacements was a godsend, and these facilities eagerly welcomed the institutional service units.

Many of the leaders of the peace churches acknowledged that the CPS model influenced the organization and oversight of these institutional service units. As a matter of fact, recruitment and administrative responsibilities for these units more often than not were placed in the hands of men who had been recently discharged from the CPS program. These men not only provided leadership and guidance to the institutional service units, but also aided in enlisting hospitals and training schools to take advantage of the resources offered through this program.

Just as the sponsoring church groups had provided the CPS units with recreational, cultural, and religious leadership during their off-duty time, so too were the institutional service units given access to such support. To help foster group morale, the sponsoring church agencies tried to arrange, wherever possible, for the students affiliated with these units to be assigned common living quarters and to have the opportunity to dine as a group.

Although members of these units rarely served more than four months at a time, a considerable number did reenlist for subsequent periods. The total number of students who served in these units from 1945 through the mid-1960s (when the hospitals were no longer facing personnel shortages) has been reliably estimated at approximately 10,000, more than three to four times as many individuals as served in the entire CPS mental hospital program. John D. Unruh, in his history of the Mennonite Central Committee titled *In the Name of Christ,* reported that more than 700 students were enrolled each year in the Mennonite-sponsored institutional service units from 1945 through 1950.[2]

Just as the CPS mental hospital program has been credited with generating 3,000 lifelong advocates on behalf of the mentally ill, the approximately 10,000 young men and women who took part in the institutional service units over a period of two decades also provided a highly literate and motivated support base for the mentally ill.

Before winding up their stints in the mental hospital service, participating students were invited to reflect on their experiences. Typical of many of the responses was the following:

> I always thought once someone was admitted to a mental hospital, they were there for life. . . . I also came to realize that mental illness was no more to be ashamed of than a physical illness. . . . I came to realize that the early treatment for a mental disorder was an almost sure indication for a prompt recovery.

A very common response of students who participated in the institutional service unit program was that the experience reinforced their decisions to pursue careers in the behavioral and medical

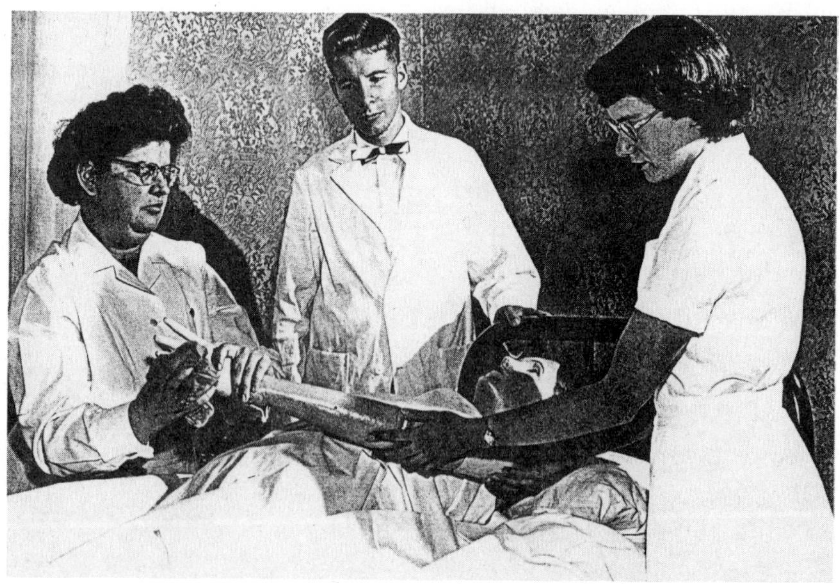

Members of institutional service unit, Indiana State Hospital at Logansport, 1952.

sciences. Another frequent reaction was that the experience had greatly broadened their social outlook and concerns. The following observation, made by one of the volunteers after her summer employment at Elgin State Hospital in Illinois, aptly summarized the impact on her and many of her colleagues of their introduction to life in a mental hospital:[3]

> . . . It made me look on mental illness with more respect and understanding than before. It gave me an idea of the kind of care they need and deserve. Made me more humble. Helped me to learn how to be patient with my fellow human beings. I found myself more and more able to learn how to keep my temper in check. It demonstrated to me the importance of growing up in a family with sound mental health values.

And finally this reflection:

> I have come to realize how many patients are cast aside and forgotten by their families. After service in this hospital, it brought me closer to my family.

The superintendents of the hospitals where these institutional service units were stationed during the postwar years were universally grateful for the contributions made by the college students who participated in this program. Silas W. Weltmer, M.D., Superintendent of the Spring Grove State Hospital in Catonsville, Maryland, echoed the observations of many other state hospital superintendents when he made the following comments in a letter to the Brethren Service Committee about members of the voluntary service unit that served at that hospital during the summer of 1948:

> . . . There is not a member of the unit I would hesitate to recommend unqualifiedly and I should deem it a privilege to do what I can at any time to promote their future interests. . . . It has been an inspiring and useful experience to have worked with the young men and women of the Brethren unit, and it is hoped that similar arrangements can be made for the summer months of next year.

Edna Thomas was a patient at Butner State Hospital in North Carolina, where an institutional service unit had been stationed for the summer. She expressed her appreciation and that of her fellow patients to this student unit in a four-stanza poem, which concluded with these words:

> . . . We'll miss you when you have gone away
> Our kindest thought will follow there with you
> Along whatever path your feet may stray,
> We need you. Please come back next summer, too!

The Mental Health Materials Center

In the fall of 1952, Alex Sareyan left the NAMH to establish a new agency—the Mental Health Materials Center. This was a nonprofit organization dedicated to facilitating the wide-scale dissemination and effective use of scientifically accurate health and mental health education publications and audiovisual aids. The rationale for setting up this organization was that many of the agencies then engaged in producing such educational resources were deeply lacking in publishing and marketing skills.

In this new venture, Sareyan was joined by Jack Neher, with whom he had been associated since they first met in the CPS unit at Connecticut State Hospital. About the same time that the Mental Health Materials Center was getting under way, Dr. Nina Ridenour (who had been serving as the director of the Education Division of the NAMH) decided to leave that organization to take a part-time assignment as a consultant with the fledgling Mental Health Materials Center as its educational consultant. The Mental Health Materials Center was chartered as a nonprofit, tax-exempt organization in March 1953. The Grant Foundation—which had been established as a charitable foundation by W. T. Grant, founder of the nationwide network of variety stores—was extremely supportive with several financial gifts in helping the new organization get on its feet during its early years.

In most instances, the services of the Mental Health Materials

Center were rendered to organizations in the role of an agent rather than that of a principal. This arrangement enabled the organizations to derive maximum benefits from their association with the educational resources they had created. It also generated more revenue for them than otherwise would have been the case. Over a period of 37 years, the Mental Health Materials Center facilitated the publication and dissemination of more than 500 educational resources, of which over 200 were book-length works. Total distribution of book titles published under Mental Health Materials Center management exceeded 2 million copies. Trade and foreign-language editions of these same works licensed to other publishers accounted for sales of more than 800,000 additional copies.

Among some of the more prominent agencies for which the Mental Health Materials Center performed these publishing services were the following:

- American Orthopsychiatric Association
- American Psychiatric Association
- American Public Health Association
- Connecticut State Board of Education
- Group for the Advancement of Psychiatry
- National Association for the Education of Young Children
- National Conference on Social Welfare
- National Center for Health Education
- National Council on Aging
- National Mental Health Association
- World Federation for Mental Health

The Mental Health Materials Center's expertise in marketing educational materials was not limited to publications. Many agencies turned to the center for assistance in finding appropriate audiences for both audio and audiovisual aids intended for use in health and mental health educational activities. In 1970, the Mental Health Materials Center was awarded a competitive contract by the National Institute for Mental Health to introduce a major drug abuse prevention program—The Social Seminar. Nearly 100 organizations, including many universities, had competed for this assignment.

The Social Seminar was a multimedia educational effort designed to assist teachers, youth workers, police, and a wide range of other professionals in educating children, parents, and adults about the underlying causes of drug abuse. In cooperation with state departments of health, education, and mental health, the Mental Health Materials Center introduced the program with a series of two-day demonstrations scheduled in 36 major cities throughout the nation. These showcase presentations were followed by five-day training sessions for those who were designated to apply the program in local settings. The Mental Health Materials Center was also awarded the contract to conduct these training seminars. Over a period of six years, a special staff recruited by the Mental Health Materials Center for this purpose succeeded in training 7,500 educators in the application of this program. All 50 states participated in this project.

Because of its expertise in the audiovisual arena, the Mental Health Materials Center was selected by the American Psychiatric Association's Hospital and Community Psychiatry Service to present a showcase of the year's outstanding mental health films at its annual institutes over a period of 25 years. The Mental Health Materials Center was asked by Encyclopedia Britannica to recruit a panel of child mental health authorities to assist in overseeing the development of an 18-volume *Young Children's Encyclopedia*. The National Institute for Child Health and Human Development awarded a contract to the Mental Health Materials Center to produce the *Selective Guide to Films of Excellence in the Teaching of Reproductive Biology*. This assignment was completed with the aid of nationally respected authorities in the biological and medical sciences. The widely disseminated guide was directed to those teaching reproductive biology at both the undergraduate and graduate levels.

Under a grant from the National Institute of Mental Health's Center for the Studies of Suicide Prevention, the Mental Health Materials Center (again in collaboration with a panel of experts) developed the *Basic Library on Suicidology*. This was one of the first authoritative collections of its kind and was quickly oversubscribed. For the National Institute on Alcoholism, the Mental Health Materials Center produced the *Selective Guide to Films of Excellence on Alcohol and Alcoholism*. Other similar guides were developed for the National Institute of Mental Health and the National Institute of Education.

For over 25 years, the Mental Health Materials Center served as the publishing arm of the Group for the Advancement of Psychiatry, a highly regarded organization concerned with the application of psychiatry to many current social concerns. For this prestigious study group of 200 psychiatrists, the Mental Health Materials Center published over 90 titles, most of which were book length. As a result of the Mental Health Materials Center's creative marketing, most of the publications of the Group for the Advancement of Psychiatry received extensive coverage in both the professional and the mass media press. During one six-week span, two separate Group for the Advancement of Psychiatry titles were given front-page coverage in Sunday editions of *The New York Times*. This publicity led to one of the titles (*Sex and the College Student*) being chosen as an alternate selection for the Book of the Month Club and to its release in a mass paperback edition that sold over 300,000 copies.

Perhaps one of the greatest contributions made by the Mental Health Materials Center to the field of health and mental health education was its development of the "Selective Guides to Mental Health and Family Life Publications and Audiovisuals of Excellence" series. In the early 1950s, the Mental Health Materials Center pioneered in developing criteria that could be used to assess the potential usefulness of educational materials in a wide variety of settings. Over a period of 30 years, these guidelines were used by the Mental Health Materials Center in reviewing nearly 40,000 publications and approximately 14,000 audiovisuals. Fewer than 20% of these met the organization's standards for excellence.

One other area in which the Mental Health Materials Center pioneered was in offering seminars for professionals engaged in mental health and health education programs. Over an 11-year period, 30 five-day seminars were conducted in collaboration with state health, mental health, and education departments and many distinguished universities.

On the occasion of the 25th anniversary of the Mental Health Materials Center in 1978, Robert E. Switzer, M.D., superintendent of the Eastern State School and Hospital at Trevose, Pennsylvania, made the following observation about the organization's influence:

> . . . I do know that your organization has touched the lives of millions of people over the last 25 years. Not only has it played a significant role in psychiatric education, but has been a prime mover in furthering efforts to promote a primary prevention. . . .

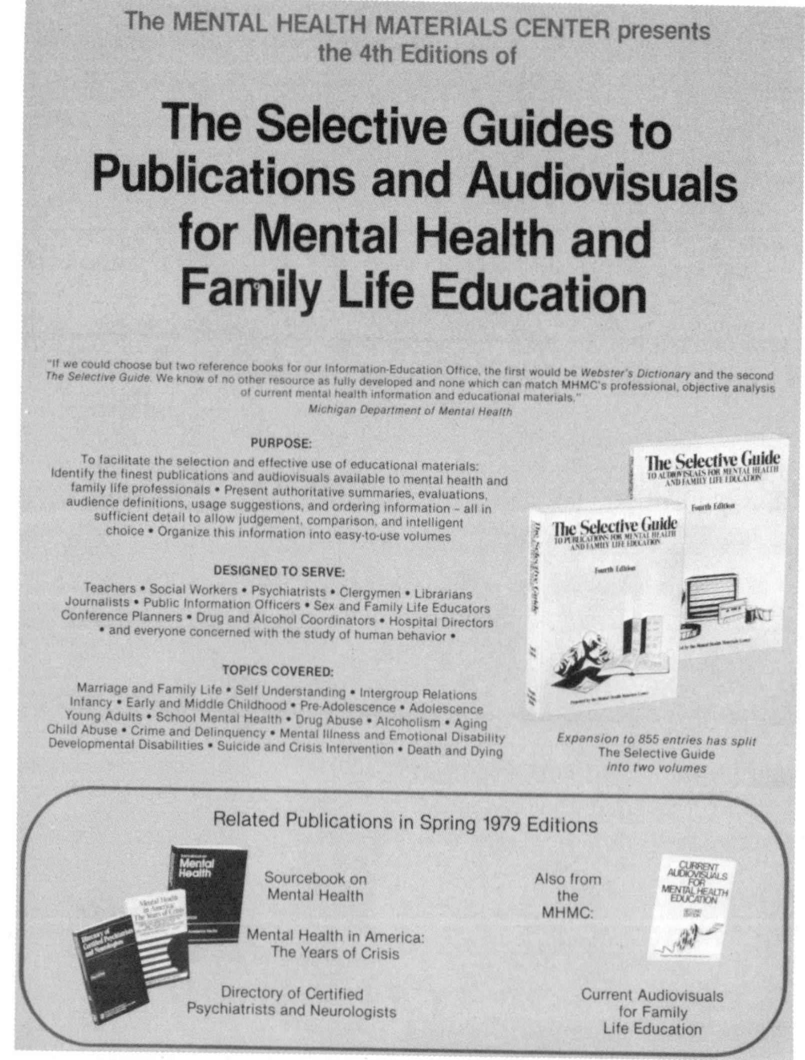

"Unless You Have a Vision of Where You Want to Go, Your Program Is Not Going to Move"

Those prophetic words were attributed to Elmer Ediger, a former CO and one of the chief architects of the Mennonite mental health centers (see Chapter 10).[4] These centers emerged in the post–World War II era as a direct consequence of that church's experience in the CPS mental hospital program.

As a CO, Ediger had been assigned by Selective Service to work in a soil conservation CPS camp. After a brief stint in this program, the Mennonite Central Committee placed him on detached service to direct the church's educational services to the men in the 62 CPS units that it had agreed to oversee.

Ediger's responsibility in this post was to visit each of the Mennonite-sponsored CPS units and to provide assistance in developing educational and other extracurricular activities helpful in sustaining the morale of their members. He was also a liaison between the Mennonite Central Committee and the men in the CPS units for which it had assumed responsibility. This experience gave him a unique vantage point for relating to and understanding the problems that were being faced by the men who had volunteered for service in the mental hospital and state training school units.

When the war came to a close, Elmer Ediger was invited by the Mennonite Central Committee to lead its newly formed Mennonite Mental Health Services program. With the firsthand knowledge he had gained from his previous assignment, he found himself in a strategic stance from which to espouse a daringly bold plan for the church to undertake in meeting the needs of the mentally ill. In this new undertaking, he had the strong backing of those Mennonite COs who knew from firsthand experience that it was necessary to bring new understanding and hope to the mentally ill. As reported in Chapter 1, a large number of those who had been exposed to conditions in state hospitals had redirected their postwar careers to the helping professions as a result of this experience.

Once the Mennonite Mental Health Services program was launched, it didn't take long before eight church-sponsored mental health centers were established. The first of these centers was located at the Mennonite-owned, 105-acre farm near Leitersburg, Maryland. It was opened in 1949 as a 23-bed hospital, designed to serve the acutely mentally ill. Two years later the second of the eight Mennonite mental health centers was dedicated in Reedley, California, and in quick succession the other six soon became realities.

In 1951, Ediger drafted a 10-page document in which he set forth the guidelines for establishing a comprehensive mental health services facility based in Newton, Kansas. This new institution opened in 1954. In the spring of 1957, when Ediger was serving as chairman of the center's board of directors, he was asked to take on the role of administrator of the center for an interim period of six months. This temporary assignment soon became permanent. In 1974, he became executive director of the center, a post that he held through the early 1980s.

During the 1950s and 1960s, when the Mennonite mental health centers were emerging, the concept of community-based mental health centers as an essential component in the delivery of mental health services also was beginning to take shape. Shortly after the Kennedy administration had taken over the White House, federal legislation was enacted that provided the necessary funding to make these centers a reality. This development marked the beginning of a dramatic new era in delivering mental health services to the public.

The arrival of community-based mental health centers precipitated a severe and continuing cutback of services to the chronically mentally ill by the state hospital systems. State hospitals began limiting their services to those who were acutely mentally ill and who had good prospects for recovery after short-term treatment. As this trend began accelerating, large numbers of chronically mentally ill people found themselves being returned to the community, where few, if any, services were available for them.

Ediger, who in the spring of 1957 had taken on administrative responsibility for the Prairie View Mental Health Center at Newton, Kansas, was among the very first to recognize the plight of these displaced mentally ill persons. He submitted a grant application to the federal authorities to set up a model aftercare program for those who were being returned to their communities by the state hospitals because their prognosis for recovery was deemed to be poor. Ediger's request was approved, and his proposed model program was soon implemented. As it gained momentum, this program was soon acknowledged to be making a measurable impact in dealing with those mentally ill Kansas residents who were being returned to their communities and, in many cases, to the streets.

Federal funds proved to be a bonanza to the burgeoning community mental health centers in the 1960s and 1970s. However, Ediger was also among the first to realize that the proverbial day of reckoning was coming soon—the day when they could no longer rely on Washington to provide funds for sustenance and growth. He also recognized that it would be unrealistic to expect that client fees alone could make up for the loss of federal support when that eventuality became a reality.

In anticipation of this certainty, he decided to establish a development office at Prairie View Mental Health Center. His objective in taking this action was to put in place a mechanism for raising sufficient funds to stimulate the development of new and innovative mental health services, in much the same manner as the federal grants had enabled the mental health centers to begin functioning in their early years. Other administrators soon began taking similar steps.

By the early 1980s, Prairie View's mental health services had been extended to cover several states. Besides Kansas, these included individual and community programs in Iowa, Nebraska, Colorado, and Oklahoma. Because of the excellence of its wide variety of mental health services, Prairie View attracted a large number of mental health professionals from all over the country. They came to observe and learn about the many innovative programs and ideas that had been fostered there under Ediger's leadership.

In recognition of Prairie View's outstanding services and excellence of its program, in 1968 the American Psychiatric Association presented the facility with its prestigious Gold Award. In 1984, the National Association for Private Psychiatric Hospitals made a posthumous Presidential Award for Excellence in Mental Health Administration to Elmer Ediger.

One of the most apt tributes given to Elmer Ediger came from a former medical director of the Prairie View Mental Health Center, Dr. Mitchell Jones. In a letter cosigned by two of Prairie View's executives, he is reported to have said:[5]

> Elmer is a man of first-rate intelligence, even temper in crisis, sensitivity, and sense of humor. . . . Elmer is the "adult" that many of the rest of us would like to be—a person open-eyed to the inconsistencies of mankind and the problems of the world, who nevertheless moves ahead optimistically, practically, and with good-natured persistence to change what he can.

Bold Experiment Aids Retarded Children

On November 21, 1949, the *Chicago Daily News* heralded a never-before-attempted program with a banner headline across the top of its front page—"Bold Experiment Here Brings Aid to Retarded Children."[6] The ensuing story described how a group of Chicago parents, "faced with the heartbreaking fact that their mentally retarded children could not be educated in the normal way, decided to do something about it themselves."

The parents had been brought together at Association House by its resident director, Alfred Rath. Only a few years earlier Rath had served with distinction as assistant director of the CPS unit at the Lyons, New Jersey, Veterans Administration Hospital. Rath's training and solid credentials in the practice of social work had prompted the board of directors of this prestigious settlement house to seek him out as its director when an opening had developed a few years earlier.

In the *Chicago Daily News* story about the new program for educating mentally retarded children, Rath was quoted as saying:

> This is not a school but an experiment. Our program is completely uncharted. No one can tell us what way to go because no one has gone this way before. . . . The mothers for whose children no training facilities were available came to us in desperation. They wanted their children educated within their capabilities, but were helpless to direct them.

Rath and colleagues designed a training program that involved the children's parents. It was so successful that training groups based on the Association House model began to spring up throughout the state. Inquiries about replicating the program also began pouring in to Association House from communities throughout the nation.

In a recent communication describing the scope of that project, Rath observed:[7]

> What began as a three-year demonstration project was extended to eight years. By then we had established the feasibility of educating retarded children at public expense, in their own school districts. Our agency had fulfilled its function as initiator, demonstrator, and advocate.

From the Association House, Rath moved on to an assignment with the National Office of the United Presbyterian Church, U.S.A., where he took on administrative responsibilities for two limited-income residential facilities for the aging in Lakeland and Orlando, Florida. From there, he went to the Mental Health Center of Polk County, also in Florida, where he became involved in the planning and establishment of the first mental health forensic unit, which became a model for replication within the state. For the same agency, he also planned and negotiated the opening of a residential facility for emotionally impaired children, which has since expanded into three separate units. Before leaving the Polk County facility, he took on the chore of preparing several grant applications that led to the development of a comprehensive mental health center serving a three-county area.

In the early 1980s, Rath moved into the voluntary sector when he accepted the presidency of the Mental Health Association for Polk County. In effect, he went back to a program that had been spawned by the NMHF, the National Committee for Mental Hygiene, and the Psychiatric Foundation when they joined forces in 1950 to establish the NAMH. In the mid-1980s, he devoted six years to the Polk County Area Agency on Aging. For two of these years he served as president of the organization. One of his special interests with this group was promoting mental health services to the area's elderly population.

Ralph Burns the Mortgage for the Building in His Honor

May 9, 1990, was an eventful day in the life of Ralph S. Lehman. That was the day that he burned the mortgage for the building dedicated in his honor for 22 years of administrative service to the Edgewood Children's Center of Webster Groves, Missouri. He had retired as that agency's executive director in the previous year, after having led the agency through a long series of accomplishments for which he had received official recognition by the Missouri State Legislature.[8]

The Edgewood Children's Center, a rehabilitative facility for emotionally disturbed children, had a long history going back to 1834, when it was first opened as an orphan asylum. In the early 1940s, it was transformed into one of the finest children's residential treatment centers in the Midwest.

In 1945, Ralph Lehman had volunteered for service in the CPS unit located at Hudson River State Hospital in Poughkeepsie, New York. In reviewing his CPS mental hospital experience for a newspaper reporter for the *West County Journal* just before his retirement from the Edgewood Children's Center, Lehman revealed that he and three other COs in the unit had threatened to quit when they became outraged by the abusive treatment that some of the regular attendants gave the patients. When they addressed their concerns to the hospital superintendent, Lehman recalls that they were admonished with the response: "If you really have the courage of your convictions, you'll go back to duty, and keep a careful log on what you observed."[9] The rest of this story was told in Chapter 5 of this book.

In the summer of 1947, Lehman was asked to direct a Mennonite-sponsored voluntary service unit made up of college students at Pueblo State Hospital in Colorado. He then enrolled at Bethel College at North Newton, Kansas, where he majored in Education and the Social Sciences. He and his wife were invited to codirect a voluntary service unit of 24 young people at the Topeka State Hospital at Topeka, Kansas. This was a year-long assignment. In reviewing that experience, Lehman commented in a recent letter:[10]

> Both of us worked in the Reception Hospital's intensive treatment section as charge psychiatric aides. We were in daily contact with psychiatrists, psychiatric nurses, psychiatric social workers, and psychologists for a firsthand exposure to all the professional disciplines in mental health. That was a particularly meaningful experience for us as the Menninger Clinic had been asked by the state to establish a model psychiatric aide training program at Topeka State Hospital. The objective of this demonstration project was to prove that a highly trained and motivated psychiatric aide staff could have a successful impact on the treatment program for patients.

The Topeka experience led Lehman to get a master's degree in psychiatric social work, as well as further training in psychotherapy. Then followed a succession of jobs as clinical director in several residential services and related services for emotionally disturbed children. In 1968, he was invited to join the staff of the Edgewood Children's Center in an administrative capacity. At that time, the center was only serving 18 children. Under his leadership, Edgewood established innovative treatment techniques such as diagnostic and emergency shelter care, safe intensive treatment (residential psychiatric treatment for the most seriously disturbed children), day treatment, intensive family therapy and support services, on-campus special education, and respite care. At the time of Lehman's retirement, the active case load had risen to 86 children.

Among his peers, Lehman was named Social Worker of the Year in 1988. He had been extremely active in both local and state as well as national assemblages of the Child Welfare League and the National Association of Social Workers.

The Kings View Center—How One Man's Vision Became a Reality

February 15, 1945, was a prophetic day for the yet-unrealized Mennonite Mental Health Program.[11] It would be another several months before Selective Service would initiate the slow process of demobilizing the CPS program in response to the war's end. But on that day the Mennonite Central Committee held a symposium in which nine participants addressed the topic, "Should the Churches Establish and Maintain Hospitals for the Mentally Ill?" The participants, who included state mental health commissioners, psychiatrists, social workers, and members of the CPS mental hospital units, presented papers that were published in July 1945 by the Mennonite Central Committee. One of the presenters was Arthur Jost, a member of the CPS unit then serving at the Utah State Hospital at Provo. In his paper he stated:

> While much has been done to alleviate physical suffering, very little has been done by the churches in providing care for the mentally ill. . . . Was Christ any less interested in healing the demon-possessed than he was in healing the withered hand? We have as yet made very little practical application of this single standard of Jesus' healing mission. . . . As science makes great strides in psychiatric discoveries, now that psychiatrists realize the need for the cooperation of ministers, educators, social workers, and lay people to promote mental health both outside and inside a mental institution, there unfolds a great field of opportunity for Christian service by the churches.

Within two years of the release of that report on the symposium, the Mennonite Central Committee, headquartered at Akron, Pennsylvania, had made a commitment to authorize the establishment of three homes for the mentally ill. These were to be located in the eastern, midwestern, and far western regions of the United States.

Jost joined the staff of the Mennonite Central Committee after his discharge from the CPS mental hospital program in January 1946. Early in 1948, the Mennonite Central Committee asked him to assist in the planning and construction of Brook Lane Psychiatric Center at Hagerstown, Maryland, which was originally named Leitersburg. This was the first of the eight mental health centers to be administered under the aegis of that agency.

Shortly after beginning this assignment, Jost was transferred to Reedley, California, where he was directed to select a site and oversee the planning and development of a mental health facility.

Despite considerable community opposition toward the establishment of a psychiatric facility there, Jost was successful in finding an appropriate site. By February 1951, a 30-bed facility had been completed and was given the name Kings View Hospital.

In 1952, Jost was directed by the Mennonite Central Committee to go to Newton, Kansas, and become involved in an educational and fund-raising effort directed to the midwestern Mennonite churches. The primary objective of this campaign was to enlist support for the development of the Mennonite Central Committee's third planned mental health facility, which eventually became known as the Prairie View Mental Health Center.

This turned out to be only a temporary assignment for Jost, and he was soon on his way back to Kings View Hospital to resume his administrative duties there. To accommodate an increasing number of patients from the southern San Joaquin Valley, he worked out arrangements with the Greater Bakersfield Memorial Hospital to build a mental hospital on an adjacent site, as well as establish a formal affiliation with that institution. Eventually, the Kern View Psychiatric Center, another of the Mennonite Central Committee's mental health centers, emerged from this development. An independent board of directors was created for this facility, and its oversight was turned over to a local Mennonite community.

Getting the mental health centers operational was a major achievement. But seeing to it that they were fiscally sound presented even more challenging difficulties. Arthur Jost was equal to meeting these roadblocks. In the mid-1950s, the California legislature was considering adoption of a community mental health law that would have permitted counties within the state to contract with private psychiatric facilities to provide mental health services to their respective constituents. Despite strong opposition, this legislation was passed as introduced. Jost was given credit for playing a major role in the lobbying effort that led to passage of this bill.

It took seven more years after the passage of that legislation before the first contract for mental health services with a private psychiatric institution was successfully concluded. This was an arrangement negotiated between nine counties in central and northern California and the Kings View Hospital, under which the latter was to provide mental health services for their populations under a cost-reimbursement system provided by the legislation.

As the Kings View service network expanded, the institution needed additional funding to enlarge its physical plant to accommodate its increased caseload of patients. Jost had become aware that the Hill-Burton Act, recently passed by Congress, provided financial assistance to hospitals that needed to expand their acute treatment facilities. When he first applied to the state agency administering this program in California, he was told that provisions of this bill did not apply to psychiatric hospitals. Undaunted by this rebuff, Jost researched the history of the legislation and successfully proved that it did indeed cover psychiatric facilities. Kings View was the first mental hospital in the state to receive Hill-Burton funds. A subsequent building grant was also awarded to Kern View Psychiatric Center.

When Congress established the community mental health center program during President Kennedy's administration, another funding opportunity was presented to Kings View. A grant that Kings View received under this new program gave it the muscle to develop an expanded range of community mental health services throughout the region it was serving. What emerged from this development was a model community-based program that earned national recognition for Kings View Center.

In 1972, Kings View was invited by a local agency to take over the responsibility for developing a program to meet the needs of its mentally retarded. This led to negotiations with the state of California for Kings View to deliver services to the six counties in central San Joaquin Valley. For the next 10 years, Kings View managed the delivery of a wide range of services to more than 9,000 retarded individuals in this region.

Throughout his career, Jost was heavily involved in local, state, and national hospital associations, where he was a persistent spokesperson for the significance of mental health in the larger field of health care. In 1974, he received the signal honor of being the first person whose work experience came from outside an acute medical treatment facility to be elected as president of the California State Hospital Association.

At the time of Jost's retirement from Kings View Center in the late 1980s, it had grown from a modest 30-bed mental hospital to a nonprofit system delivering a wide range of mental health services in 23 counties in California. By that time, the Kings View Hospital itself was offering a broad spectrum of mental health services from its 43-acre rural site 25 miles southeast of Fresno. Among these services were inpatient, day treatment, and outpatient programs for adults, adolescents, and children. Throughout the nearly 30 communities in California's Central Valley and North Coast, Kings View Center was operating a wide variety of integrated programs for mentally ill, developmentally disabled, and chronically addicted people. It had opened the Rio Vista Residential Treatment Center, a halfway house designed to ease the recovering patient's return to an appropriate form of living in his or her home community. Through an affiliated agency, Menno Care, it had developed three group homes for persons with serious prolonged mental illness.

The spark that had ignited Jost's lifelong drive and commitment

AMERICAN PSYCHIATRIC ASSOCIATION
HOSPITAL & COMMUNITY PSYCHIATRY SERVICE

Achievement Award

GOLD AWARD

PRESENTED THIS 14th DAY OF SEPTEMBER 1971 TO

Kings View Community Mental Health Center
Reedley, California

For its effective delivery of mental health services
to rural counties in central California

PRESIDENT, AMERICAN PSYCHIATRIC ASSOCIATION

CHAIRMAN, ACHIEVEMENT AWARDS BOARD

SECRETARY, AMERICAN PSYCHIATRIC ASSOCIATION

MEDICAL DIRECTOR, AMERICAN PSYCHIATRIC ASSOCIATION

to help people cope constructively with their emotional needs and problems certainly came out of a deeply ingrained set of Christian values. In retrospect, it is fair to surmise that the intensity of that spark might not have been as great if he and other COs like him had not been intimately involved in the CPS mental hospital program during World War II. The compulsion to do something positive and meaningful as a result of that experience was certainly greatly reinforced by the fact that 3,000 others had been part of that experience, too.

For his creative and outstanding achievements in bringing new hope and compassion for those troubled with emotional ills, Arthur Jost was given the Presidential Award of the National Association of Psychiatric Hospitals in 1989. Several years earlier, his facility had been honored by the American Psychiatric Association's Hospital and Community Psychiatry Service with a Gold Achievement Award for its effective delivery of mental health services in rural counties in central California.

If ever there was a turning point in the life of Arthur Jost, it had to be the day in March 1943 when as a CO, he volunteered for service in a state mental hospital.

Chapter 12

Looking Back

. . . When the war ended and the men who had served in these CPS units were discharged, there was also released a highly articulate and concerned group of advocates for the patients they had left behind. . . . While CPS can hardly claim credit for all the advances that have been made in behalf of the mentally ill over the last half-century, it can certainly claim that it "stirred the pot" and forced American society to look at this problem from a new perspective and with greater concern for the individuals involved.

From a respondent to the 1988 questionnaire sent to those who were in the Civilian Public Service mental hospital program during World War II.

In the spring of 1988, in preparation for this book on the Civilian Public Service (CPS) mental hospital program, a questionnaire was mailed to 1,277 of the approximately 3,000 conscientious objectors (COs) who had served in one or more of the 61 mental hospital or training school units authorized by Selective Service during World War II. (For a copy of this questionnaire, see Appendix A.) Current addresses for these individuals were located through the good offices of individuals affiliated with the American Friends Service Committee, the Brethren Service Committee, and the Mennonite Mental Health Service Committee.

Replies were received from 435 individuals, for a response rate of 34%. There were no follow-up mailings. Considering the fact that nearly 50 years had lapsed since the recipients of this questionnaire had served in the CPS program, the number of responses received was gratifying beyond expectations. Several noteworthy findings and observations emerged during the tabulation of the questionnaires. Among them were the following:

- One in four reported that as a direct result of their participation in this program, their postwar studies had been redirected toward their preparation for entry into one of the helping professions.
- One in three noted that their postwar careers had been redirected into the helping professions because of their CPS experience in mental hospitals and training schools for the retarded.
- Nearly 45% observed that their social and political outlook had been considerably broadened in response to their CPS experience.
- By early 1988, one in four respondents was still active or had retired from a career in the field of education. The overwhelming majority had been or were still engaged as professors at the college or university level.
- Nearly 40% were still involved or had been involved in the delivery of services in the fields of medicine and the behavioral sciences.
- About 10% advised that they had been or were still serving as clergymen, or were working in an administrative capacity with a church or religious agency.
- About 10% had pursued careers as artisans, had played major roles in the construction industry, or had worked in the fields of engineering and chemistry.
- About 10% had devoted their careers to farming or some aspect of agribusiness.

As was stated earlier, when the first COs were drafted in June 1941 to do work of national importance under the umbrella of the CPS program, the service opportunities were largely restricted to projects under the management of the Soil Conservation Service of the Department of Agriculture, the Forestry Service, and the National Park Service. Although many of these projects did meet the criterion of "national importance" from the perspective of Selective Service, in the eyes of many of the CPS conscripts, they did not.

In addition, large numbers of COs in the program felt uncomfortable about their financial dependence on the three peace churches that were paying to maintain them in these CPS units. Underwriting these expenses cost the peace churches an average of $35 per month per man. Those who were able to do so were encouraged to reimburse the particular church agency under whose auspices they had been assigned to serve. The funds soon ran out for many who had opted to contribute toward their own maintenance.

When Selective Service authorized the opening of voluntary detached service opportunities in state mental hospitals in June 1942, it offered an important incentive to those who were unsatisfied with work projects of questionable importance in the base camps. Because the sponsors of these new detached service projects were required to assume responsibility for the monthly maintenance of those who volunteered, these programs also were attractive to COs who wished to free the peace churches from the burden of their care.

From the perspective of 1988, many of those who participated in the CPS mental hospital program during World War II offered a wide variety of pithy observations and recollections. These observations and recollections provide a special insight into that experience, which came at such a critical time in the lives of these men, and therefore are an important part of this book.

Reasons for Volunteering

Typical reasons that many reported had prompted them to volunteer for service in a mental hospital or state training school for the retarded included the following:

> The work in base camps was not seen as a service to our fellow man. I found it difficult to spend my time away from people and their needs. I felt that work in a psychiatric hospital could be so much more meaningful and needed.

> In the camps we were mostly isolated from communities. In the hospital setting, we were part of the hospital community as well as the surrounding neighborhood.

> To trim trees in the forests so that visitors could have a better view of the countryside did not seem like essential work of national importance.
>
> I volunteered for service in a mental hospital because I felt I could make a much more effective witness for our beliefs than was possible in the setting of a forestry or soil conservation camp to which I was originally assigned. A chapel we had been asked to construct at the forestry camp where I initially served was torn down a few years later along with all the other buildings at this site.
>
> I felt that much of the work assigned to us while in base camps was "made work"—not always of great significance. In these settings my skills were only partially used to advantage. On the other hand, during my experience at the CPS units at Vineland Training School and at Kalamazoo State Hospital we were not only appreciated, but the work was much more satisfying to me as an individual.
>
> The work we were required to do at the base camp was constructive but far from urgent: it consisted of building a roadside park on the Blue Ridge Parkway in North Carolina at a time when gas and tire rationing prevented cars from using this recreational highway. The only urgent work occurred when we were called out to fight a forest fire. . . . Also, I was supposed to pay $35 a month to cover my expenses for room and board. . . . Under this obligation, my financial resources soon ran out and I did not wish to be a burden to the Quakers who were sponsoring our unit. For this reason, I welcomed the opportunity to "volunteer" for detached service at a school for delinquent boys where I could earn my room and board plus a monthly allowance of $15.

Initial Fears

For most COs who had volunteered for service in mental hospitals, the most traumatic period was the first day they reported for duty. Almost without exception, none had ever been within the walls of such an institution. An undeniable sense of fear accompanied each man as he entered the doors of the institution for the very first time. Some of these feelings were vividly recalled by a number of the respondents to the survey.

> One of my greatest concerns when I first reported for duty at Byberry was the fear of being physically hurt. My first assignment was to report to a restraint room in which 15 male patients had been shackled to their beds. As I entered the ward, a young worker-patient came up to me and punched me in the stomach . . . "just to let you know where you stand."

> At the time of our unit's arrival at Marlboro State Hospital, the nursing staff was so distrustful of our presence that contrary to usual practice, no passkeys were issued to us for a period of six weeks after our arrival. . . . Finally, when they saw we could be trusted, we were given keys.

> At first I was afraid of the patients and the job. But I had to lose my fears and inhibitions pretty fast because on my first night, I was placed in charge of a ward with 250 men—alone! The nurses and other COs were very supportive.

> Within a few weeks of my arrival at Williamsburg, I found myself as the lone attendant on the night shift of the admissions ward. I had to change in a hurry from a terrified boy "locked up with raving madmen" to a combination nurse, teacher, father, priest, confidante, Mr. Fix-it, and guide to 60 disturbed people. I grew up!

Hostility Experienced

A common experience shared by the men in most CPS mental hospital units was the almost universal social hostility directed at them by the hospital community when they first reported for duty. This hostility was echoed, although to a lesser extent, by members of the surrounding community. In some units, these feelings gave way after a period of time to almost complete acceptance, whereas in other units, hostile attitudes were muted to a point where civility (if nothing else) reigned. In a few instances, there was no ground-giving. Some idea of the range of these feelings may be gleaned from the following recollections:

> At the opening of our unit at the Medical State Hospital in Washington, there was a great deal of opposition, even enmity, directed at our CPS unit by both the hospital staff as well as the community. We were socially rejected, both at the hospital as well as the community. The Methodist minister who was supportive and friendly to us lost his post because of his support for us. . . . By the end of two years the unfriendly climate in which we found ourselves had turned to nearly cordial.

> If at mealtimes we would sit at a table where regular staff members were seated, they would get up and move to another table. . . . Being shunned by others gave us a better perspective on what it must be like for those who are subject to discrimination because of their race or creed.

> The hospital community had no idea of what to expect when our CPS unit arrived. Their impressions of us, in general, were that we were "traitors—cop-outs, and the like." Their initial impressions gave way and became more accepting of us as they saw us in action with the patients.

> For the year and a half that I was at Cherokee State Hospital, we never went to the dining hall but were greeted by other hospital attendants with jeers like "yellow-belly" and "Cee-O." At first the patients echoed the employees' taunts, but within a few months that ceased. Though the administration made feeble attempts to make us welcome, the hospital staff continued to be uniformly negative toward us.

> Some of the attendants resented our presence at Fort Steilacoom State Hospital as a matter of patriotic principle, and also because they considered us as "scabs," and as such kept them from strengthening their union's bargaining position with the administration. . . . On one occasion when a regular member of the staff and one of our CPS men were working together, the former severely beat the latter, causing him to sustain a serious head injury. Though

> the employee was immediately dismissed, he transferred to another state institution where he was hired without question.
>
> During the second year of our stay at Medical Lake State Hospital, several wives of the CPS men who had been hired to fill staff vacancies were dismissed because they refused to buy war bonds.

But there was another side to the story of how CPS units got along with the hospital and local communities. This story differed radically from the incidents described above. For example, one member of the Kalamazoo State Hospital CPS unit reported a very different welcome for his fellow COs:

> Upon our arrival at Kalamazoo, our CPS unit was greeted with enthusiasm and support by the hospital's administration. The commendable reports which they had received about the work performance of the CPS unit at Ypsilanti State Hospital triggered their receptivity to a similar unit for their institution. Notices had been placed on bulletin boards throughout the hospital advising members of the regular staff who felt they could not work with COs in their midst to turn in their keys rather than stay and make trouble. Some opted to leave. Most stayed.

At Mount Pleasant State Hospital in Iowa, the hospital superintendent's initial hostility toward one CO was transformed into respect:

> A most unusual discriminatory stance was reported to have been taken by the superintendent of the Mount Pleasant State Hospital in Iowa when interviewing prospective candidates for inclusion in a CPS unit to be assigned to his institution, from among a group of Mennonite young men. The particular young man he was addressing had a beard. The superintendent offered to accept the young man, provided he would agree to remove his beard. The CO replied that if the superintendent wanted him, he would also have to take his beard. The superintendent relented and approved his application. Three months later, when the two had a chance meeting, the superintendent remarked that at the time he was interviewing for the unit, he did not want any bearded men in his group. He then remarked, "But as of now, if you want to have a beard that grows

down to your belt, that's okay with me. You've proved to me that you've worked out well, and have earned the respect of the hospital community."

Major Challenges Encountered

Questionnaire recipients were asked to describe some of the challenges they faced at the time of their introduction to work in a mental hospital. A great many respondents mentioned the serious staff shortages that prevailed in so many institutions during the World War II era. It wasn't at all uncommon to read a response to the effect that "at times we were so shorthanded, I was the only attendant covering a building with 800 to 900 patients." One young CO physician who had been assigned to Norwich State Hospital in Connecticut reported that at the time of his arrival at that institution, the medical staff was at a severely marginal level because several staff physicians had resigned to join the military service. Within 10 days of his arrival at the hospital, he had been asked to assume responsibility for 1,600 patients, which represented about 60% of the institution's total patient population. Within a short time, his patient load had been increased to 2,300 patients. This same physician noted:

> Many of the members of the CPS unit served in a variety of administrative responsibilities at the institution, and performed in a highly satisfactory manner in carrying out their duties. Many of the wives who accompanied members of the CPS unit were given supervisory and managerial roles in the hospital and added their expertise in uplifting the quality of patient care. Among the unit, three of the members had professional qualifications in psychology and social work. Their skills were welcomed by the administration and used to good advantage in serving patients.

At a number of mental hospitals, staff shortages had become so acute that members of the CPS units were drawn into assisting in a wide range of assignments that normally would have been reserved for individuals with some professional training.

> We were active participants in processing new admissions, dispensing medicines, giving injections, writing medical reports, assisting in electro-shock therapy, and in other special treatments in addition to our regular duties in overseeing patient activities. Our recommendations for transferring patients from one ward to another were generally accepted by the medical staff.

Many CPS men were greatly upset by prevailing practices that were overlooked in many institutions by the administration but that were patently inimical to patient welfare. Typical of these practices were those reported in the following responses:

> The men in our CPS unit had a very hard time getting the hospital to abandon the use of clubs by attendants in controlling patient behavior.

> At the time of our arrival at Byberry, there was a custom when patients were being transferred from Philadelphia General Hospital to our hospital, to tell them that they were being taken home rather than to a mental hospital, which then had the justifiable reputation of being the "end of the road." Perhaps it was only a small gesture, but we succeeded in putting an end to this deceitful practice.

A frequently recurring complaint that appeared in the responses had to do with the personal problems that were brought about by the trying circumstances in which the COs were endeavoring to maintain their own mental well-being. This complaint is aptly reflected in the three following responses:

> One of the greatest challenges I faced while a member of the CPS unit . . . working with patients who were often miserable and tormented, was trying to maintain my own mental health. Another acute concern was trying to keep my "cool" while witnessing examples of patient abuse by the regular attendants.

> I believe that one of the greatest challenges we faced as attendants at the Philadelphia State Hospital was working under the distressing conditions we faced. There was a minimum of therapeutic help available to the patients—many were in a deplorable psychological

> condition—the prognosis for others appeared hopeless. About all we could offer was custodial care at a very inadequate level. And then there was the constant level of stress, all too common in the face of disease. In response to this regime, most of us reached a point of personal psychological crisis within six months. In order to cope and to be able to offer some help to our patients, we had to develop a degree of psychic distance from the patients. At that point some of us were no longer able to function and had to transfer out of the unit. . . . Another and equally pressing concern for me as a pacifist was the old bromide—"you can't reason with a mad man." There I was, virtually alone with 450 violent patients. I soon confirmed that only nonviolent attitudes and approaches were appropriate in relating to the patients.
>
> The major problem was to try to keep your own mental balance in an atmosphere decidedly untherapeutic. Patients were routinely treated as objects rather than as human beings. The general stress that prevailed in the institution may have been a major factor in the hospitalization of five regular attendants during my two-year assignment at the hospital. It was particularly difficult to start each day with a fresh supply of tolerance and optimism when you could not look to the administration, the nursing staff, and the regular attendants for support. As more CPS men were assigned to duty on the violent ward, we were able to devote more attention to individual patients, and in so doing, found that we were able to relate to them with greater effectiveness. Some of the patients would ask me to sing a song which happened to be a particular favorite of theirs. Many of the regular attendants frowned upon this practice as mollycoddling the patients.

Another respondent reported that in addition to patient abuse, which was rife in nearly every mental hospital during that period, members of their CPS unit were particularly distressed about the extent to which it was a common practice for many of the employees at their institution to steal from the institution.

> Employees stole supplies of all kinds—food, clothing, medical accessories—and sold them. Don't forget, wartime rationing was in place. And that made this a very lucrative practice.

> Then too, there was the devastating experience of being exposed to the fraternity of "bug-housers" who moved from one state hospital to another and made a clique of extortionists, thieves, and sadists. To make matters even worse, the hospital itself was a political plum, rife with payoffs for political favors and nepotism.

During the war era, the medical personnel of most state mental hospitals had been drafted to meet the needs of the military establishment. Those who remained were reported by one respondent to include doctors who had flunked out of medical school or who had failed to make it in private practice. Very few of the physicians serving in mental hospitals at that time had been certified as psychiatrists. Many state hospitals did not have even one psychiatrist among their medical staffs. One former CPS man remarked: "The doctors were the biggest problem I had to face. We had to carry on in spite of their incompetence. On the other hand, the nurses were very helpful. . . . There were numerous cases of misdiagnosis and neglect of duty by the physicians."

To illustrate the insensitivity that often characterized the level of care provided by the medical department at one state hospital, another former CPS man recalled the following incident:

> Frank, one of our elderly patients, had been in the hospital for about 25 years. When I first saw him, his belly was extended beyond anything I'd ever seen. For a long period of time, he had been experiencing excruciating pains because of gas that kept accumulating in his stomach. We used to try relieving him but it didn't seem to help. A few days before he died, two hospital doctors came to see him at the insistence of one of the nurses. They stood in front of Frank and began punching him in the belly to see if that offered any relief. Finally, one of the doctors turned to the other and said, "Well, I guess he has a malignancy." The other responded, "Well, I guess he does have a malignancy." From the tone of their remarks, it appeared as though they had been engaged in discussing a bag of grain. After all those years of careless attention, there was now this casual and useless diagnosis.

Most state hospitals in the 1940s were almost completely self-sustaining communities. They often had their own water systems, power plants, farms, and police and fire protection services. Any breakdown in these essential services could have devastating consequences for the hospital's well-being. Like all other personnel services in the hospital, the ranks of these ancillary departments had also been depleted by the demands of the war. In many institutions to which CPS units were assigned, the administration found it necessary to place COs in these services. Following is an illustrative anecdote:

> The hospital powerhouse was the last stronghold of the old guard at the institution—engineers, ex-soldiers, ex-cons, winos, and others of their ilk. They were all super-patriots and wanted to have nothing to do with the fellows in the CPS unit. Finally, they too became desperate for help and even though unhappily and reluctantly, agreed to try just a few of the COs. After each payday, it was almost a ritual for several of the powerhouse crew to go on a binge and disappear for a few days. Or, if they did return to duty as scheduled, they would be in such a state that they could not be depended on.
>
> The most devastating experience for the engineer on duty was to find that the water in the boiler was getting so high, and the steam getting so low, that the buildings would begin to get cold and the hot water throughout the system would turn cold. Supervisors in the laundry and the kitchens would start screaming. And if the water level got too low and the steam began getting excessively high, an even worse scenario would develop. The increased pressure would cause the whistle on the safety valve to start screaming so that it could be heard throughout the entire hospital. And that would mean that excessive amounts of coal and oil would have to be used to bring the system back into order. The engineers soon began to notice that when the COs were covering a shift, these worries disappeared. They knew that when the so-called "worthless, unpatriotic intellectuals" were on duty, all would be well.

The most distressing of all challenges that greeted COs when they were first introduced to the mental hospital world was the pervasive brutality directed at the patients by many of the attendants. Several observations about this practice have already been accounted. To report or not report these disturbing practices posed a very difficult problem for virtually all men in the units. One of these dilemmas surfaced at the Lyons, New Jersey, Veterans Administration Hospital. A former CPS man who served in that unit recalled:

> There was a wholesale exposé of brutality toward the patients, engineered by one of the men in our unit whose exact name I have forgotten. He was a quiet-spoken, pale-faced young man who was privately burdened with a powerful conscience. He was so revolted by the atrocities that constantly occurred on the wards that without telling anyone exactly what he was up to [he] began compiling detailed descriptions of brutality incidents instigated by regular attendants. In addition to those incidents which he personally witnessed on his own tours of duty, he collected additional accounts of abuse from after hours' conversations and mealtime chit-chats. Without their knowing it, everybody in the institution was providing grist for his mill. For some time, he industriously recorded what he had picked up into a several-hundred-page document. One day, he suddenly packed his duffle bag and left Lyons in a paroxysm of do-gooder enthusiasm. He brashly informed the authorities that he was refusing to participate further in his assignment, thereby earning for himself a prison sentence, but not before presenting the authorities and the press with copies of his documented abuses at Lyons.
>
> In due course, a federal investigator who looked and behaved exactly like an FBI man appeared at the hospital and began taking sworn depositions from everyone named in his document. I found myself in the anomalous position of being asked to inform on my co-workers in an institution where we, the ward attendants, were forced to rely on each other for maintaining some semblance of order for the sake of our patients and ourselves. Needless to say, the submerged tensions between the men in our unit and the regular attendants were greatly heightened at this time. . . . Had he stayed on at Lyons instead of opting for prison at the time of his exposé, he would have been in great personal peril. Some of the patients at this facility were convicted murderers in civilian life and had beaten the rap by pleading insanity. These individuals were

often the quietest and best-behaved among our charges. Several of them would have been able and willing to permanently "erase" our friend from the scene in return for past and future favors.

Reflections on the Positive Side

Another episode of violence that was reported by one member of a CPS unit had quite a different spin. In this instance, one of the patients was the perpetrator of a violent act—this time directed at a physician. As the physician approached the patient, the latter grabbed a chair and was about to smash it over the physician's head. One of the CPS men who happened to be on duty was quick enough to subdue the patient and thus averted what might have turned into a tragic event. For this act of bravery, the attendant received a military citation, possibly the only award of its kind given to a CO serving in a civilian setting during World War II.

From the foregoing anecdotes, one might assume that there was a constant state of tension between the COs in the CPS mental hospital units and their co-workers. However, that was not the case. Many employees among the regular staff were very exceptional and caring in their relationships with the patients in their charge. Many of those who responded to the questionnaire reported that they had learned much from these caring individuals and had developed a relationship with them based on mutual respect.

The wives of the CPS men who joined them at the various state hospitals where they were assigned made significant contributions in helping to maintain these hospitals during one of the most critically difficult periods the institutions faced. In many hospitals where CPS units were assigned, the work done by the wives of the CPS men was highly regarded by the hospital authorities.

As the CPS units got oriented to and comfortable with their institutional settings, important changes began to occur in the daily hospital routines. The men began to find that they were gaining new insights into their own behavior and outlook on life. One man reported:

> It was the test I needed. It nearly broke me emotionally. Our presence at Cherokee provided me with an opportunity to introduce a healing climate into what had been a brutal environment. I know we saved many patients from merciless beatings and demeaning verbal abuse. And it helped to convince me beyond all argument that there is far greater strength in "loving concern" than there is in "the club and fist."

Another responded with this comment: "The presence of our unit at Augusta State Hospital served as a 'moral governor' to the rest of the hospital staff."

Among other responses in a similar vein were the following:

> While working at the Ypsilanti unit, I came to understand that Mennonites could make an impact on society and on institutions. The CPS unit at this hospital was, in itself, a power-block and proved it could be effective in bringing about positive changes in institutional life. . . . We were respected for our work performance and this might have been the beginning of helping me to become less timid and actually start feeling good about being a Mennonite.

> Within a month or so from our arrival at the Lima State Hospital, some of us were taking the places of two or three regular staff attendants, because our approach in dealing with the patients earned their respect. Rather than trying to control patient behavior, our approach had been to lend a helping hand. As a consequence, many patients improved in a relatively short time. . . . We were trusted by the medical staff and some of us were given the opportunity to become familiar with individual cases and even invited to enter into treatment decisions.

> The growing affection that developed between the patients and the men in our unit, and the greater patient loads we were able to handle, gave the hospital medical and nursing staff new visions of how custodial care could become therapeutic influence for the betterment of their patients.

> The CPS unit at Duke aided in the process of achieving racial integration of the patients at this medical facility.

> One day, one of the younger patients came up to me and said: "I like being around you fellows. You don't swear and neither do I when I'm around you."
>
> At the time of our discharge from the Highland Hospital Division of the Duke unit, the returning employees from military service were confounded at the behavior of the patients and the total absence of black eyes and bruises on the patients which had been so characteristic of the period when they had been members of the attendant staff.

In a great many state hospitals where CPS units had been assigned, hospital directors encouraged the men to join the staff as regular employees when the war ended and they were released by Selective Service. Although the overwhelming majority chose to pursue interrupted educational programs or to explore new career directions, many did stay on in a variety of supervisory and other roles in these institutions. For many CPS men who did leave the hospitals when their discharges were approved, it was a poignant time. At one hospital, the director of nursing remarked to a group of CPS men who had been discharged,"Too bad we didn't enroll all of you in the nursing program. If we had, you'd all be going home with R.N. degrees." One former CPS man gave this account of his discharge: "At the time four of us were being discharged in conformance with Selective Service regulations, the head nurse turned to us and said: 'If any of you ever want to come back to Marlboro, there will always be a job for you here.' While sharing this farewell with us, tears were streaming down her cheeks."

Effects of the Experience on Career Directions

The CPS mental hospital experience had a profound influence on the lives of a significant number of those who participated in this program. New and more socially significant career choices were plotted to reflect new concerns for taking more active roles in helping people cope with the problems of daily living. Those who came out of this program were perceptibly more tolerant of the disenfranchised—the emotionally and mentally disabled—and those whose beliefs were different. And there was personal growth—lots and lots of personal growth. As the men looked back on their CPS experience from the perspective of 1988, here's a sampling of what they had to say:

> I found that I too could be courageous. That change, if it comes, is a result of somebody doing something—standing up for something, or some principle, and that sometimes it was my turn to do just that. And I've been doing just that ever since.
>
> I learned that change is slow and requires patience. I learned that nonviolence can work on an individual level, but it demands courage, emotional control, and respect for one another . . .
>
> I saw people get better—persons who responded to care and ministrations of love. I saw catatonic patients come out of their withdrawal and violent and paranoid patients become meek, amiable, and outgoing. Love works better than drugs.
>
> As a result of my experience at Howard State Hospital, I decided that in my postwar career, I would rather work with and for people, rather than other choices that were open to me. My work there also led me to become a more gentle person in dealing with others.
>
> In a real sense, I grew up during my stay as an attendant at Medical Lake. I moved away from being a war protester, and instead became an agent for social change.
>
> As our church leaders came to visit our CPS units . . . we told them that the church should become responsive to the needs of the mentally ill and get involved in relating to these needs—and they did.
>
> This was a time of personal growth for me. Before my arrival at the Medical Lake unit, I had had little contact with the real world of pain, illness, deprivation, and emotional turmoil. Within the

> first month of my arrival at the hospital, I was ambushed and beaten by two patients. Through the support of others in our CPS group and sympathetic patients, I lost my fears. By not retaliating against my attackers, I became in fact, as well as theory, a nonviolent person.
>
> The CPS experience made me realize that for the rest of my life I am a part of mankind's fabric and mosaic, and there, but for the Grace of God, go I. . . . It exposed me to an aspect of life which I scarcely knew existed. It was society at "rock-bottom." I felt, and still believe, that if love works at "rock-bottom" levels, it proves its effectiveness at all levels.
>
> As a result of my CPS experience at Harrisburg, I now feel that I have a more finely tuned social conscience.
>
> . . . The CPS experience gave a number of outstanding persons a chance to "evolve" in extremely diverse ways. Is this not the essential and important remainder of the experience, rather than the effect on the patients?
>
> Coming from a Roman Catholic background into the multi-denominational fellowship of the CPS camps made me realize the identity, under various labels, of the Christian tradition.

Impressions of Former COs Who Made Return Visits to the Institutions They Served During World War II

Long after their discharge from CPS and well into their postwar careers, many who had participated in units assigned to either state mental hospitals or training schools for the retarded made return visits to these institutions. For most, the changes that had occurred were almost beyond belief. In the 1970s, a return visit to the Connecticut State Hospital revealed that the patient population had declined from 3,300 in the CPS era to about 800 and that the attendant staff had increased from 300 to about 1,200. In this latter period deinstitutionalization of mental patients had reached its peak. Most state hospitals had discharged their chronically mentally ill patients and were limiting their services to those whose prospects for a positive response to treatment were favorable.

Many of those who commented about return visits to the facilities in which they once had served observed that they had been given warm welcomes by residents, staff, and administration. Typical responses included the following:

> I returned to the hospital for a visit in 1983. One of those with whom I visited was the chaplain. She remarked how thrilling it was for her to meet one of the men who had helped to make such a turnaround in the care of the mentally ill. She observed that even current textbooks on caring for the mentally ill made mention of the gains attributed to the work performed by the COs in mental hospitals during World War II. It made me feel good to know that I had been part of this history.

> I visited Pennhurst Training School in 1975—some 30 years after leaving this institution. I found it nearly unrecognizable. It was now patient-oriented to an extent that was unbelievable from that which had prevailed in the war era. . . . I like to think that the presence of our CPS unit at that time must have played some role in achieving this transformation.

> Strong personal friendships had been formed by the men in our unit at the Vineland State Training School and the "students" confined to this facility for the developmentally disabled. Nearly 40 years later, I returned for a visit and met some of my former students. They still remembered the personnel of our CPS unit. They were eager to learn about the former members of the unit who had tutored them and with whom they had built warm and long-lasting friendships.

> Several years after my discharge, I went back to Concord State Hospital to visit a patient. A doctor who did not know me was polite and helpful but reserved. He offered to walk me to the ward where the patient I was visiting was then living. As the doctor unlocked the door to the ward, a patient rushed up to me (not the

> one I was planning to visit) and exclaimed with obvious joy: "I haven't seen you for seven years. . . ." The doctor's attitude toward me immediately changed from reserve to warmth. The patient who greeted me so effusively had not been on the ward on which I had been stationed during the war. He had worked in the laundry where I used to see him casually on a daily basis. I was glad that he, whom I could scarcely recall, remembered me with such affection. It made me feel good to see how much pleasure I had brought to someone whose life I had touched so briefly so many years earlier.
>
> A few years ago, my wife and I stopped in at the Exeter State Training School to find an institution that was completely different than it had been as we remembered it from the CPS era. Everything that we had tried to put into effect and even dreamed about was now a reality. The current chief administrator told us that the CPS unit experience had marked a major turning point in bringing about this change.

Not all return visits evoked such positive responses. A former CPS couple had this observation on the occasion of a visit to Howard State Hospital some 25 years after their departure from that institution:

> We were disappointed to find some of the staff bitterly complaining about the deterioration of the hospital as a result of its having become a politicized institution. The welfare of the patients no longer appeared to be a high priority for the institution. They seemed to be longing for a revival of the climate of caring and compassion which we had tried to instill during our tenure there. We left with a feeling that we had sown some seed that had turned out to be not entirely unproductive.

CPS Experience Broadened Social Outlook of Its Participants

One of the very significant changes that occurred in the postwar lives of many who took part in the CPS mental hospital program was a commitment to seek social change through the political process. This commitment was evidenced by the responses of many of those who returned the questionnaire. A frequently expressed comment was to the effect that "those who served in the CPS mental hospital units gave the mentally ill in the postwar period thousands of advocates who championed their cause . . . and continue to do so." One former CPS man reported that after his discharge from the CPS program, he had been well received by those in his home community, including returning veterans. He decided to run for election to the city council and won by a wide margin. And he continued to campaign for successive terms with great success.

Here are the comments of several former CPS men describing their enlightened involvement in the political arena:

> I have come to believe that our national policies are predicated on greed, hatred, and war as a method of resolving our international conflicts. I regularly write to the editor of the *Augusta-Kennebec Journal* in opposition to such issues as "star wars," aid to the contras, and many other similarly related topics. The editor calls me one of his favorite correspondents.

> Any attempt on the part of the Congress or my state legislature to act on legislation relating to the care of the mentally ill receives my careful attention. When I see such matters on the agenda of these bodies, I make sure to write to my representatives, urging their support for measures that will promote their welfare.

> I have gained strong convictions about the government's responsibility for caring for indigent people. I have also come to realize that the government must plan more wisely in meeting their needs.

> The strong resistance which I developed to the Reagan administration's negative approach in dealing with social issues and concerns is attributable to the influences awakened in me as a result of the CPS experience in which I was involved.

> My political and social outlook has changed substantially from the days when I was a 20-year-old CO, working in a state hospital. My worldview has been greatly expanded as a result of that exposure

> to a growing concern for the disadvantaged and social outcasts, not only in our country, but throughout the world. . . . Clearly, I have become an advocate of social change rather than maintaining the status quo. It was also instructive to have worked in such an institution where I could begin to understand the entrapments and inertia that are so inherent in the operation of these facilities.
>
> In Ohio we are closing state mental hospitals and throwing many mentally incompetent people out into the streets. (We call it "returning them to their communities.") It is claimed that about two-thirds of the homeless street people are mentally ill or mentally retarded. No one wants to accept responsibility for them. In our community, one shelter for these people was closed because neighbors complained that it didn't meet zoning requirements. The present-day attitude of most people seems to reflect the axiom, "out of sight, out of mind." And let someone else bear the responsibility for their care.

CPS Experience Had Profound Influence on Career Choices

The CPS mental hospital experience had a profound influence on the career directions of one out of three men who participated in the 1988 survey. Many had been planning to resume careers in business, the arts, farming, and other fields outside the arena of the helping professions when they were discharged. Many of those whose education had been interrupted by the draft had no thoughts of preparing for careers in medicine, nursing, religion, psychology, social work, or education. But as the war came to an end, their pre-CPS career directions no longer seemed relevant. Their intense involvement with human beings whose lives had been shattered by emotional ills and developmental disabilities triggered new values and new insights. These served as a basis for rethinking what they wanted to do with the rest of their lives. One man offered the following succinct observation on the change that occurred in his life on his discharge from CPS:

> Prior to my induction into the CPS program, I had only completed my schooling at the 8th grade level and my only work experience had been as a farmhand. At the completion of my CPS mental hospital experience, I was moved to pursue a medical career and fulfilled all the necessary educational requirements to become a physician.

Another commented:

> I credit the hospital experience with leading me toward a people-oriented vocation instead of taking over my father's profitable "meat and cheese business." I became involved in mental health agencies in the Chicago area for more than 30 years.

One CPS man reported that after his discharge from the hospital where he had been assigned, he entered college at the age of 40. He went on to earn a Ph.D. degree and became a full professor of education at Lock Haven State College in Pennsylvania. In his response, he noted:

> My CPS experience led me to realize that I had talents for human service that could be developed. I became much more interested in all political and social matters, and was eager to see what I could do to help the poor, the imprisoned, and the mentally ill. To facilitate my inclinations, I decided to join the Society of Friends.

Several men who came out of the CPS program moved on to do important work in the mental health field at national as well as state governmental levels. One man, trained as a psychiatrist, became engaged in a number of projects as a member of the staff of the National Institute of Mental Health. He went on to serve as a regional director for the National Institute of Mental Health in two different regions. He then joined the California Department of Mental Health. Another was the recipient of several grants from the National Institute of Mental Health, all related to the development of community mental health centers. He also helped formulate and write a model code for local mental health authorities for the state of Illinois.

Even though only a small number of CPS men chose to redirect their postwar careers to people-oriented services, they nevertheless were able to touch the lives of tremendous numbers of people. This was particularly so because many of them became teachers to others seeking to enter the helping professions. They served as role models. They rose to leadership roles in citizens' and professional organizations engaged in bringing about social change. Here are a few illustrations of what happened:

> My whole life became involved in programs that related to meeting the emotional and mental health needs of people. After CPS I took courses in social work and earned master's and doctoral degrees in this field. Eventually, I became a Professor of Social Work as well as a Dean of a School of Social Work. Following my retirement, I continued to be active as a board member of several mental health and family service agencies. And I continue to spend at least half my available time in activities related to family life education.

> I decided to do graduate training in psychology, and have had a career as a psychologist in the U.S. Public Health Service, the National Institute of Mental Health, a major medical school, and a university. I've been active as an executive director and as a volunteer in several local and state mental health associations, as well as serving as a delegate to national and international mental health meetings.

> I became a psychiatrist, and have spent 25 years promoting welfare through my work as a clinician in private practice in two different psychiatric clinics for children. For an extended period of time, I served as a volunteer with the Mental Health Association of Southeastern Pennsylvania and also with the World Federation of Mental Health.

> In the five years immediately following my discharge from CPS, I was employed by the Pennsylvania Citizen's Association for Health and Welfare. My particular area of concern was on the delivery of mental health services. In this capacity I worked in areas related to public education and legislation. It was also part of my assignment to visit every mental hospital, both public and private, in the state.

> Subsequently, I was engaged in administrative work with the Baltimore City Health Department and stayed with this program until my retirement.
>
> My CPS institutional experience had a profound influence on my life. Clearly, God had me on a ward where I developed an interest in pursuing medicine as a career, a move I had not clearly envisioned prior to CPS. I am forever grateful to the Lord for pointing me in this direction.

Perhaps one of the more influential roles played by CPS men during their postwar careers was in the field of religion. Among those who returned the questionnaire, one in 10 had opted to become pastors of local congregations or to accept administrative positions with one of the denominations or other church bodies. The following account given by one man who started out to complete his seminary training after the war, but whose career took a different twist, makes a few points that deserve a hearing:

> Following CPS in 1946, I continued my education toward the ministry. . . . After two quarters of seminary training I reached an impasse, and decided to take time out to reassess my life. I went to work in a local mental hospital. I found my work there in the in-service training program to be so satisfying that I never took another direction to my life. When the Illinois state mental hospitals started shutting down, I transferred to the state prison system where I continued in my nursing career until my retirement. . . .
>
> One of the worst results of closing down the state hospitals was most apparent in the prison system. A large minority of the inmates I found to be suffering from mental illness. Prior to the shift in the state mental hospital program described above, a judge had the option of committing a mentally disturbed defendant to a state mental hospital, if this seemed to be warranted. At the present time, a judge has no choice but to sentence a criminal to prison. And in prison, the mentally ill inmate is subject to almost constant abuse.
>
> I would like to see the mentally ill and retarded prisoners currently in our criminal justice system isolated from the other inmates. Then, as they respond to treatment, they could be trans-

> ferred to halfway houses. Because of their antisocial behavior, many of these individuals may never be able to return to normal society, but they do deserve a better fate than is now the case.

One of the men who had served in the CPS unit at the Connecticut State Hospital at Middletown was invited to join the Psychology and Biology Department faculties at Wesleyan University after his discharge. In time, he became a full professor. He also had the unusual distinction of being invited to serve as a member of the Connecticut State Hospital Advisory Board, a post that he held for many years. In recounting his experiences as both an adviser to the hospital and as an educator, this is what he had to say:

> In my postwar career as an educator, I found that the work I performed working with the mentally ill as a member of the CPS unit helped me understand much about teaching the "normal" student. . . . Our presence at the hospital during the war helped bring about an increased involvement in that institution's affairs by the community.
>
> Following our departure when the unit was disbanded, a Mayor's Task Force was established to lobby for better pay and housing for the hospital's employees. The local Friends' Meeting arranged for students at Wesleyan to volunteer for weekend service at the hospital. Students were given an opportunity to work on the wards and to attend lectures given by the staff on various aspects of mental disorders. One student participant became so motivated by his experience that he decided to pursue a career in psychiatry. . . . Children of the families of the Friends' Meeting were encouraged to visit elderly female patients at the hospital on a weekly basis. Though the hospital administration was initially dubious about the benefits of this program, they were soon delighted when they observed how much these visits meant to the patients.

Final Reflections

Before signing off on their responses to the CPS mental hospital experience nearly 50 years after it ended, many respondents assessed the impact of that program. Many were critical of what had happened in recent years as a result of deinstitutionalizing chronically mentally ill patients. The following was a typical reaction:

> Public sidewalks are not much better than the old-time mental institutions to which we were exposed in CPS, when the mentally ill were warehoused and ignored.

On a more positive note were observations like these:

> I am profoundly impressed by the fellows who made medicine, psychology, social work, the ministry, and other helping professions their life work, no doubt as a result of their CPS experience. Perhaps this contributed more to the advances in the state of mental health care in America than the CPS mental hospital program itself.
>
> I believe that we did have an impact and perhaps something did happen to awaken the public's concern for the mentally ill. But perhaps this would have come along, anyway. If we did help to speed this process, that's fine! In a sense, this is an irrelevant consideration. We did the best we could and we really did help, and if society allows a deterioration within the structure of care for the mentally ill, then perhaps there are cultural and economic aspects of the whole society that now need to be addressed. . . .
>
> I perceive that with the end of World War II, a turning point was reached with respect to the care of the mentally ill. It is my perception that since then, fewer mentally ill persons are hidden away in shame by their relatives. There is far less stigma at present associated with the need for seeking psychiatric help. And drug and alcohol treatment centers are now integral features of the expanded network of socially acceptable mental health centers.

EPILOGUE

Compared with conscientious objectors (COs) during the Korean and Vietnam wars, men in the Civilian Public Service (CPS) program had a unique characteristic. They were banded into distinct units and were easily identifiable as an "alien" group within the institutions they served. To meet the various daily challenges they faced, often in stressful and alienating settings, they had to reach out to each other for counsel and support. They soon learned they had to work together to develop strategies to cope with problems they faced as individuals or as a group. With the passage of time, they not only learned to improve their skills in facing challenges but also gained new insights into and experience with the power of group dynamics.

It was out of this give-and-take process that emerged the forces that sparked the most influential crusade on behalf of the mentally ill that occurred in this century. The CPS mental hospital experience was truly a turning point, not only for the mentally ill, but also for those young men whose beliefs in the sanctity of life had not permitted them to bear arms at a critical period in their lives.

On May 6, 1946, *Life Magazine* published an article by Albert Q. Maisel titled "BEDLAM 1946—Most U.S. Mental Hospitals Are a Shame and Disgrace." As reported in Chapter 2, publication of that piece had been directly inspired by the collected reports of some 3,000 COs who had become deeply moved by and concerned with the unspeakable conditions that they had observed during their work assignments to 61 state institutions for the mentally ill and mentally retarded. Release of that historically significant article triggered the publication of other journalistic exposés of horrific and inhumane conditions then prevailing in similar institutions throughout the country. All of these exposés so touched the conscience of the American public that they marked the dawning of a new and enlightened era for these hospitals and the patients they served.

Five years after the appearance of Maisel's first article, he decided to revisit the institutions about which he had written in 1946 to learn whether anything had happened to these facilities in the intervening years. He reported his findings in *Life Magazine* in November 1951 under the headline: "Scandal Results in Real Reforms."[1]

In his opening paragraph, Maisel observed:

> Five years ago shock and revulsion swept the country as one reporter after another dug up evidence proving that most of the public mental hospitals of the U.S. were little more than filthy, brutish concentration camps. Newspapers, magazines (*Life,* May 6, 1946), books and movies backed the exposures with demands for reform. Such crusades have been seen before in the U.S., but all too often they have quickly run down, leaving things pretty much as they were before. This time it was different.

As the United States moves into the last decade of the twentieth century, once again all is not well for large numbers of the mentally ill. In 1990, *The New York Times* published an article titled "U.S. Returns to 1820s in Care of Mentally Ill, Study Asserts."[2] In part this is what it said:

> The United States has taken a leap backward in mental health care and more people with serious mental illness are in prisons and street shelters than in hospitals, according to a report issued today.
>
> Not since the 1820s have so many mentally ill individuals lived untreated in public shelters, on the streets, and in jails. . . .
>
> Of the 250,000 with serious mental illnesses, the report estimated that 100,000 are in jails or prisons. The largest "de facto mental hospital" in the country is the Los Angeles County jail, where there are 3,600 inmates who are seriously mentally ill on an average day, 700 more than in the nation's largest mental hospital, the report said. . . .
>
> In Idaho, the report said, it is standard practice to bring the mentally ill to jail first, where they are fingerprinted before seeing an "examiner."

> The waiting list for South Florida State Hospital is six months long, according to the report, and at emergency rooms at Broward General as well as in Tampa, mental patients are routinely shackled for hours or even days while waiting for a bed. . . .
>
> The failure of the system has come about after the movement of the 1960s and 1970s to move mental patients out of mental institutions, with the idea that they would be treated at mental health clinics in the communities where they resided. From 1955 to 1984, the number of patients in public mental hospitals dropped from 552,000 to 119,000.
>
> Whatever was supposed to happen did not happen, and deinstitutionalization was a disaster, the report concluded.

The news story cited above attributed the findings of the report to the Public Citizens Research Group and the National Alliance for the Mentally Ill, consumer and advocacy organizations and frequent critics of mental health care in the United States.

As once again the nation finds itself facing a major crisis in the care of its mentally ill, some new and innovative forces need to be brought to bear in coping with this serious dilemma. In considering new approaches to solving this problem, it may be useful to recall some historical efforts that did result in progress in mental health care.

Perhaps one of the oldest examples of dealing constructively and compassionately with the mentally ill occurred many hundreds of years ago when families in Geel, Belgium, decided to open their homes to the mentally ill when no other institutional facilities were available to care for their needs. To this day, the villagers of Geel have sustained this tradition.

In the nineteenth century, a selfless and dedicated ex-schoolteacher, Dorothea Lynde Dix, had her conscience stirred to action when she happened to discover a number of severely mentally ill persons confined under wretched conditions in a Massachusetts prison. Exposure to that tragic scene motivated her to mount a one-woman crusade throughout the United States, Canada, and Europe, where she lobbied before legislatures and governmental authorities. Before she was through with her campaign, her efforts had led to the establishment of 32 mental hospitals. She even succeeded in getting the U.S. Congress to pass a bill appropriating 10 million acres of public land, proceeds from the sale of which were to be earmarked for the construction of new mental hospitals. Unfortunately, President Pierce vetoed that legislation, and a tremendous potential benefit for the mentally ill was lost.

Early in this century another champion of the mentally ill, Clifford W. Beers, was the spark plug who set in motion a chain of events that led to the establishment of the first national citizens' mental health movement in this country. This was the National Committee for Mental Hygiene, which was later to merge with the National Mental Health Foundation and the American Psychiatric Foundation to become the National Association for Mental Health. Beers's involvement in this crusade had been prompted by his experiences as a patient in several mental hospitals.

The Turning Point describes in detail how another revolution in mental health care in the United States was accomplished by a band of COs. Because of circumstances they did not anticipate, these men found themselves in a world in which their hearts and minds were troubled by the sights and sounds around them. They were so moved that they finally were impelled to find creative ways to bring their concerns to the attention of the nation. And they set about to do so.

To underscore the point already made—that just a few highly motivated and energized individuals can reach for and attain impossible goals—one needs only to recall how a small handful of young Mennonite "graduates" of the CPS mental hospital program were instrumental in bringing about the growth and development of the several Mennonite mental health centers described in Chapter 10 of *The Turning Point*. Some of these men were not only the dreamers whose visions moved their church to establish a network of mental health facilities steeped in the traditions of their faith, but also the administrators who guided these centers so that they became role models for similar facilities throughout the nation.

The men who came out of the CPS mental hospital experience cannot be given sole credit for the dramatic turnaround in the care of the mentally ill in the post–World War II era. But time and again, mental health professionals held in high public and professional esteem have acknowledged the significant contributions to mental health care made by men whose story has been recounted in these pages.

The homeless mentally ill, who have become a major societal concern of the 1990s, represent as great a human tragedy as did those patients who confronted the first CPS units in the early to mid-1940s. If these young men were able to accomplish what they did for mentally ill people despite the severe handicaps with which they had to contend, there has to be dormant within the current generation the capacity for reaching out to the present-day forgotten mentally ill with the kind of helping hand that will restore the dignity and well-being of these poor souls.

The important consideration is that small bands of dedicated individuals can initiate and facilitate social change on a grand scale. Once again in this century, a major crusade on behalf of the mentally ill is wanting. Another major turning point is at hand. Where are the architects and builders to implement the plan of action that is now so desperately needed?

References

Chapter 1

1. The Reporter, August 15, 1944. A publication of the National Service Board for Religious Objectors (later the National Interreligious Service Board for Conscientious Objectors), Washington, DC.
2. Howard Moore: The CO in World War I . . . The Compass, Vol. 1, No. 3 (Spring 1943), pp. 4, 6, 46–47. Published by Men in Civilian Public Service. Archived at Swarthmore College Peace Library, Swarthmore, PA.
3. The Reporter, November 15, 1945.
4. Directory of Civilian Public Service, May 1941 to March 1947. A publication of the National Service Board for Religious Objectors (later the National Interreligious Service Board for Conscientious Objectors), Washington, DC.
5. Adrian E. Gory and David C. McClelland: Characteristics of conscientious objectors in World War II. Journal of Consulting Psychology, September–October 1947, pp. 245–257.
6. Directory of Civilian Public Service, May 1941 to March 1947.
7. Eric Schmitt: They served country and conscience. The New York Times, May 29, 1989, p. 8 L.
8. The Reporter, April 15, 1943; June 15, 1943; July 1, 1943; July 15, 1943; November 15, 1943; March 1, 1944; April 1, 1944.
9. Archives, National Interreligious Service Board for Conscientious Objectors, 1601 Connecticut Avenue, N.W., Washington, DC 20009.

10. Robert A. Clark and Alex M. Burgess: The work of conscientious objectors in state mental hospitals during the Second World War. The Psychiatric Quarterly Supplement, Vol. 22, Part 1, 1948, pp. 128–140. Reprinted by permission of Human Sciences Press.

Chapter 2

1. The story of what inspired the *Life Magazine* article "BEDLAM 1946" by Albert Q. Maisel may be of interest to readers of *The Turning Point.* In the early days of 1946, Leonard Cornell, then Executive Secretary of the National Mental Health Foundation and his colleagues were planning to launch a major public education and fund-raising campaign in the latter part of the year to provide the necessary momentum for their drive (see Chapter 8).

   It was their hope that they could interest the editors of *Reader's Digest,* at that time a very influential periodical, in running a story on the disgraceful conditions then prevailing in many of the nation's public mental hospitals. Bolstered with an introduction from Mrs. Eleanor Roosevelt, then one of the foundation's sponsors, Cornell arranged for an interview with one of the senior editors at *Reader's Digest.* When he arrived at the appointed time, he learned that the editor was dashing from a luncheon meeting to a conference and could spare only five minutes. Cornell, realizing that it was an almost impossible task to tell his story in such a brief space of time, pulled out from his briefcase a handful of graphically explicit photos that illustrated the bedlam-like conditions then prevailing at the Philadelphia State Hospital and many other similar institutions throughout the country and simply said: "This is what I wanted to talk to you about."

   The editor, after glancing from one shocking photo to another, became responsive. The editors of *Life Magazine* made a commitment to publish Maisel's article in their May 6, 1946, issue. As was their practice, *Reader's Digest* followed up with a condensed version of that story under the title "The Shame of

Our States" as their lead article in the July 1946 issue. The publication of these two articles triggered a massive public reaction, as well as a proliferation of similar exposés at the state level from coast to coast.
2. The Annual Report of the National Committee for Mental Hygiene, 1944.
3. Frank L. Wright, Jr.: Out of Sight, Out of Mind. Philadelphia, PA, National Mental Health Foundation, 1947. Used by permission of the publisher and the author.

Chapter 3

1. Excerpts from letters are reprinted by permission of Warren Sawyer.

Chapter 4

1. The Reporter, October 1, 1943. A publication of the National Service Board for Religious Objectors (later the National Interreligious Service Board for Conscientious Objectors), Washington, DC.
2. The Reporter, October 1, 1943.
3. The Reporter, May 15, 1944.
4. Robert A. Clark and Alex M. Burgess: The work of conscientious objectors in state mental hospitals during the Second World War. The Psychiatric Quarterly Supplement, Vol. 22, Part 1, 1948, pp. 128–140. Reprinted by permission of Human Sciences Press.
5. Permission to use excerpts from letter of Van Cleve Geiger granted by his brother, Calhoun Geiger.
6. The Reporter, July 15, 1944.
7. The Reporter, July 15, 1944.
8. Kenneth Hetrick: Exchange Bulletin—Camp Series, February 10, 1945, p. 6. A publication of the Mental Hygiene Program of Civilian Public Service, Philadelphia, PA.

9. Gordon Zahn: An open letter to the Board of Visitors, Rosewood Training School, Owings Mills, MD, April 5, 1946. Reprinted by permission of the author.

Chapter 5

1. Louis E. Swanson and James F. Gifford, Jr.: Conscientious objection and clinical care: a history of Civilian Public Service Camp No. 61 at Duke University, 1942–46. North Carolina Medical Journal, Vol. 46, 1985, pp. 419–423.
2. Elizabeth Rosenthal: That person in the white smock is not a doctor. The New York Times, January 10, 1991, p. B11.
3. Statement that was appended by John Burrowes to the questionnaire sent to him and other men who participated in the CPS mental hospital program. (See Appendix A for a copy of this questionnaire.)
4. News columns. Poughkeepsie New Yorker, May 14, 1945.
5. Eleanor Roosevelt: My Day. Poughkeepsie New Yorker, July 10, 1945.
6. Editorial. Poughkeepsie New Yorker, July 15, 1945
7. Editorial. The Hartford Courant, January 21, 1946.
8. Need they wander in darkness? The Hartford Courant Sunday Magazine, February 24, 1946, pp. 6–7.
9. The New Haven Register Sunday Supplement, January 20, 1946.
10. Editorial. The Hartford Times, January 21, 1946.

Chapter 6

1. Letters to the editor. Norwich Bulletin, January 5, 1944.
2. Letters to the editor. Norwich Bulletin, January 10, 1944.
3. Letters to the editor. Norwich Bulletin, January 12, 1944.
4. Letters to the editor. Norwich Bulletin, February 5, 1944.
5. The Providence Rhode Island Bulletin, as cited in The Reporter, January 15, 1944. A publication of the National Service Board for Religious Objectors (later the National Interreligious Service

Board for Conscientious Objectors), Washington, DC.
6. The News Tribune (Tacoma, WA), as cited in The Reporter, September 15, 1943.
7. The Times (Seattle, WA), as cited in The Reporter, September 15, 1943.
8. The Philadelphia Inquirer, as cited in The Reporter, May 1, 1945.
9. The Times (Martin's Ferry, OH), as cited in The Reporter, March 15, 1945.
10. The Bergen Record, as cited in The Reporter, May 15, 1945.
11. The Commercial Appeal (Memphis, TN), as cited in The Reporter, October 15, 1945.
12. The Evening Tribune (Albert Lea, MN), as cited in The Reporter, October 1, 1944.
13. The Lakewood Log (a Washington State weekly), as cited in The Reporter, October 1, 1944.

Chapter 7

1. Symposium—the use of force. The Attendant, Vol. 1, No. 2, July 1944, pp. 3–7. A publication of the Mental Hygiene Program of Civilian Public Service, Philadelphia, PA.
2. Marvin K. Weisbord: Some Form of Peace—True Stories of the American Friends Service Committee at Home and Abroad. New York, Viking Penguin, 1968, p. 36. Copyright © 1968 by Marvin K. Weisbord. Used by permission of Viking Penguin, a division of Penguin Books, USA Inc.
3. Some Form of Peace, pp. 36–37.
4. Some Form of Peace, pp. 36–37.
5. The Reporter, May 15, 1945. A publication of the National Service Board for Religious Objectors (later the National Interreligious Service Board for Conscientious Objectors), Washington, DC.
6. The Reporter, May 15, 1945.
7. The Reporter, May 15, 1945.
8. The Reporter, May 15, 1945.

Chapter 8

1. Joseph F. Nolan: Drive opens to assist mentally ill. The Philadelphia Inquirer, May 6, 1946.
2. Help for mental cases. The Philadelphia Evening Bulletin, May 7, 1946.
3. Nina Ridenour: Mental Health in the United States: A Fifty-Year History. Cambridge, MA, Harvard University Press, 1961, p. 78.
4. The Barry Bingham letter was conceived and drafted by the author of *The Turning Point* in the spring of 1949, at which time he was the public relations director of the National Mental Health Foundation. All the replies received by Mr. Bingham were turned over to the National Mental Health Foundation and subsequently to the National Mental Health Association. Although a few of these responses survived several moves of the latter organization, unfortunately the bulk of them were inadvertently destroyed.
5. Budget figures were provided by the Planning and Financial Branch, National Institute of Mental Health, Rockville, MD, during a telephone call in the spring of 1992.
6. Variety, January 1, 1947.
7. The three series of radio dramas described in this chapter are in the archives of the Hornbake Library, Non-Print Media Services Section, University of Maryland, College Park, MD 20742.

Chapter 9

1. The National Mental Health Bulletin, Spring 1950. A publication of the National Mental Health Foundation, Philadelphia, PA.

Chapter 10

1. Elmer Ediger: Influences on the origin and development of Mennonite Mental Health Centers. The Mennonite Quarterly Review, January 1982, p. 35.

2. William Klassen. The role of the church in community psychiatry. McCormick Quarterly Review, July 1967, p. 23.
3. Klassen, p. 24.
4. Klassen, p. 24.
5. Klassen, p. 26.
6. Ediger, p. 36.
7. Vernon Neufeld: The Mennonite mental health story. Mennonite Quarterly Review, January 1982, pp. 20–21.
8. Neufeld, p. 23.
9. Ediger, p. 37.
10. Neufeld, p. 21.
11. Neufeld, p. 22.
12. Lucy Ozarin, quoted in If We Can Love: The Mennonite Mental Health Story. Edited by Vernon Neufeld. Newton, KS, Faith and Life Press, 1983, pp. 305, 307.

Chapter 11

1. Institutional Service Units Files, Archives of the Brethren Church, Elgin, Illinois.
2. John D. Unruh: In the Name of Christ—A History of the Services of the Mennonite Central Committee, 1920–1951. Scottdale, PA, Herald Press, 1952.
3. Institutional Service Units Files, Archives of the Brethren Church, Elgin, IL.
4. Information presented in this section is based on data provided by the Prairie View Mental Health Center, Newton, KS.
5. Letter from Laban Peachey, Chairman, and Larry W. Nikkel, Administrator, Prairie View Mental Health Center, to Dr. Samuel Feder, Chairman, National Association of Private Psychiatric Hospitals Annual Awards Committee, June 29, 1981.
6. Norine Foley: Bold experiment here brings aid to retarded children. Chicago Daily News, November 21, 1949, p. 1.
7. From a statement prepared by Alfred Rath for Alex Sareyan, July 1, 1990.
8. Information presented in this section is based on data provided

by Edgewood Children's Center, Webster Groves, MI.

9. Letter from Ralph Lehman to Alex Sareyan, June 20, 1990.
10. Letter from Ralph Lehman to Alex Sareyan, June 20, 1990.
11. Information presented in this section is based on data provided by the Public Relations Office, Kings View Center, Reedley, CA.

Epilogue

1. Albert Q. Maisel: Scandal results in real reforms. Life Magazine, November 12, 1951.
2. Philip J. Hilts: U.S. returns to 1820's in care of mentally ill, study asserts. The New York Times, September 12, 1990, p. 28. Copyright © 1990. Used by permission of The New York Times.

Appendix A

Questionnaire sent in 1988 to men who had been in Civilian Public Service (CPS) mental hospital or training school units during World War II

1. What CPS base camp were you first assigned to? How long were you there before reassignment?
2. To what other base camps were you assigned and how long did you serve in each?
3. What prompted you to volunteer for service in a mental hospital or training school unit?
4. In which mental hospital or training school unit/s did you serve and how long in each?
5. In what capacity/ies did you serve in the above unit/s?
6. What position or job did you hold prior to your induction into CPS?
7. What was your religious affiliation at the time of your induction?
8. What was your political affiliation at the time of your induction?
9. What was your educational status at the time of your induction?
10. What was your marital status at that time?

(Please answer the following questions from the viewpoint of the hospital or training school at which you served the longest period of time.)

11. How did the patients perceive your unit?

	At arrival	After 1 year	By the time I left
Positive	______	______	______
Neutral	______	______	______
Negative	______	______	______

(Please check one response in each of the above columns and the following three questions.)

12. How did the community in which your unit was located react to your unit's presence?

	At arrival	After 1 year	By the time I left
Positive	______	______	______
Neutral	______	______	______
Negative	______	______	______

13. How did the attendants and nursing staff react to your unit?

	At arrival	After 1 year	By the time I left
Positive	______	______	______
Neutral	______	______	______
Negative	______	______	______

14. How did the institution's administration react?

	At arrival	After 1 year	By the time I left
Positive	______	______	______
Neutral	______	______	______
Negative	______	______	______

(If there are any special observations you would like to make concerning responses to the above questions, please do so at this point.)

15. What were the greatest challenges and/or opportunities faced by your unit? Please list in order of importance.
16. What were the greatest challenges and or opportunities faced by you as an individual at the institution?
17. Did the presence of your unit at the institution bring about any benefits to the patients? Yes ______ No ______ If yes, please describe.

18. Can you recall any major institutional changes for which your unit was responsible?
19. Do you now feel that your service in a hospital or training school satisfied your need to be involved in work of greater importance than provided in your base camp assignment?
20. During the CPS era, were you aware of its Mental Hygiene Program and did you participate in its program? If so, please describe.
21. In 1946 the above program was succeeded by the National Mental Health Foundation. Were you aware of its existence? If so, did you participate in any of its activities? If so, please describe.
22. In the postwar era did you participate in any local, state, or national organizations engaged in promoting the welfare of the mentally ill or retarded? If so, please describe.
23. Looking back, do you feel that the gains made in behalf of the mentally ill or retarded as a result of the CPS program were:

    Of short-term duration? Yes ______ No ______
    Of moderate duration? Yes ______ No ______
    Of long-term duration? Yes ______ No ______

    On what do you base your conclusions?

24. What is your present occupation?

    If retired, what was it prior to retirement?

    If retired, what are your current major interests?

25. In what ways, if any, did your CPS institutional service influence

    Your postwar studies?

    Your postwar career?

    Other aspects of your life?

26. Did any changes take place in your postwar political or social outlook as a result of your CPS institutional experience? If so, please describe.

27. If there are other observations you would like to offer about your CPS experience, please share them below.

Appendix B

Summary of responses to the questionnaire sent in 1988 to men who served in Civilian Public Service (CPS) mental hospital and training school units during World War II

- Total number of questionnaires mailed: 1,277
- Responses received: 435 (34% return)
- Number of respondents who indicated that gains made in behalf of the mentally ill as a result of the CPS experience were

  Of short-term duration: 30 (7%)
  Of moderate duration: 52 (12%)
  Of long-term duration: 286 (66%)
  No response: 67 (15%)

- Number of respondents who indicated that their postwar studies were redirected to helping professions: 114 (26%)
- Number of respondents who indicated that their postwar careers were redirected to helping professions: 144 (33%)
- Number of respondents who indicated that their political and social outlooks were considerably broadened by their CPS experience: 191 (44%)
- Occupational status of respondents in spring 1988 or at time of retirement:

  Education: 107 (24.6%)
  Medicine, public health, and counseling: 89 (20.5%)
  Religion: 43 (9.9%)
  Business and commerce: 69 (15.8%)
  Farming and agribusiness: 40 (9.2%)

Miscellaneous: 79 (18.2%)
No response: 8 (1.8%)

Editor's Note: It is significant that 55% of the respondents reported that at the time of this survey they were or had been engaged in careers related to education, medicine and the behavioral sciences, or religion. As noted above, 33% of the respondents indicated that their postwar career choices had been influenced by their involvement in the CPS program.

APPENDIX C

Roster of men who served in the Civilian Public Service mental hospital program and who participated in the survey that led to the writing of The Turning Point

Ralph J. Adlesic
James E. Albrecht, M.D.
William F. Anderson
Paul Andreas, M.D.
Roland Austin

Roger Bacon
Rufus Baehr
C. Lloyd Bailey
John G. Bailey
Marriner R. Bailey
Leo Baldwin
Meredith E. Barkley
Merrill H. Barneby
Hugh E. Barrett
Eugene Basinger
Paul W. Beard[a]
Harvey W. Beier
B. Tartt Bell
Merrill Benner
Peter G. Bennett, M.D.
Morris Berd
Lewis E. Berg
Milton M. Bergey, Jr.[a]
James Bixel
Robert L. Blake
Gerald L. Bleile[a]
Delbert Blickenstaff, M.D.
Henry D. Blocher
Howard Blosser
Roy L. Bomberger[a]
Robert A. Bone
Charles C. Booz
Waldo Brandt[a]
George Breneman[a]
Charles K. Brown III
Claude Brown
Roy C. Bucher
Elmer Buhler
Leland C. Bullen
Leo Buller[a]
Samuel B. Burgess, M.D.
Laurence Burkhalter
Kenneth Burnham
John H. Burrowes[a]

---

[a]Indicates financial contribution in support of expenses required to complete *The Turning Point.*

William Cable
Alan B. Campbell
Benjamin L. Candee
James R. Carlson
John R. Chittum
Theron Christophel
Robert H. Clark
Peter Classen, M.D.
Edgar Clemens
Whitfield Cobb
Joseph Coffin
Jacob Conner
Lloyd Conrad
John E. Corbett
Leonard G. Cornell[a]
Robert M. Cox
Owen E. Crosbie
Richard H. Crum
Robert N. Currier
Herbert J. Curtis

George Davidhizar
Joseph Davis, Jr.
Robert A. Davison[a]
LeRoy Detweiler
Jake A. Dick
Robert Dick
Daniel Diener
Arthur A. Dole
Theodore W. Donovan
Allon Dourte
Roger Drury
Harold P. Dyck[a]
Reverend L. Herschel Dyer

Elon Eash[a]
J. Wilbert Edgerton
Paul Ediger
John Elliott
Theodore R. Emory
Aaron R. Epp
Frederic W. Errett
James Eshleman

E. Lee Feller
James F. Finucane
William E. Finley
Elmo L. Fischer
Carlyle Frederick
Ed Freyenberger
Willard Friesen
Darrell Fryman

James Garber
Calhoun Geiger
Leland W. Gerber[a]
Irvin Gerig
Philip C. Gifford
Seth K. Gifford
John W. Gilbert
Delmar Gingerich
Lester Glick
J. Hobart Goering[a]
James D. Good
Richard C. Goodwin[a]
Raymond L. Gorden[a]
Ronald D. Gordley
Ezra Graber
Harold Graber
Ora A. Graber
Robert W. Gray
Harry E. Graybill
Lawrence Greaser
Floyd I. Greenleaf

Chauncy Grieser
D. Thurston Griggs
Edward V. Gulick[a]

Loris A. Habegger
Herbert M. Hadley
Henry B. Hall
Ralph P. Hallowell
Russell A. Hammar
James Harnish
Percy Harris, Jr.
Neil H. Hartman
Ralph W. Hartzler[a]
Wilton Hartzler
LeRoy Hawthorne[a]
H. Lee Hebel
Jesse Heddings
Jesse Heise, M.D.
Andrew J. Helmuth
Emery J. Helmuth
E. Eugene Hershberger
Earl Hertzler
William G. Heusel, M.D.[a]
C. William Heywood
William Hiebert
Irvin Hiebner[a]
William W. Hobbs
Jonas Hochstetler[a]
John A. Hockman
John H. Hoffman, Jr.
Verle Hoffman
Leonard W. Holden
Robert D. Hood
Clarence D. Hooley
Theodore D. Horner, Ph.D.
Samuel Horst
Dan Hostetler
John Hostetler
C. Nelson Hostetter
Stanley Hostetter
Arthur Householter
Earl Householter[a]
Richard Hunter[a]
Earl R. Hurst

Paul E. Illick
Alan C. Inglis

Elden Johnson
J. Edwin Jones
Arthur Jost

Lee Kanagy
Daniel Kauffman
J. Howard Kauffman
Paul E. Kauffman
Gordon Kaufman
Vernon Kaufman
Rev. William F. Kautz
William Keeney
Norman A. Keller[a]
Mahlon V. Kennel
Calvin B. Kenty
Carl E. Kime
Robert L. Kirk, D.O.
Luther H. Kirsch
Warren Kissinger
Herman B. Klassen
Paul Klassen
Marvin Kline
Clarence Klingenberg
Walter Koehn[a]
Vincent Krabill
Arthur Kraybill

Delmar Krehbiel
William B. Kriebel
Clarence E. Kuszmaul

Robert L. Lam
Gabriel W. Lasker
Paul Leatherman
Warren Leatherman
Harold D. Lehman[a]
Nevin Lehman
Ralph S. Lehman
Tedford P. Lewis
Paul E. Libby
Leonard Lichti
Paul S. Liechty
Wallace W. Littell
George T. Little
Robert H. Llewellyn[a]
W. Raymond Long
Rev. Charles R. Lord
William H. Ludlow
Charles H. Ludwig[a]
Harry Ludwig[a]

Eliot E. Macy
Eugene Maier
A. William March
Ross T. Marquis
James M. Martin
Russell Martin
Stanley L. Martin
Mark Martzall
Adelbert Mason
David P. McAllester
Richard G. McComb
Preston McCracken
William A. Meeh[a]

Samuel B. Mellott
Paul H. Metzger
Lowell E. Metzler
Dean Meyer
David P. Michener, M.D.
Ward Miles, M.D.
D. Paul Miller
Daniel Miller
Elmer A. Miller[a]
Jacob A. Miller
John A. Miller
John O. Miller
N. Emerson Miller
Ralph W. Miller
Vernon Miller
Waldo E. Miller
Dorsa Mishler[a]
Hugh Moore[a]
Robert M. Morgan
Clyde Mosemann
Theodore H. Moshos
Jonas L. Mullett

Mervin Nafziger
Theodore Neff[a]
Jack Neher
Allan Neubauer
Harold A. Nolte[a]
Irvin A. Nussbaum

Paul D. Olmstead
Philip Orpurt[a]

Robert H. Painter, M.D.
Carl Paulson
Herbert Penner
Fay D. Peters

Gerhard M. Peters
David S. Platt
Harold Plenert
Jake Plett
Robert J. Poorman
Dale Porter
John S. Pullman

Warren P. Quensel

Edward G. Ramberg
Eugene A. Ransom
Alfred Rath[a]
John Ratzlaff
Elwood P. Reber
Ferman Rediger
Everett Refior
Benjamin L. Reid
Alfred Reindl
Daniel Reinford
Robert Reuman
Floyd Rheinheimer, M.D.[a]
Gilbert L. Rice
Sam Richert
Richard Ricklefs, M.D.[a]
James Riddles
John D. Riebel
Harold E. Riegger
E. Lowell Rife
James Rinner
Ed Ritter[a]
Ross Roby, M.D.
S. Milford Roupp[a]
Cecil Rust, M.D.

Nathan Sadowsky
David R. Salstrom
Ross Sanderson
Amos Sands
Alex Sareyan
Isaac L. Sauder
Warren Sawyer[a]
Charles Schilling
Alva Schlabach[a]
Leonard Schmucker[a]
Rev. Dr. Howard Schomer[a]
Karl Schultz, Ph.D.[a]
Dwayne Schweppe
Stuart Shank
Elmer E. Shaw
Morris Sherk
Thomas E. Shipley
Doyle Short
William Sinden
Roland F. Smith
Robert R. Solenberger
Ralph Sommer
Ray Spicher[a]
Harold Steiner
Rev. Arthur M. Stevenson
Albert Stewart
Vernon H. Stinebaugh
Roscoe Swank
Louis E. Swanson
Stanley Swartzendruber

Merlin Taber
Richard W. Taylor
Ian Thiermann[a]
Stephen Thiermann
George Thorman
Amos Tilton
William Timberlake, M.D.
Wilmer Tjossem

Francis C. Troyer
Lotus Troyer
Lester Tyson[a]

Philip C. Vail
Harry R. Van Dyck
Robert G. Vessey
Rev. Carl A. Viehe[a]
John Vogt
Orville L. Voth[a]

Arlie Waggy
Roland Warfield
Marvin H. Wasser
Asa D. Watkins
H. Earl Weagley, Jr.
Arthur Weaver
Clyde Weaver
James O. Weaver[a]
Richard S. Weaver
Robert Wehmeyer
Gilbert Weldy
Wayne E. Wheeler
Orville J. White

Leonard Wiens[a]
Edward Wildman, M.D.[a]
Harmon Wilkinson
Abe Willems
Max W. Wilson
Marlin Wine
John W. Winters
Lauren Wispe
Clifford Wolfe
Avery Wood
Frank L. Wright[a]
Mahler Wyse

Amos W. Yoder
David Yoder
John Mark Yoder
Karl Yoder[a]
Ralph Yoder
Samuel L. Yoder
Swami Yogeshananda

Gordon C. Zahn
Ray M. Zercher
Melvin A. Zuck

APPENDIX D

Civilian Public Service mental hospital units in service during World War II under the sponsorship of religious agencies

American Friends Service Committee

Unit 41: Eastern State Hospital, Williamsburg, Virginia
Unit 49: Philadelphia State Hospital, Philadelphia, Pennsylvania
Unit 69: Cleveland State Hospital, Cleveland, Ohio[a]
Unit 75: Medical Lake State Hospital, Medical Lake, Washington
Unit 81: Connecticut State Hospital, Middletown, Connecticut[b]
Unit 83: Warren State Hospital, Warren, Pennsylvania
Unit 84: Concord State Hospital, Concord, New Hampshire
Unit 87: Brattleboro Retreat, Brattleboro, Vermont

Brethren Service Committee

Unit 47: Sykesville State Hospital, Sykesville, Maryland
Unit 51: Fort Steilacoom State Hospital, Fort Steilacoom, Washington
Unit 68: Norwich State Hospital, Norwich, Connecticut
Unit 70: Dayton State Hospital, Dayton, Ohio
Unit 73: Columbus State Hospital, Columbus, Ohio
Unit 74: Cambridge State Hospital, Cambridge, Maryland
Unit 80: Lyons VA Hospital, Lyons, New Jersey
Unit 82: Fairfield State Hospital, Fairfield, Connecticut
Unit 88: Augusta State Hospital, Augusta, Maine
Unit 109: Marion State Hospital, Marion, Virginia

---

[a] In 1944, this unit disbanded at the request of the hospital director.
[b] In 1945, administration of this unit was transferred to the Selective Service.

Mennonite Central Committee

Unit 44: Staunton State Hospital, Staunton, Virginia
Unit 58: Delaware State Hospital, Farnhurst, Delaware
Unit 63: Marlboro State Hospital, Marlboro, New Jersey
Unit 66: Norristown State Hospital, Norristown, Pennsylvania
Unit 69: Cleveland State Hospital, Cleveland, Ohio[c]
Unit 71: Lima State Hospital, Lima, Ohio
Unit 72: Macedonia State Hospital, Macedonia, Ohio
Unit 77: Greystone Park State Hospital, Greystone Park, New Jersey
Unit 78: Denver State Hospital, Denver, Colorado
Unit 79: Provo State Hospital, Provo, Utah
Unit 85: Rhode Island State Hospital, Howard, Rhode Island
Unit 86: Mt. Pleasant State Hospital, Mt. Pleasant, Iowa
Unit 90: Ypsilanti State Hospital, Ypsilanti, Michigan
Unit 93: Harrisburg State Hospital, Harrisburg, Pennsylvania
Unit 110: Allentown State Hospital, Allentown, Pennsylvania
Unit 118: Wernersville State Hospital, Wernersville, Pennsylvania
Unit 120: Kalamazoo State Hospital, Kalamazoo, Michigan
Unit 122: Winnebago State Hospital, Winnebago, Wisconsin
Unit 143: Catonsville State Hospital, Catonsville, Maryland
Unit 144: Hudson River State Hospital, Poughkeepsie, New York
Unit 147: Tiffin State Hospital, Tiffin, Ohio
Unit 150: Livermore State Hospital, Livermore, California
Unit 151: Roseburg State Hospital, Roseburg, Oregon

Disciples of Christ

Unit 139: Logansport State Hospital, Logansport, Indiana

Evangelical and Reformed Church

Unit 137: Independence State Hospital, Independence, Iowa

Methodist Commission on World Peace

Unit 61: Duke University Hospital, Durham, North Carolina
Unit 131: Cherokee State Hospital, Cherokee, Iowa

[c] In 1945, this unit reopened under Mennonite Central Committee auspices.

Appendix E

Civilian Public Service state training school units in service during World War II under the sponsorship of religious agencies

American Friends Service Committee

Unit 62: Cheltenham State Training School, Cheltenham, Maryland
Unit 119: State Colony for the Feebleminded, New Lisbon, New Jersey
Unit 124: Delaware State Colony, Stockley, Delaware
Unit 129: Pennhurst State Training School, Spring City, Pennsylvania
Unit 130: Pownal State Training School, Pownal, Maine
Unit 132: District Training School, Laurel, Maryland

Brethren Service Committee

Unit 91: Mansfield State Training School, Mansfield, Connecticut
Unit 95: Buckley State Training School, Buckley, Washington
Unit 105: Lynchburg State Training School, Colony, Virginia

Mennonite Central Committee

Unit 92: Vineland State Training School, Vineland, New Jersey
Unit 117: Exeter State Training School, Lafayette, Rhode Island
Unit 123: Union Grove State Training School, Union Grove, Wisconsin
Unit 127: American Fork State Training School, American Fork, Utah
Unit 142: Woodbine Colony for the Feebleminded, Woodbine, New Jersey

American Baptist Home Mission Society

Unit 136: Skillman State Training School, Skillman, New Jersey

Association of Catholic Conscientious Objectors

Unit 102: Rosewood State Training School, Owings Mills, Maryland

Appendix F

Religious affiliations represented in Civilian Public Service (CPS) program

Affiliation	No. of men in CPS program
Mennonites	4,665
Church of the Brethren	1,353
Society of Friends	951
Methodist	673
Jehovah's Witnesses	409
United Church of Christ[a]	310
Church of Christ	199
Presbyterian, U.S.A.	192
Northern Baptist	178
German Baptist, Brethren	157
Roman Catholic	149
Christadelphian	127
Lutheran	108
Episcopal	88
Disciples of Christ	78
Nonaffiliated	449
Unclassified as to denomination	709
Miscellaneous[b]	1,201
Total	11,996

[a]Includes men who were affiliated with the Congregational and Evangelical and Reformed Churches at the time of their induction.

[b]Men classified in this group totaled fewer than 75 for any one religious affiliation. Most of the sects included in this category had fewer than 10 members each. In all, 215 different religious affiliations were identified in this group.

Source. Directory of Civilian Public Service, May 1941 to March 1947. A publication of the National Service Board for Religious Objectors (later the National Interreligious Service Board for Conscientious Objectors), Washington, DC.

ANNOTATED BIBLIOGRAPHY

A considerable number of books have been published about the World War II Civilian Public Service (CPS) program. One of the more extensive collections of these works is at the Swarthmore College Peace Library, Swarthmore, Pennsylvania.

Listed below are selected books that offer insights additional to those contained in *The Turning Point*. Also included are a few recent releases that provide a broader perspective on the total CPS program than the reader will gain from *The Turning Point*.

The CPS Story: An Illustrated History of Civilian Public Service. By Albert Keim. Intercourse, PA, Good Books, 1990

This is a pictorial history of the broad CPS experience. Its many brief descriptive passages serve to enlighten the reader about all aspects of the program. An excellent overview, attractively presented.

If We Can Love: The Mennonite Mental Health Story. Edited by Vernon H. Neufeld. Newton, KS, Faith and Life Press, 1983

Neufeld, who for a long time was executive director of Mennonite Mental Health Services, offers an insider's viewpoint on the origins and development of the mental health centers that emerged in the post–World War II era out of the Mennonite experiences in the CPS mental hospital program.

Pathways of Peace. By Leslie Eisan. Elgin, IL, Brethren Publishing House, 1948

The author offers a Brethren-oriented perspective on the range of CPS projects overseen by the Brethren Service Committee. This book also has a major section detailing the experiences of men who served in both state mental hospitals and state training schools for the retarded.

Service for Peace. By Melvin Gingerich. Scottdale, PA, Herald Press, 1949

The author describes the CPS program from the Mennonite viewpoint. Brief histories are provided of the activities of many of the individual CPS units stationed in both mental hospitals and state training schools for the retarded.

To the Beat of a Different Drummer: A Decade in the Life of a World War II Conscientious Objector. By J. Henry Dasenbrock. Winona, WI, Winona Press, 1989

Unlike the books previously cited, this one is written from the viewpoint of one individual conscientious objector (CO). Although the author participated in several CPS programs, he did not serve in the mental hospital program. This book is included here because it sheds light on how one person responded to this experience, both at the time and during the five years after his discharge from CPS.

We Would Not Kill. By Hobart Mitchell. Richmond, IN, Friends United Press, 1983

The author recounts, in a very compelling narrative, how he and 160 fellow COs responded to being assigned to a canal-drainage project for the U.S. Department of Agriculture under sponsorship of the American Friends Service Committee. He describes the wide range of pacifist views held by his fellow campers, as well as provides a very realistic picture of how COs lived, worked, studied, played, and tried to maintain some semblance of connection to the world from which they had been conscripted.

Index

The Author

Alex Sareyan was born in New Haven, Connecticut, in 1913. After high school, he was accepted at the University of Pennsylvania's Wharton School, from which he graduated in 1934 with a B.S. in economics. He had pursued majors in both journalism and accounting. Though jobs were scarce in the Great Depression, he managed to land a position as business manager of a quarterly journal on economics located on New York's prestigious Wall Street. He started at $15 per week and worked seventy- and eighty-hour weeks. About a year later, he was offered a chance to be a merchant marine cadet on one of the Robert Dollar Line's round-the-world passenger-freighter liners, the *President Garfield.* The offer was irresistible, especially since difficult working conditions for the magazine caused a staff turnover of 400 percent a year. Soon he was flying cross-country in a ten-passenger airliner to embark at San Francisco.

When Sareyan returned to New York City, he found employment with the Anaconda Wire and Cable Company, first as an accounting clerk and later as a statistician. During this period, he affiliated with the Broadway Tabernacle, a historic and prestigious

Congregational church. Its pastor, Dr. Allan Knight Chalmers, had been an assistant minister in New Haven during Sareyan's boyhood. The Tabernacle fostered deep concerns for seeking and promoting social justice and a strong commitment to world peace. This setting nurtured Sareyan's pacifism and personal commitment to nonviolence as a means of resolving conflictual situations. With the advent of World War II, he applied to his local draft board for conscientious objector (CO) status.

Sareyan was drafted by Selective Service and assigned to work of "national importance under civilian direction" in a soil conservation camp under the U.S. Department of Agriculture at Coshocton, Ohio. After his brief stint there as a statistician, the camp's sponsoring peace church, the American Friends Service Committee, called him to help in opening a new Civilian Public Service (CPS) camp under the auspices of the Forestry Service in New Hampshire's White Mountains.

After a year as business manager of that camp, Sareyan volunteered with the initial group assigned to the Connecticut State Hospital at Middletown (Conn.) soon after Selective Service had agreed to permit COs to serve in the nation's mental hospitals. The Quakers also sponsored this unit, and shortly after it was opened, Sareyan was named its assistant director. He was a liaison between the members of the unit, the hospital's superintendent, the American Friends Service Committee, and Selective Service.

Sareyan devoted half his fifty-four-hour work week to the required paperwork and coordination, and half as an attendant on a male ward. When the superintendent asked him to develop a monthly house newsletter for the hospital community, he was relieved of ward duties. After about eighteen months at the hospital, Sareyan prevailed upon the new superintendent to permit him to devote full time to developing a public relations office for the hospital. At the time, it was the first such office initiated by a state hospital in this country. During that era, public mental hospitals were notorious for the low regard in which they were held. Public knowledge and perception about mental illness and the mentally ill were also abysmally deficient.

Shortly after Selective Service discharged him from the Connecticut State Hospital's CPS unit in January 1946, Sareyan was invited to join the fledgling Connecticut Department of Mental Health as its first public relations director. About the same time, he received an offer to take a similar assignment with the National Mental Health Foundation. This new citizens' movement had just emerged on the national scene from the CPS Mental Hygiene Program. It was able to pay an executive staff member only $200 per month, but Sareyan was attracted by the challenge of operating at a national level. Even though the new agency was headquartered in Philadelphia, he was allowed to establish a New York City base for his activities.

During following months, Sareyan commuted between New York and Philadelphia. In New York, he built a network of relationships with many of the nation's key science writers stationed there. Many of the nation's service organizations also had offices in New York, and he enlisted their participation in the Foundation's effort to bring about a better day for the mentally ill.

Sareyan arranged to visit most of the major regional, state, and voluntary mental health agencies throughout the country to explain the objectives of the Foundation. He encouraged them to take advantage of various educational resources the Foundation had developed to enlighten the American public about the mentally ill. At that time, the Foundation was not trying to build an independent support base. Instead, it was enlisting the aid of existing networks such as churches, religious agencies, and service and other organizations concerned with health and welfare issues. As these relationships strengthened, the Foundation soon found an extensive market for educational materials it was developing to win public support for its efforts.

A shift came to Sareyan in the fall of 1950, when the National Mental Health Foundation, the National Committee for Mental Hygiene, and the American Psychiatric Foundation merged to form the National Association for Mental Health. He was asked to direct the new agency's public relations program. One of his first tasks was to plan and coordinate activities for National Mental Health Week.

In 1953, Sareyan left the National Association for Mental Health and cofounded the Mental Health Materials Center, primarily designed to assist other nonprofit health and mental health agencies in developing and distributing their publications and educational resources. Over the years, the MHMC has provided such services to more than thirty national organizations, several university presses, and many state and other governmental and voluntary agencies. MHMC was soon asked to manage publishing and marketing duties for the Group for the Advancement of Psychiatry. During twenty-five years, it handled ninety titles for GAP. Most were book-length studies and sold more than ten thousand copies each. Several sold more than fifty-thousand each, and a few sold more than 250,000 each.

In addition to publishing services for agencies, MHMC pioneered in offering seminars and workshops on the skillful and effective use of educational resources to health and mental health educators. These were conducted for one-week periods, usually in collaboration with various schools of public health. Over a ten-year period, MHMC conducted over sixty such training sessions for a total of more than 1,200 health educators. All these seminars were held with grant support from the National Institute of Mental Health.

Another unique service developed by MHMC was a series of selective guides identifying educational resources of excellence, publications and audiovisuals useful in implementing mental health and health education objectives. Resources listed in these guides were carefully screened by MHMC staff and by an elite panel of experts. Many authorities credited this service with playing a major role in raising the quality of health and mental health education.

One way to assess an organization's imprint on society is from the perspective of those who have seen it function at close range. Here then are a few reflections from some who have observed it:

> In reminiscing your many years of outstanding contributions to the mental health field, I am impressed by the number of times the MHMC has helped the American Psychiatric Association. . . . *The Psychiatric Glossary* certainly owes a large measure of its success over these many years to the initial large distribution of over sixty thousand copies you helped us to arrange. . . . I wish that more people could have had the opportunity I have had to see how your hard work and dedication have accomplished so many things for the mental health field.
>
> Robert L. Robinson, Director of Public Affairs
> American Psychiatric Association, 2/13/78

For this past quarter of a century, the Mental Health Materials Center has been the outstanding information resource center for mental health and family life education.

C. Cameron Macauley, Director, Extension Media Center
University of California, Berkeley, 3/15/78

Since that bold beginning, you have enriched mental health education substantially by the identification and promotion of materials which have reached audiences that otherwise could not have been exposed to important mental health messages.

Richard Hunter, Deputy Executive Director
National Mental Health Association, 1/24/78

Your organization was well-versed in the principles and practice of mental health education long before most of the mental health enterprise had even begun to consider it! . . . We at the NIMH have enjoyed and learned from our long-standing work with you, and we sincerely appreciate the innumerable contributions you have made to the entire field of mental health.

Jacquelyn Hall, Ph.D., Chief, Mental Health Education Branch
National Institute of Mental Health, 3/1/78

I do know that you and your organization really have touched the lives of millions of people over these past twenty-five years, and that probably more than anyone else in the whole country, you've had a real hand in doing what has been done in terms of all kinds of psychiatric education and all sorts of primary prevention.

Robert E. Switzer, M.D., Superintendent, Eastern State
School and Hospital, Trevose, Pennsylvania, 5/31/78

The wide influence that GAP enjoys in the behavioral science world in this country and abroad is in part due to the creative stewardship of GAP's publishing program by the Mental Health Materials Center.

Jack A. Wolford, M.D., President
Group for the Advancement of Psychiatry, 4/18/78